Kay,

My prayer is that these words bring understanding, hope, healing and peace.

A STRANGER IN MY BED

Warmly,

Debbie Sprague

"I have known Debbie and Randy Sprague for several years. I had no idea the impact PTSD had been having on their family, though, upon reflection, it should not have surprised me. Randy, a Vietnam combat veteran, had been fighting the effects of PTSD for thirty years, as have so many of our Vietnam vets. As in most of their cases, little was available in assistance until literally the last decade. And while there is now assistance for our veterans, there is little assistance for their families, who are living through this hell with their veteran.

"Debbie Sprague ignored the therapists who said to walk away from Randy. Instead, she walked away from the therapists and did her own research, resulting in a book that should be required reading for every military chaplain and VA counselor. She has grasped the reality of the effects of PTSD on a family and found a solution that can work.

"After thirty years in the Marine Corps and multiple combat tours, I can attest that what she has written about in *A Stranger In My Bed* will work if you follow her 8 Steps. And if your family is worth time and effort, you will find this book a revelation."

—Carl Bott, Lt. Col. USMC (Ret.)

"Having known Debbie for several years now, it's no surprise that she approaches this topic with a genuine tenderness and warmth, but also provides real, actionable ways for those who love someone with PTSD to walk forward in this life. This book is a beautiful, though at times hard, look at what PTSD can do in our homes, but also at what love can do in response. I found myself teary-eyed at some points, nodding in recognition at others, and then cheering in my heart for her and Randy as I watched their story unfold. Truly a wonderful, honest look at this thing called Post-Traumatic Stress Disorder, how it impacts our families, and ways we can cope."

—Brannan Vines, Founder and President, Family of a Vet

"The effects of Post-Traumatic Stress Disorder on our veterans and their families are tragic. We cannot continue to keep this epidemic hidden. Debbie Sprague brings this topic to life by courageously sharing her story, providing powerful information, insight, and hopeful solutions for those caring for their veteran. *A Stranger in My Bed* is a valuable resource, not just for spouses of veterans, but also for all who care about the well-being of our veterans and their families."

—Dr. John Gray, bestselling author,
Men Are from Mars, Women Are from Venus

"A must-read for anyone who cares about veterans! Debbie Sprague breaks the stigma of Post- Traumatic Stress Disorder by bringing us into her world for a glimpse of the pain that it created in her family and their journey toward healing. She shares how the families of those who are struggling from PTSD are affected. Written with courage and love, *A Stranger in My Bed* takes a giant step in bringing about greater understanding, compassion, and support for our veterans and their families."

—Marci Shimoff, #1 *New York Times* bestselling author,
Happy for No Reason and *Chicken Soup for the Woman's Soul*

"This book is a perfect read for any combat veteran wife or those who have a loved one who has PTSD. I personally feel that for those who really want to look at the issues of PTSD and who are seeking help, this book is a door opener into finding your answers. I felt in many parts the book took me to the life I lead, and that is what many wives are looking for. *A Stranger in My Bed* will be a suggested read for all members of Vietnam Veteran Wives Organization."

—Danna Hughes, President/Founder Vietnam Veteran Wives/Ferry County Mountain Veteran Center, www.vietnamveteranwives.org

"An absolute must-read (and reference) for all family members who live with anyone suffering with PTSD. Debbie has not only researched her subject thoroughly but also has first-hand experience. As a wife of a Vietnam vet living with PTSD for years, I say thank you, Debbie, for finally offering us help!"

—Barbara Cocchi, Southern Director, World Relief, Ret.

"This book should be required reading for every coach, healer, and health professional working with veterans and their families. *A Stranger In My Bed* provides practical information and will help you deepen your understanding of Post-Traumatic Stress Disorder and what to do about it.

—Christian Mickelsen, CoachesWithClients.com

"Congratulations and many thanks to Debbie Sprague for her generosity in sharing her story as the spouse of a veteran with PTSD, so that many other spouses and caregivers can take heart and have hope for a better future. *A Stranger in My Bed* chronicles how PTSD can overwhelm caregivers, who themselves often decline to the point of losing themselves altogether, abandoning their own vital needs in their service to others. Being the spouse/caregiver of someone with PTSD can be overwhelming, but Debbie provides the ultimate workbook/action plan to combat the "overwhelm" and set a course for a happier and healthier existence for all concerned. If you are a spouse or caregiver for a dear one afflicted with PTSD, read this book from cover to cover. You can be happy again, and you will be a better and more effective caregiver for everyone in your family, once you acknowledge your own importance and take care of yourself."

—Stephanie Richmond, Certified Life Coach
and Executive Director, Stand Beside Them, Inc.

A
STRANGER
IN MY BED

8 STEPS TO TAKING YOUR LIFE BACK FROM
THE CONTAGIOUS EFFECTS OF YOUR VETERAN'S
POST-TRAUMATIC STRESS DISORDER

DEBBIE SPRAGUE

NEW YORK

A STRANGER IN MY BED

8 Steps to Taking Your Life Back from the Contagious Effects
of Your Veteran's Post-Traumatic Stress Disorder

ISBN 978-1-61448-574-2 paperback
ISBN 978-1-61448-575-9 eBook
ISBN 978-1-61448-576-6 audio
Library of Congress Control Number: 2013939476

Morgan James Publishing
The Entrepreneurial Publisher
5 Penn Plaza, 23rd Floor,
New York City, New York 10001
(212) 655-5470 office • (516) 908-4496 fax
www.MorganJamesPublishing.com

Cover Design by:
Chris Treccani
www.3dogdesign.net

Interior Design by:
Bonnie Bushman
bonnie@caboodlegraphics.com

To my husband Randy, with all my love, honor, and respect,
for his service to our country
and for his strength and vulnerability in allowing our story to be shared,
so all veterans and their families might find a place of peace.

For all the warriors who have fought through the ages,
and their loved ones who have and continue to hold them up
with selfless love and care.

Most importantly to the Lord, who has been my constant strength
and ever-present guide throughout this journey,
answering my prayers for help
and letting me feel the solid rock of his support beneath my feet.

CONTENTS

PART 2: Getting to Know the Stranger: Post-Traumatic Stress Disorder

PART 3: Helping the Stranger: Treatments for Post-Traumatic Stress Disorder

PART 4: Living with the Stranger

PART 5: Secondary Stress Disorder: 8 Steps to Taking Your Life Back from the Contagious Effects of the Stranger

FOREWORD

Debbie Sprague's honest approach to telling the story of her Vietnam era husband Randy's PTSD is very timely and important.

Though the challenges and struggles of dealing with a loved one suffering from PTSD are different for everyone, this account conveys a powerful and compelling message that can be translated to families of all eras, especially to the generation of Iraq and Afghanistan warriors.

Debbie is not a Washington-insider, and her humility, insights, suggestions, and resources will resonate and inspire hundreds of thousands of military, veterans, and family members all across the country. This personal story of overcoming not just her husband's diagnosis of PTSD, but her own, is needed more than ever as our Nation struggles to deal with over twelve long years of war. We are learning that the wounds of war are contagious in ways we did not previously understand. They affect the warriors, their families, caregivers, and communities very profoundly.

We should never forget the service and sacrifice of the one percent of our citizens who have defended our great country. One of the ways the other 99 percent can honor them is to provide the support and services their families need to not only survive, but thrive in ways meaningful to them.

On behalf of the 380,000 members of the Military Officers Association of America, we appreciate and applaud Debbie's willingness to speak directly and put a personal face on her family's situation and the challenges of living with PTSD.

We believe that caregivers must first and foremost not give up and lose hope for a better future. They don't have to go it alone.

We hope that many other families can find strength from reading Debbie's inspiring story.

VADM Norbert R. Ryan, Jr. USN (ret)
President & CEO
Military Officers Association of America (MOAA)

ACKNOWLEDGMENTS

To my mom and dad for bringing me up in the Lord and giving me a rock solid foundation on which to grow. Thank you for being an exemplary example of what commitment to marriage means. And for teaching me the value of hard work and giving me the confidence to go after my dreams.

To my daughter, Andrea, for standing next to me through the most difficult times my life. In addition, for her support in telling our story. And to her wonderful husband Randal for his patience with Randy, his kindness through all the difficult times, and holding up my daughter when I wasn't able to.

My utmost appreciation to my amazing editor, Jennifer Read Hawthorne. I realize it is not easy to take on a first-time author. You believed in my mission and the importance of this book—and in me . . . even when I did not believe in myself. Thank you for your patience, your flexibility, and your guidance in making *A Stranger in My Bed* the best book possible. You provided the incentive and the support to keep me moving forward even during the times when the process seemed overwhelming and never-ending.

With gratitude and love to my mastermind coaches and mentors Marci Shimoff, Janet Bray Attwood, Chris Atwood, and Geoff Affleck. Thank you for your confidence and your help in bringing this book to reality by sharing your knowledge, your contacts, and your love.

David Saywell, thank you for allowing me to share your work from *The Beginning* and for your confidence, support, and friendship both during and after our mastermind group. And to my fantastic photographer, Michael Sauer, for sharing his time and talents.

To Brannan Vines, founder of Family of a Vet, for providing me with the opportunity to begin learning about PTSD, helping me find the support I so desperately needed, and opening my eyes to the magnitude of the problem. You gave me the inspiration to reach beyond myself and begin giving back all that I've learned. I would also like to acknowledge all the wonderful volunteers at Family of a Vet for their friendship, support, and insight into their lives, their problems, and their love and commitment to their wounded warriors.

To all my experts who so graciously gave of their time and their knowledge to add such valuable content to this book: Roberta Mittman, Dawson Church, Dr. John Gray, Dr. Chet Sunde, Dr. Joe Rubino, Nancy Forrester, Barbara Stanney, Marci Shimoff, Janet Attwood, and Chris Atwood.

To my dear lifelong friends who have provided support and encouragement to me throughout this journey: Mary Warnock, Cindy Yerger, Pamela Hanford, Mary Hale, Colleen Charters, and Lyn Davis. In addition, to my dear friend and fellow Vietnam vet wife Barbara Cocchi, who daily kept me motivated and accountable to my writing and fitness goals throughout this journey.

To David Hancock and Morgan James Publishing, who saw the value and the need for this book and made it possible to put it out into the world. And to Rick Frishman and Author 101 University for the wonderful learning and networking opportunities.

INTRODUCTION

It began as a love story, a fairytale about love at first sight, a perfect wedding, and the dream of *living happily ever after.*

But far too soon, the dream ended. Lying next to me at night, my beloved husband began thrashing out in the darkness, screaming in anger, speaking in a tongue foreign to me—a stranger in my bed. His vivid nightmares were of a place and time that I knew nothing about; our world was overcome by fear, anger, and traumatic memories.

Through the grace of God and a "coincidental" meeting with another vet, my husband was eventually diagnosed with Post-Traumatic Stress Disorder (PTSD), a result of two tours of duty in Vietnam over thirty years before. But having a diagnosis didn't make the symptoms go away. And as if nights weren't bad enough, during his waking hours, he now became silent, cold, and angry. Vietnam had stolen the warm, charming man that I had fallen in love with.

As he became consumed in his own world, I too slowly began to change. I felt isolated from everyone around me. Subtle changes began to happen: I felt numb, depressed, consumed by anger and resentment, hopeless that my life would ever change. This was an unknown world for me—a world that no one seemed to understand, much less want to talk about.

My family and friends would question me about the absence of my husband at family gatherings, social events, and church. I tried to tell them about his PTSD, but I would get blank stares in return—even worse, devastating comments: He's playing the system. He's trying to get money. PTSD is a bunch of BS.

I was working from home, living 24/7 in this world of darkness. On the few occasions that I had to emerge from the house, I would put on my "happy" face, so no one knew the numbness that encased me. I, too, had become a stranger—and I didn't like the person I had become. I desperately wanted my life back. But I had no idea what had happened to me or where to begin.

I sought professional help. And learned that I, too, had PTSD.

I was advised to walk away from my marriage. But how could I walk away from a man who had been nineteen when he put his life on the line for our country? How could I turn my back on the man I had promised to care for "in sickness and in health?" Had my vows been meaningless?

I began learning everything I could about PTSD. I found tools and knowledge to help heal the wounds that this life had created. I realized that, in order to care for my husband, I needed to take time to care for my own mind, body, and spirit. I learned how to have love, compassion, and forgiveness for my husband and myself. And I've been able to joyfully honor the marriage vows that I made before God, my family, and my friends.

Then, when I learned about the millions of loved ones also caring for their veterans, I knew that I could make a difference in their lives. I could share what I had learned to help others get to a better place much quicker and easier than I had.

Who Can Benefit from This Book

My original intent was to write *A Stranger in My Bed* for spouses and loved ones caring for their veterans. However, as I became more aware of the needs, I saw benefits that could spread far beyond the spouses. While there is a growing awareness of PTSD today, there is still a huge stigma attached to it and lack of understanding of what Post-Traumatic Stress Disorder really is. Few people are aware that PTSD is "contagious," that those living with it can begin to take on the symptoms.

A Stranger in My Bed will support everyone touched by PTSD, especially the following people:

Veterans can learn how their PTSD is affecting their spouse and family. This may motivate them to seek out or stay in treatment. They will also learn that supporting their spouses for self-care will benefit them as well. They may learn about treatment options not currently familiar to them.

Friends, Relatives, and Loved Ones need to be educated in order for our veterans to receive the support they need—they need an education to remove the fear of the unknown and replace it with a community of supporters that understand how to show compassion for our warriors suffering from the invisible wounds of war.

Medical and Mental Health Professionals will gain a greater understanding of what is happening on a day-to-day basis inside the life of a family of a veteran suffering from PTSD. Greater understanding will lead to better support for both the veteran and the spouse with physical, mental, and emotional issues that are caused by living with PTSD.

Clergy and Marriage Counselors will be able to have a greater understanding of PTSD and the common spiritual and marital issues suffered by veterans. This will enhance their effectiveness in providing support, and spiritual and marital guidance.

Helping Professionals such as Social Workers, Recreation Therapists, and Coaches will gain a greater understanding of all aspects of PTSD, so they are better prepared to help spouses and families.

Substance Abuse and Domestic Violence Workers will gain a better understanding of PTSD and the effects on the family, to better identify when PTSD is in the picture and recommend proper treatment.

If PTSD becomes a chronic condition for those serving in current conflicts, as it has with Vietnam veterans, we are looking at many decades that our caregivers will be serving. It is crucial that they begin today to care for their own well-being, so they have the strength required for a lifetime of care for their veteran.

Please note that this book is written from the angle of female spouses and caregivers of male veterans with PTSD. However, we want to acknowledge that women soldiers can be equally affected by the trauma of war; this book is meant equally for male caregivers whose lives have been torn apart by PTSD.

What You'll Find in *A Stranger in My Bed*

Consider this your guidebook for navigating the treacherous and often mysterious road of living with your veteran's PTSD. Throughout the five sections, you will find information that will sometimes sadden you, but also enlighten, guide, and inspire you.

The journey begins with a love story. In part 1, I pull back the curtains to share the most intimate thoughts, feelings, even what I call the "jackass moments" from my own life with PTSD. The stories shared are of typical behaviors, symptoms, triggers, and problems that are part of everyday life with PTSD. Things that other spouses living in this world might read and think, *That sounds like my life—and I thought I was the only one.*

The goal of part 1 is to help you open up conversations about PTSD with someone you care about. It is often easier to start by saying, "Look at this couple," rather than revealing your own problems. I also want to give you hope that, with faith, work, and determination, life can get better.

Parts 2 and 3 give you the nitty-gritty specifics of PTSD, including what it is, what it looks like, how long it's been around, how it affects spirituality, how it's treated, and how many are affected. I have invited experts to give you a real-life perspective on both traditional therapy models and alternative therapy treatments.

Part 4 digs into the issues and problems that PTSD brings to a relationship— the why's and how-to's of living with normal relationship problems, how they become exaggerated by PTSD, and the unique problems brought into a relationship by PTSD. Top experts in the area of relationships and money add valuable information and tips in this section.

Part 5 is all about the spouse and caregiver. In "Secondary Stress Disorder: 8 Steps to Taking Your Life Back from the Contagious Effects of Your Veteran's PTSD," I have enlisted some of the best self-help experts in their respective fields to specifically address the needs and concerns of caring for *you* while living in the world of PTSD. This section will introduce you to Secondary Traumatic

Stress and the crippling effects of caregiver overwhelm. Eight strategic steps are then provided to give concrete information and help you step into action by:

1. Increasing knowledge and acceptance of your veteran's PTSD.
2. Uncovering your personal power.
3. Building your support system.
4. Moving away from pain, fear, and guilt to love, compassion, and forgiveness.
5. Treating the side effects of stress and overwhelm.
6. Cherishing your need for health and wellness.
7. Adding the sparkle of fun, happiness, and passion back into your life.
8. Learning how to put it all together.

In the final step, you'll be able to take the tools, tips, knowledge, and strategies that work for your unique situation and create your own GPS—goals, plans, and support system—to guide you on a detour to your "new normal"—a life that you have designed to meet your needs and your dreams.

An Invitation

In *A Stranger in My Bed*, Randy and I have opened up our lives to you, sharing things that family and friends will learn for the first time when they read the pages of this book. I kept it hidden; I was afraid to share the emotions of anger, fear, and loneliness that were destroying my life. I was afraid to let anyone know that I was "less than perfect." I am sharing this with you to encourage you to take action and to show you that a better life is truly possible.

Randy had no idea how deeply this world of PTSD had affected our entire family. I am not casting blame but offering compassion. Randy was lost in his own world of fear, anger, and pain—reliving horrors that I cannot even begin to imagine. He lost the ability to have compassion or concern for anyone other than himself. He was in survival mode.

And the good news is he survived. I survived. And our marriage survived. Our hope and prayer is that those who read this book will be helped to survive as well.

The purpose of this book is to address what our veteran's trauma will do to his family and his future. The particulars of Randy's experience are not shared because we believe that every veteran's story is equally important. We would like to acknowledge all soldiers for their service, their valor, their courage— even their fear.

Each veteran has a story that has become deeply embedded in his mind, a story that continues to affect his life today. Each of our veterans suffering from the trauma of war deserves to be honored and cared for. Each deserves our compassion and support for his service to our country.

Living in the world of PTSD is not the life that Randy and I had dreamed of—it's a life that challenges us every day. However, we are here, and we have found peace in the path that God has chosen for us.

Our prayer for you is that you will find hope in these pages and help to find peace within your own hearts and your own lives as well. It is also my heartfelt prayer that anyone caring for a wounded veteran be supported and inspired by what I have learned and so gratefully share in this book.

PART I

A STRANGER IN MY BED: OUR STORY

... to have and to hold from this day forward, for better for worse,
for richer for poorer, in sickness and in health,
to love, honor, and cherish, until death do us part.
This is my solemn vow.

Traditional wedding vow

CHAPTER I

IT BEGAN AS
A LOVE STORY

In 1991 my life was everything I had ever dreamed of. I was married to a tall, dark, handsome, Christian man, and we had two beautiful children, Aaron and Andrea. We lived in a beautiful, comfortable home, in a nice family neighborhood where the kids attended private Christian school. I had a prestigious job as executive director for a nonprofit organization that provided services to over 10,000 people, disabled adults and the elderly. My job was meaningful and provided a great sense of satisfaction.

I also served on numerous boards and advisory councils and was well respected in my community. I was active, healthy, able to find time to exercise and enjoy my family and friends. I had great friends, many of them since my childhood. I was active in our church, taught Sunday school, served on the school board. Our entire family attended church together every Sunday. I managed to balance work with being a mom, attending every track meet, basketball game, field trip, and school play. Yes, I had a full, balanced, and blessed life.

But then my dream ended, and I woke up to the harsh reality of a failed marriage. It turned out he had never really been in love with me: I was a rebound romance, attractive to him for my house, new car, job, and money in the bank. Our mutual interests began to disappear. He stopped going to church—and wanted the kids and me to stop also. Our relationship was cold and empty. We didn't talk, we didn't laugh, we weren't friends. I continued to hold on because of our kids, until one night the words just came out of my mouth that I didn't want to be married to him anymore. A huge weight was lifted from my shoulders.

I found myself in a new life as a single working mother. Seeing my children every other week. Struggling to keep them in their school, in the home they loved, and in the neighborhood filled with their friends. My neighborhood girlfriends, whom I had become very close to, suddenly became distant and hurtful. I was now a divorcee and no longer fit in. Their husbands became fearful of having me near their wives, thinking that this affliction of divorce might be contagious.

★ ★ ★ ★ ★

Dating after thirteen years of marriage was a very new experience. My first shot at it was with a man that had two children, close in age to my own. He was ambitious, strong, and caring. He held one of the most powerful positions in the county. He made me feel important, secure, and loved—everything that had been missing in my marriage.

But after a year, I realized that dating a man with kids was not a good idea. Despite his love for children, and the focus we put on making lots of time for the kids when we were together, I could see how difficult this was on Aaron and Andrea. Their dad had become engaged to a woman with two children, and I could see how the loss of attention from both of us was affecting them. Having to share the time and fight for the attention of their parents was not fair to these two innocent children, whose lives had been torn apart through no fault of their own.

My next attempts at dating resulted in lots of first dates—until I met Steven. Although he had never married, he had an eighteen-year-old daughter who was living with him and would soon be off to college. He was quite fine seeing me every other week; he enjoyed his alone time and had no intention of getting into a committed relationship.

He shared with me that he had recently gone through a very serious scare with cancer, and so far had beaten the odds. He still required check-ups every six months and didn"t want to get involved with anyone, fearing that his cancer would return. My response to him was, "You know there's no guarantee for any of us, and I could get hit by a truck tomorrow."

Steven was an attorney. He was smart, polite, and ethical. He revived my love of skiing and golf, which had been set aside since early in my marriage. He took pleasure in attending social events with me at his side. He was a gourmet cook and took great delight in "entertaining me."

This was a workable situation for my life as a single mother. One week totally committed to my children, the next week delegated to working late, caring for my house and half-acre yard, with a healthy dose of an adult social life, fun, and recreation tossed in.

So when my fortieth birthday arrived, although I wasn't living the life I had dreamed of, it was working and I was content.

But two days later, my life turned into an unimaginable nightmare that fully engulfed me the next five months. Ten-year-old Aaron suddenly became ill, and overnight we were faced with the diagnosis of an inoperable, malignant brainstem tumor. Five horrible, indescribable months later he died in my arms.

★ ★ ★ ★ ★

During that time Steven became my rock. We had barely been dating six months, but he stood by me, an invaluable ally, helping me through what seemed like insurmountable obstacles that continued to arise throughout the five-month battle.

When Aaron was first diagnosed, he was immediately flown to University of California San Francisco (UCSF) Medical Center; I was told that he might not even survive the flight. He had surgery immediately upon arrival to insert a shunt to ease the pressure from the fluid on his brain. But the bigger problem was the tumor, which was inoperable. The only possible treatment was experimental, which Aaron's health insurance did not cover.

My parents, Steven, and my best friend, Mary, all drove the four hours to San Francisco to be with me. When Steven learned what was happening, he immediately took action. As an attorney familiar with the process, he was able to have the case reviewed—and Aaron's treatment was approved for insurance coverage.

Two months later Aaron's treatment was stopped. It was not working. The doctors put us in contact with the Make-a-Wish Foundation, which granted Aaron's wish for a trip to Disney World. But while in Orlando, Aaron's condition worsened and he went into a coma. Because no further treatment options were available, the hospital in Orlando wanted to discharge Aaron. The insurance company was not willing to pay to fly him home to California, because the trip had been for "social reasons."

So there I was, in Orlando, alone with my child in a coma, and no viable options in sight. Fortunately, Steven, at home in California, again went to work, and within a few days we were on a Learjet bringing Aaron home.

My family was steadfast in their love, devotion, and care during Aaron's illness. My church family was faithful with their prayers and support. My friends, as well as total strangers, offered unbelievable gifts of kindness. My staff was amazing in their generosity and concern. But most important was the gift of faith and support I received from my Lord. He gave me the confidence to put the outcome of Aaron's illness in his hands, giving me the strength to get through the most horrible experience of my life.

Each day I would pray for strength, and somehow each day that strength was there to help me make it through. Aaron's faith, too, stayed strong to his dying breath. He went through his journey with strength and courage, never questioning or complaining about the lot that had been given him. I could not have asked for a greater gift than to know without a doubt that at the moment of Aaron's death he went directly from my loving arms into God's.

★ ★ ★ ★ ★

Andrea's entire world was rocked. For five months she had been pushed back and forth between relatives. Her life was put on the back burner as Aaron became foremost in everyone's thoughts, prayers, and actions. When it was all over, and everyone was back to their own lives, it was my beautiful little seven-year-old daughter who showed up with wondrous strength, faith, and wisdom.

Andrea gave me hope, courage, love, and faith to go on, even though a part of me had died with Aaron. We missed him beyond words, but we had such comfort in knowing that he was safe with God, and that we could go on.

Andrea's vision of Aaron in heaven, building Lego castles while eating spaghetti and chocolate mint ice cream, warmed my heart and replaced the   vision of his suffering, embedded in my mind. Together, Andrea and I could share our memories of Aaron. We could talk about him freely, without the discomfort that those around us would show when his name was spoken. Together we healed and continued to keep Aaron in a very special place in our hearts.

It was difficult to return to work, not only because of my sadness over the loss of Aaron, but because of all the sadness that surrounded me. What had previously been a job filled with so much satisfaction, despite the constant struggles raising money to continue programs and services, changed after Aaron's death. Seeing people who were sick, suffering, hungry, and poor, struggling to buy medication and to keep a roof over their head, became much more difficult for me with each passing day.

★ ★ ★ ★ ★

One morning in March 1995, a client came in to see me who had been a customer years before when I had my travel company. She related how embarrassed she was to have to ask for help, but her husband had had a stroke and was now in a convalescent hospital; she just couldn't make ends meet.

As she looked at me with tears in her eyes, she said, "You know I see Harvey every day. He doesn't remember much of our life, but he does remember our Alaska cruise and what a wonderful time we had. Every day our life is now brightened by the cruise that you took us on."

Her words touched my heart, and my tears joined hers. I held very vivid and fond memories of her husband, and that cruise. I remembered how even in their seventies they looked like newlyweds experiencing life and love for the very first time. I recalled watching them and thinking, *I want that; I want what they have.*

When I got home that evening there was a message from a man I had met over ten years before. He was the owner of a large tour and motor-coach company. To my amazement, his message relayed that he had a business opportunity that he wanted to discuss with me. He wondered if I would have time for a dinner meeting, if he made the five-hour drive from Nevada. Having no idea what to expect, I called him back and accepted his request for a meeting.

A few days later I was having dinner with William, the president of the company; Dennis, the vice-president; and Leo, the manager of the motor coach division. To my amazement, William knew more about me than I knew about myself. Every accomplishment, every job, even things that I had no idea how he might have learned about. All good things!

I actually felt a bit uncomfortable with his knowledge—as if he had had me investigated prior to our meeting. But he had tracked me down to offer me a job. He was planning to open a new division in Northern California and wanted me to set it up and run it for him.

It was an offer I couldn't refuse. A higher salary, company car, opportunity for travel—he even threw in a golf membership at the local country club. Not to mention this position would be working with people that were happy, healthy, fulfilling their dreams, and creating memories that would last a lifetime.

The job was exactly what I needed right then. As difficult as it would be to walk away from all the people who had supported me through such a painful time, I knew that my answer to William would be yes. God's perfect timing had brought me Ann and Harvey's story—on the same day as William's call. It was time to see joy and happiness in our life again.

★ ★ ★ ★ ★

Life eventually settled back into a routine for Andrea and me. She was happy, excelling academically, and had become very close to her friends at school. She loved my new job. William, the president of the company, was very family oriented and allowed me to take her on trips with me. She got to experience things that I would never have been able to provide for her otherwise: Broadway plays, famous art museums, professional sports events, the Pasadena Rose Parade, and many more extraordinary happy times. It was a very positive change for the two of us.

Over the past few years Andrea had grown apart from the kids in the neighborhood. Some had moved away, others attended different schools, and they rarely saw each other. When Andrea was twelve she told me that she was ready to move from the neighborhood she had grown up in. We had talked for several years about getting a smaller house with a yard that was easier to maintain. I didn't want to move her from this house and this neighborhood until she was ready. It wasn't just a house; it was here in this living room that we had said good-bye to Aaron. She had had enough in her young life to deal with; staying in this house was the least I could do for her.

We loved our new house; our yard looked out over a pond and a golf course—a beautiful view that someone else got to maintain. It was time to leave the memories of our broken family and our broken hearts behind.

★ ★ ★ ★ ★

Another year came and went, and Steven was again in the picture. He had been in and out of our lives for seven years, unable to make a commitment. He continued to break my heart over and over with his disappearing acts.

In the meantime I had dated and kissed a lot of frogs—none turning out to be even remotely close to a Prince Charming. Steven had taken a new job with better pay in another city. He talked about a future together, but I didn't hold much hope for that to happen. Besides, Andrea never really connected with him, and his constant trampling on my heart did not endear him to my family and friends.

February 14, 2000 was another disappointing Valentine's Day. I went to sleep resigned to the fact that I would never marry again, never feel the love my heart yearned for. It had been absent in my marriage and seemed destined never to be. That love I felt only in my dreams, from a stranger whose face was so familiar, though I had never met him.

Suddenly, there he was, standing in front of me, that same familiar face, his arms reaching out to hold me, his eyes assuring me that he was ready to love me just the way I needed. The church bells were gently ringing in the background . . . the feeling of love engulfed me with a calm I had never felt before.

BUZZZZZZZZZZZZZZZZ.

Startled by the noise, I jerked awake. I glanced around my familiar room. My heart sank. His familiar face was in my mind—I could still feel the tenderness of his touch—and the love in his eyes was still warming me. Overcome by feelings of immense sorrow and disbelief, I slowly climbed out of bed.

My alarm had rudely awakened me to reality and the day in front of me. I was not looking forward to this trip. It was our annual VIP customer appreciation event in Reno, which involved long days in which I had to provide lots of TLC to my customers. That part would have been fine had I not had to jump on a plane at the end of the event, leaving my customers alone for their trip home. Due to someone else's poor planning, I would have to leave the group in Reno to fly to San Francisco to meet another group that I was escorting on a trip to New York City.

I had been up late the night before preparing for the bus trip to Reno, and the New York trip. I was so excited that I was able to take Andrea along to New York, because the trip included a performance of *Lion King*, just out on Broadway. I had also gotten tickets for Andrea and me to see the Broadway performance of *Beauty and the Beast*, one of her favorite Disney stories. My mother and some of her friends were also going on the trip, so I had no worries of Andrea traveling with the group to San Francisco without me.

I arrived at the bus yard just before 6:00 a.m. It was still dark, with hard, cold raindrops bouncing off my windshield. I reluctantly climbed out of my car and pulled the hood of my coat a little bit tighter around my head, trying to stay dry in the downpour before having to greet my customers.

As I walked through the parking lot dodging mud puddles, I saw that the bus lights were on. I was relieved to see that the driver was here preparing for the trip. I never knew what to expect with our drivers, but this morning, so far, so good. As I rounded the corner I saw Ed, my favorite driver, tall and lean, with distinguished gray hair and a smile as big as his heart. I could always depend on him to do a great job. In this industry the favorite saying was "a bad driver is easy to find," and our company had found plenty.

As I got closer, I saw another man step out of the bus. He was dwarfed standing there next to Ed's six-foot-four frame. Rather than the company navy blue winter coat, he wore a brown leather bomber jacket. I couldn't see his face in the gloomy light. My heart sank as I thought, *Looks like Ed's not my driver after all.* I joined them, and the three of us stood in the pouring rain as Ed introduced me to the new driver, Randy.

As our hands touched for the obligatory handshake we looked up at each other for the first time, and our eyes met. There, standing in front of me, dazzling baby blue eyes looking into mine, was the man from my dreams.

★ ★ ★ ★ ★

Year after year men came and went in my life. I did not recognize them; none had the familiar face, the warmth in their smile that came with the man in my dreams. But in that moment, standing in the pouring rain, on that cold and gloomy morning of February 15, 2000, there he was, the man I had dreamed of all those years, standing in front of me. He had finally arrived. I say it was love at first sight, but actually I had been in love with him long before our eyes finally met.

I had given up on love. Thirteen years of marriage to a man that I never felt love from. Nine years of dating, seven of those on and off with a man who was incapable of commitment, unable to say the words "I love you." I had been waiting, and hoping. Another disappointing Valentine's Day and then—there he was.

My customers had all met Randy months before I did, and they loved him, especially the little elderly ladies. He fondly referred to them as "blue hairs." And they lovingly referred to him as "blue eyes" in their letters and phone calls requesting him as their driver. Somehow for months he had eluded me, until that rainy morning.

When the trip began, I tended to my customers and Randy to his driving. I just couldn't get him out of my mind as I sat directly behind him on the four-hour drive across the mountains. He was so close I could have reached out and touched him, yet so far away. It may have just been my imagination, but it seemed that he held my hand just a little too long each time he helped me off the bus. Every time, that touch was electric. It warmed me to my core on that cold wintry day.

I had a full schedule of events to attend that evening in Reno. When Randy dropped us off, I said good night and joked about him being single. I said I had someone "in mind for him." To my disappointment he smiled and said that would be nice—when could he meet her? I had meant me.

Later that evening, when I finished up with everyone, I gathered my courage and called Randy to tell him that I had left something on the bus. The drivers were staying across town at a different hotel, but without hesitation he quickly said, "I'll be right there." He must have flown, because I had no more walked out the front entrance of the hotel than he was there, smiling at me and asking, "What did you leave on the bus?"

Embarrassed by my boldness, I answered, "You."

★ ★ ★ ★ ★

We found a quiet place in the lounge and talked and laughed for hours. I can still remember the smell of his leather jacket, the scent of his cologne, the twinkle in his blue eyes, the smile that lit up his entire being, his handsome tanned face, the cute dimple in his chin, the dishwater blond hair—everything so new, and yet so familiar. The exact man that had been in my dreams all those years.

The next day, Randy and my fifty VIP customers dropped me off at the Reno airport. One hundred eyes were upon us as he helped me off the bus, and I waited on the sidewalk for him to retrieve my suitcase. And then, blind to those one hundred eyes, he hugged me good-bye.

As I flew across the country, I wondered what the future would bring. Randy was a driver, and I was a regional sales manager. Not the best combination for a relationship, and not one that the company we worked for would look kindly on.

Six days later I arrived with my group at the San Francisco airport. With thirteen-year-old Andrea at my side, I scanned the baggage claim area looking for our driver. To my surprise, there was Randy. My heart stopped. What would my daughter think of him? She had not liked one single man I had dated in nine years.

We walked towards each other, then Randy's arms went around me, not in a quick friendship greeting, but a powerful, make-my-knees-shake-and-my-heart-tremble kind of hug. The kind of hug that made my daughter and my mom, who were standing nearby, stop and take notice.

"Who is that?" Andrea demanded.

"Just the driver," I replied.

"Hum," was her response, the sound of disbelief in her tone.

To my surprise the bus was filled with drinks and snacks. Questioning, I looked at Randy.

"Oh, I knew it was a long trip and thought it might be nice for the passengers," Randy nonchalantly whispered.

He was right. Our flight from New York, with forty-six people in our group, had been canceled that morning. Finally, twelve long hours later, we had arrived in San Francisco, and still had a four-hour bus trip home. A long day was putting it mildly, but instantly Randy had made it better. I was amazed by his thoughtfulness and generosity. That just wasn't the kind of thing that drivers did, especially on their own initiative.

We talked all the way home, as the passengers dozed off after the long day. When we arrived at the final stop, I was nervous. I wasn't really sure what would happen next—whether Randy would call, if we would we see each other again, or what the future would hold for us.

Randy had to leave the next day for another trip that would take him away for a few days, but he promised to call when he got home. True to his word, he called and invited me to dinner. I wondered how something that felt so right could also feel so wrong.

We were both seeing someone else. For Randy, it was a relatively short-term relationship, and she lived three states away in Colorado. He had only seen her a few of times since moving here four months earlier.

And then there was Steven. Our on-and-off again relationship over the course of nearly seven years. I thought that I loved him. I had great appreciation for him and the way he had stood by me through Aaron's illness. But I also knew I was settling for less than the kind of love I needed and desired—and that I was worthy of.

As I watched Randy lovingly serve the dinner he had so carefully prepared for me, I knew that there was an undeniable connection that had to be explored. Here in front of me was a man who quickly warmed my heart with his care and consideration for all those around him. His wonderful sense of humor kept us laughing for hours on end. And his looks melted me from the first moment I laid eyes on him. He was the most charming man I had ever met.

We talked about us, our possibilities, and our feelings. We agreed that if we were to explore a relationship, we both needed to be free. Our connection had happened so quickly, we were amazed at how real it felt to both of us.

To pursue Randy, and the unknown, after such a very short time of knowing him, presented me with a very big decision. I would have to end a relationship with the man who had stood next to me during the most difficult time in my life, my son's losing battle with cancer—a man I loved, but who was incapable of returning that love to me.

★ ★ ★ ★ ★

After knowing Randy less than three weeks and only seeing him a handful of times, I chose him. However, there was one big obstacle in the way. I was scheduled to go on a cruise with Steven in two weeks. Randy begged me not to go, and even offered to pay the cancellation penalty, an expense I knew he could not afford on his driver's salary. But I couldn't do that to Steven—I knew I had to talk to him in person. I knew I had to do it the right way—if there was any right way. But I had already made my decision.

I didn't wait long to tell Steven that I had met someone else. Our trip started off rough. We met at the Sacramento airport, where our scheduled flight to San Diego was canceled, causing us a delay. When we finally arrived in San Diego, Steven's bags were lost. His impatience and lack of people skills became quite evident. The worst of him was coming out, and making the best of Randy shine even brighter.

Since he was already in a foul mood, I thought I might as well get it over with. I told him that I had met someone that I had a very strong connection with, someone I felt I might have a future with, and I needed the opportunity to know for sure.

His response was not at all what I had expected. With panic in his eyes, he looked at me and said, "I'll marry you today. I'll go talk to the ship's captain right now and make the arrangements. I had been planning to start giving you money for your house payment; I know you've been struggling, and I've been wanting to help you. With my new job, now I can. Didn't I do a good job at Christmas? I thought I did really well this year. I tried really hard, and it was actually fun."

I stood there, speechless for a moment, trying to choose my words carefully. I knew the step that Steven had just taken was huge for him. Gently, I began, "Yes, you were very generous and extremely thoughtful at Christmas. Steven, I have waited and wished for those words for five years. But not now, and not this way. If you had wanted to marry me, you would have done it before now, or at least talked about it with me. I love you, but we both know that you are not capable of loving me the way I need to be loved. I know you are doing the best you can. But I know it's just not enough for me. Seven years, and you still can't say the words "I love you."

"But I've been trying so hard this time."

With tears in my eyes, I gently said, "I know, but I'm afraid it's too late."

Steven and I tried to make the best of our cruise, each spending our days going different directions and coming together in the dining room at our assigned table for an uncomfortable dinner. He was hurt and angry, but he knew I was right. As we parted in the airport at the end of the cruise, he looked at me and said, "Well, if this thing goes to hell in a handbag, give me a call." I silently walked away and didn't look back.

I grabbed the shuttle to the long-term parking, and there, sitting on my red Jeep Cherokee, was Randy. He had been waiting four hours, after taking the three-hour bus trip to Sacramento and then a taxi to the airport. Thank goodness he had respected my request and not met me at the gate; I could not have done that to Steven.

In the meantime, he had also ended his relationship. Now we were both free to see where this would lead. We had decided it would be best to keep it from our co-workers; we needed to have time without those eyes looking on.

We quickly became inseparable whenever our schedules allowed. Andrea was warming up to him. I laughed when she told me she thought he was "quite a hunk for an old guy."

Randy was wonderful! We laughed endlessly. I couldn't remember ever in my life laughing so much. We played golf; we danced in the kitchen while we cooked. We spent hours in the hot tub sipping whatever special concoction Randy had dreamed up, and we talked endlessly about our pasts and our dreams for the future.

The fact that he had been married three times had seemed like a deal breaker at the beginning. Andrea's rules for me were simple: 1) no attorneys, 2) no bald men (Steve was bald), and 3) no one who had been married more than one time. Things can happen the first time she said, but more than that, there's a problem. She had actually written down these rules and presented them to me on one occasion. Pretty wise words for a thirteen-year-old, but Andrea was wise beyond her years and had experienced a life that had forced her to grow up quickly.

So when Randy came along he fit the first two rules, but not the third. He had just ended his third marriage when he decided to move home to Shasta County, back to where he had been raised. He did have a very good explanation for each marriage and why it had failed. And, of course, it was never his fault. I loved him and believed everything he told me. He was the man of my dreams, so no need to worry. He also shared a glimpse of his financial situation with me. That too, was understandable: after three divorces, of course he had no money.

Day after day we fell more and more in love with each other, and the more Andrea was around Randy, the more she liked him. On the six-month anniversary of the day we had met, the three of us were driving to Chevy's for dinner. My dear Andrea commented on the full moon, suggesting that it would be a great night for a proposal.

Embarrassed, I quickly said, "Andrea! Hush!"

In the middle of dinner Randy said, "Well, Andrea since you brought it up . . ." As he continued, a little blue box appeared on the table. "Andrea, would it be okay with you if I asked your mom to marry me?" He went on to say, "I know you have a dad, but I would like to be part of your life. Would that be okay?"

Her face was beaming, smiling from ear to ear. She looked at me and said, "Well, Mom, what do you have to say?"

In unison, Andrea and I both said, "YES!"

Two months later, on October 28, 2000, we were married. We had a beautiful wedding, with Andrea my maid of honor and Randy's son, Sean, his best man. All the arrangements had fallen into place perfectly, and we were amazed at the instant bond between our kids. Randy's two grown children, Sean and Rhonda, were there with their spouses, Alison and Jeremy. They all welcomed their new sister, Andrea, into their world with open arms.

My dreams had come true. I was happier than I had ever been. I felt loved as I had never felt loved before. Life was wonderful.

Our Wedding Day, October 28, 2000

CHAPTER 2

THE
CHRISTMAS
GIFT

The bliss of our honeymoon continued for six months. We loved the time we shared together, and our new family grew closer by the day. Andrea adored Randy. He was caring and supportive, attending all her games and school functions and showing genuine interest in her life. He would boast about her accomplishments and outstanding academic excellence like a proud papa to anyone who would listen.

A few financial surprises popped up from Randy's past, but I dealt with them and figured it was worth digging into my savings to clean the slate. Another ripple showed up when Randy came home one day and announced that he had just quit his job driving. There'd been no discussion with me—he'd just flat quit.

The timing was not good; I had just refinanced the house to a fifteen-year mortgage. We had discussed this in depth, and Randy had assured me that he would help with the increased house payment. This was all part of our road-to-retirement plan and living the life of our dreams.

It didn't take Randy much time to get a new job, a minimum-wage position doing manual labor at a landscape rock yard. Just like his driving, it seemed a little foreign and beneath his skill set, especially in view of his past life in the navy working in the Pentagon, then moving into the private sector of Martin Marietta Aerospace as a project manager. His explanation was that the stress of those positions had gotten to him. "Besides," he would always add, "you would not have liked me in those days."

I did look forward to having him home at nights. Although his work schedule still included weekends, with a day job he at least had normal hours now. His driving schedule had always been so erratic, with crazy schedules leaving his sleep patterns totally messed up.

Unfortunately, even with the new job his sleep was still disturbed; he often stayed up until it was time for me to get up in the morning. From the beginning of our marriage I had encouraged him to come to bed to watch TV until he fell asleep. I wanted to have him by my side. Driving kept him away from home so frequently; I yearned for the comfort of having him close. He agreed and watched his late-night war movies as I lay next to him and did my best to sleep with the sound of gunfire blaring in my ears. But at least he was there.

By our second anniversary he was on his fourth job since our wedding day, and just like the first time, he had left each job without a word in advance to me. This time, though, it was a job he loved. He was working as a court clerk in a department full of women, who fondly nicknamed him "the rooster." He seemed very happy; he even met a new friend in the Marshall's office with whom he soon began playing golf and having lunch.

★ ★ ★ ★ ★

One morning as I was getting ready for work, I felt an excruciating pain in my abdomen—as if a knife had pierced my stomach. I doubled over in agony, unable to move. When I finally caught my breath, I called Randy. He couldn't get away until lunch, and by the time he got home, I had been in pure torture for four hours. He found me lying on the couch doubled up, tears of pain still streaming down my face.

He immediately called the doctor and rushed me to his office. They discovered a ruptured ovarian cyst, which had to be surgically removed. But the pain continued so there were more tests, and more pain. A blood test showed positive for the possibility of ovarian cancer. But the test is not always accurate, and it often has a false positive; the only way to know for sure would be a hysterectomy.

I would need to be off work for eight weeks, so I called William to let him know and began to make the necessary arrangements. It wasn't a surprise to him; I had been keeping the office informed about what was going on. When I came out of surgery, I not only had the good news of no cancer, but also a beautiful bouquet of flowers and balloons from William and the staff at the corporate office. Five days later when I was released from the hospital and got settled in at home, another equally beautiful bouquet arrived from William, along with a personal call to check on my condition.

I really appreciated his concern, although it wasn't surprising that he showed so much care and compassion. Despite his explosive temper at times, he had been very kind and accommodating to me since I'd begun working for him. He'd been part of our love story, having driven ten hours in pouring rain to attend our wedding. He'd allowed me to expand Andrea's young world in many ways that I would never have been able to afford without his generosity. Truth was he'd practically become family during these past eight years since that first surprising phone call.

He also knew that I put in way beyond my required hours. He knew he could depend on me to be at every sales meeting, trade show, and special event, working long days and nights, keeping customers happy "until my smile hurt." He knew he could depend on me to step in at a minute's notice on any trip, with anyone's customers, and do a job that left every client happy.

I returned to work the week before Christmas, to my assistant's delight. Although I had kept up on as much work as I could from home, and was always available to him by phone, Jake just felt better having me back in the office to deal with the "hard decisions," as he put it.

Earlier in the week we had received a memo from the corporate office telling us that we could close at noon on December 24, 2002. It was nice to know that we could start our holiday early this year—William wasn't always that generous. I was trying to get the last project on my desk completed, so that I could actually get out of the office by noon. It was Christmas Eve and I had plenty to finish up before our family festivities began that evening.

The phone rang at 11:00 a.m., disturbing the silence in the office. Jake told me it was Bob Young, the CFO in the corporate office. I didn't know Bob very well—he was relatively new to the company and we had had only a few short conversations. It wasn't time for the monthly financial reports to be sent, so I hesitated a moment before picking up the phone, wondering why he might be calling.

Without any preamble he simply said, "William is closing your office. He would like to know what it would take for you to buy it. By the way, he needs his answer by noon today. He also said to not even consider starting up on your own. You signed a non-compete agreement, and if you say no, he will sell the business to your competitor."

Bob continued to explain that the future of the company was unknown, and that I would need to find an alternate source for motor coaches and tour products. I would be buying the customer list and the "goodwill" that I had established since opening the office eight years before.

My head was spinning. I was angry, but not surprised. I was angry and hurt that William had not had the courage to discuss this with me himself, but rather had sent a virtual stranger to do his dirty work. However, I was not surprised by the decision; four of the motor coach divisions in California had been closed within the past six months, including the one in Redding, where I lived. What had once been one of the largest bus and tour companies in the country had been falling apart piece by piece since the owner's affair and a messy divorce that had torn the family-owned company apart.

Merry Christmas to me. A great salary, health benefits, company car, country club membership—gone! I was numb. Jake poked his head into my office. I knew he was curious about the call, and generally, I freely shared with him what was going on. But at this moment I had no words. I could not send him away today with this weighing on his mind. He deserved to enjoy his holidays while I figured out what I was going to do.

★ ★ ★ ★ ★

How could I run a bus tour company with no buses? How could I pay the overhead for the office and Jake's salary while I recreated the business? How could I do all the tasks that were now fully supported by the corporate office?

The alternative was no job and no income, in a city where jobs paying above minimum wage were few and far between. Although Randy loved his job at the courthouse, he made half of what I did. With a daughter in high school and college in the very near future, I was in a very difficult situation.

But I was always up for a challenge, and this was no exception. I knew I would have to say yes and do whatever it took to make this work. But how? Now, suddenly, I was going to be all alone. I had clients, lots of clients. But I had no bus company, and no products to sell.

I moved the office to my home into a spare room and filled my garage with desks, filing cabinets, and boxes. I had a big job in front of me. I now had to do not only what I normally did on a daily basis, but also the job done by ten others, plus all the details of starting many aspects of the business from scratch. With a heavy heart, I let my assistant go. In all my years as a manager I had never had a more dependable, loyal employee.

As I worked twelve to fourteen hours a day, my pain came back. After running more tests and finding nothing, the doctor told me there was nothing wrong. He said it was stress, so he put me on Paxil to "help me cope with the overwhelm."

I was too embarrassed to tell anyone that I was not able to handle the stress and overload on my own. Not my best friend, not even Randy. Not only were the long hours taking their toll on me, but my sleep was also being affected. Randy's sleep patterns had still not changed at all, even with his eight-to-five job. He was still up until early morning hours watching war movies, and then would come home from work at 5:30 p.m. and take a nap until I went to bed. It left little time for us, and also little support for the help I needed both around the house and with the business.

After a short time, I discontinued the Paxil. I didn't like the way it made me feel, nor the weight gain it created.

We struggled; my paycheck had been twice what Randy was making at the courthouse. Now I had no salary; my income was totally dependent on commissions, and I had the extra expenses of the business. Andrea was now a senior in high school, college bound with goals and plans for her future. She had wanted to be a doctor since she was a little girl, and I had been saving her entire life for her college, but with today's tuition costs, what I had saved would barely cover her first year.

I had enjoyed the luxury of a college education without having to work, able to devote my full time and attention to learning. I had also been able to enjoy the important growth that happens in college with new friendships and college life. I wanted the same for Andrea.

Then, like a gift from heaven, a motor coach company not only agreed to move buses to Redding to service our business, but also to paying me the same salary that I had just lost to become their sales representative and manage their bus charters. There was only one caveat: they needed to have full-time driver dedicated to servicing my client base, and they wanted Randy to be that person. So just short of a year with the courts, he put his driving cap back on, as well as the crazy schedules that came with it.

CHAPTER 3

HAPPY BIRTHDAY TO ME

This new twist in our life seemed to be working out fine; working from home actually came with unforeseen benefits. I was able to spend more time with Andrea for one. It was great to be there when she got home from school, and she was a tremendous help to me in the office. Randy was staying busy driving, and I was immersed in the very busy job of managing the tour and charter business. Our schedules were crazy, but we were doing what we needed to do to make ends meet. The owners of the new motor coach company were wonderful, a pleasure to work with.

But six months after we started working with the new company, I received a fax. The company had been sold. The new owner had decided to take the business in "another direction." And that did not include Randy or me. The fax terminated our arrangement—effective immediately.

Fortunately, one of their prime competitors was standing by; they jumped at the opportunity to start doing business in the Redding area. However, they only agreed to give me discounted rates on charter buses; they had their own staff and no need for any further services. They readily offered Randy a job driving.

The day had been saved! The new company was eager to take over all of our charter business. They were concerned about whether they would be able to cover all the trips and wanted to immediately get all of our charter trip information so they could begin making the necessary plans. They even told us they would purchase additional motor coaches if necessary to be able to take care of our customers. Our business was able to continue, seamlessly providing charter services without any disruption to our customers.

We had been working with the new company for three months, and everything was going well. Our customers were happy, Randy was happy, and I was extremely happy. It was such a relief to have a reliable company with new equipment and professional drivers. The owners were easy to work with and had been very accommodating to our needs. They had even purchased a new bus exclusively for the Redding area and had assigned Randy to drive it.

One afternoon I received a call from the owner telling me they were faxing over a revised invoice for the next morning's trip. When it hit my desk, I hit the ceiling. They had increased the price of the charter eight hundred dollars! There had been no changes to the trip on my part, no extra miles or hours. I sat in disbelief, thinking this must be a mistake. I picked the phone up and called the owner, who nonchalantly said, "No, the price is correct; we have decided to increase our prices!"

"I can't ask my customer to pay this much more on the night before the trip. And we have a contract for the previous price."

"Too bad, this is what it is," he answered coolly.

Too shocked for words, I silently put the phone down. Clearly they had used me to get their foot in the door, and now after gleaning my customer list, were ready to push me out and take it over.

What was I to do now? This business had been nothing but headaches and hard work. I'd always prided myself on honesty and integrity; I just couldn't understand how I continued to have this happen.

I flashed on a memory. A while back a driver had told Randy that the owner of a small bus company in Sacramento had been asking how he could work with us. I called Randy and told him what was going on. He was furious. Frantically I asked, "Can you find out who that man was and get me a phone number?"

"I'll get back to you as soon as I can," he said, and he was gone.

My heart was pounding with anger and anticipation. I had to fix this; I could not let them get away with this.

Minutes later Randy called back. "Got it; ready to write?"

I held my breath as I dialed the number, praying he would answer and that he would have a bus and driver available on such short notice.

The phone rang again and again, until finally a man's voice, barely audible because of the static on the line, said, "Hello."

I tried to tell him who I was and what I needed, but the static on the line prevented him from hearing me.

"Can't talk now, don't have good service. I'll get back to you later."

Great! Later—what did that mean, later today, later this week? I was left without an ounce of confidence that I would get a call back, let alone have my problem taken care of.

I had no other alternative if this company was not able to help me. I would have to pay the extra $800 out of my own pocket. I could not ask my customer to pay extra money, and I could not simply cancel their trip. I felt totally violated . . . again.

Still lost in my disgust and anger, I was startled by the sharp ringing of the phone.

"Hello," said the male voice, "sorry I couldn't talk before. I wasn't in a good area."

I began to tell him who I was when he abruptly stopped me, "Oh, I know who you are. I've been wanting to talk to you."

I explained my dilemma and asked if there was any way that he might be able to help.

"Hmmm" was the answer. "Let me call you back." And with that he abruptly hung up. He had offered no words of hope—not a *maybe* or a *possibly*—just hung up the phone.

He called back in ten minutes, but to me it seemed as if it had been ten hours.

Yes, he would be able to do the trip. My heart stopped when he gave me the price. It was less than my original price with the other company.

I let out an enormous sigh of relief, "Thank you so much—that's great. By the way, are you interested in doing more trips for us?"

Without hesitation he said, "Yes, that would be good."

"Do you want all of our business?" I asked. "Can you handle all my trips?"

With that question, there was a long silent pause. Then, "Yes. I would need to get another bus, but I've been looking at one. Maybe you can go to Los Angeles with me to help pick one out."

By the time we hung up every last booking had been moved over. A leap of faith, a man I had never met, and buses I had never seen. I had just been burned, again. But this man came with good recommendations, and I chose to trust him.

I picked the phone up and canceled the next day's trip. "And, by the way, make that everything else you have booked for me while you're at it," I added with great satisfaction.

At the same time Randy was making arrangements to move over to the new company as their driver. Again we had worked as a team to make it through life's challenges together.

★ ★ ★ ★ ★

The business was running smoothly, Randy was happy driving, and life was good. It seemed as though the past three years had flown by . . . though not without headaches. We had planned a Caribbean cruise for November 2003 to celebrate my fiftieth birthday. Turning forty had been followed by the absolute worst event in my life (my son falling ill two days later), so I was approaching this next milestone with a bit of fear and apprehension.

After all the turmoil of the last few years, we were looking forward to having a great time with the family and friends that were joining us. We were delighted that even Randy's brother, Brent, and his wife, Tweedy, were coming along.

As I began preparing for the cruise, I found that all my summer clothes were suddenly too tight. I was forced to shop for the next size up, vowing that I would get back into my exercise routine as soon as I got home.

In all, forty people joined us on the cruise: family, friends, and some of my dear customers. They were all excited to help me celebrate my fiftieth birthday, as well as visit the amazing ports on our itinerary.

The second day out, our port of call was Cozumel, Mexico. Randy, Brent, Brent's friend Mike, and I went to play golf. It was a beautiful golf course moving from dense jungles to amazing ocean views. We had just finished a great first hole and were all preparing to hit our approach shot to the second green. I was walking down a steep incline to my ball, my eyes focused on an alligator lying near the green.

Suddenly, the most excruciating pain I had ever felt swept through my entire body. My head was spinning. I had no idea what had happened, but I suddenly felt as though I had been struck by a bolt of lightning. The pain was so severe it froze me; I couldn't move or speak. I had stepped in a hole that was camouflaged by the tall grass, lurched forward, hyperextended my knee, and, as I would learn later, torn my meniscus.

The guys were yelling at me to move so they could hit, but I just stood there in agony, frozen, not able to turn around and look back up the hill.

With my back still to him, I kept waving at Randy, trying to motion him to come down the hill to where I was standing. He just kept yelling at me to move so he could hit his ball. The pain had silenced my voice, and I was afraid if I tried to yell the tears would come. I motioned, he yelled, I motioned, he yelled, back and forth until, frustrated at my lack of compliance, he drove the cart down to where I stood.

When he saw my face, he knew instantly something was wrong. I pointed to my knee and managed to tell him what happened. He yelled to the others that I was hurt and to bring ice. Together they helped me into the golf cart, gently propped my knee up, and reluctantly shared the ice that had been keeping their beer cold. They packed the ice in a golf towel and gently wrapped it around my swollen knee. I blessed them and assured them that I was fine, and yes they could finish the next sixteen holes.

When we returned to the ship we headed straight to the doctor. He x-rayed my leg and promptly put me in a wheelchair for the duration of the cruise. He gave the orders to follow up with my doctor at home, telling me I would definitely need to have surgery. I was to see him every day for the remainder of the cruise, because he wanted to keep close tabs on me.

Not quite the birthday I had hoped for.

Randy hovered over me like a mother hen, tending to my every need. I felt silly riding in the wheelchair—but he insisted that we comply with the doctor's orders. I was so disappointed that I was ruining the fun we had planned. Here we were in Belize, one of the diving meccas of the world, and I wasn't even going to be able to touch the amazingly crystal clear water. The snorkeling excursion we had pre-booked was now totally out of the question.

I had resigned myself to the thought of staying on board the ship when Randy arrived at the cabin with a flyer advertising a special excursion to a small resort offering a lobster lunch and use of their private beach. Randy had already checked, and they could easily accommodate my new mobility problem.

After a delightful lobster lunch, Randy wheeled me across the street to the beach, bucket of iced drinks in hand. He pulled a lounge chair into the water, and then carried me through the water and gently placed me on the chair. The water was the perfect depth to keep me cool in the hot sun. The bucket of ice cold beverages next to me, the gorgeous azure sea, with its gentle waves in front of me . . . ah, life was good—and so was my dear husband.

During the cruise Randy's sleep patterns continued to be off kilter. Even with our active days, fun-filled nights, and the calming effect of the gentle rocking of the ship, he still had trouble sleeping.

I also began noticing subtle changes in Randy on this trip. I had always been able to count on him as my right-hand man when we traveled with a group. However, this time he seemed very uncomfortable at the airport, looking at me blankly when I was explaining how I needed him to help me. We had done this plenty of times before; it seemed to me it should just be routine. I was on crutches for the trip home; they were difficult for me to maneuver with my hands full of travel documents, making it a chore to do the running I normally did when getting a group checked in. I needed Randy's help more than ever this time.

We had a ninety-two-year-old customer with us, Oscar. He always required a bit of extra attention. Sure enough, as I was ready to hand out the boarding passes, Oscar had disappeared. With boarding passes in hand, the rest of the group headed off to the gate. I was left trying to find him, hobbling around on my crutches, with Oscar nowhere to be seen.

When I attempted to enlist Randy's help to go check in the men's room, he just looked at me with a blank stare. I decided it was easier to do it myself, and painfully hobbled away in search of Oscar. But he wasn't in the men's room, and he never answered my page, so I awkwardly made my way back across the ticket area to talk to security again.

This time I asked for a supervisor and explained my problem. He made some calls and found that Oscar was already at the boarding area. When he had tried to get through security without his boarding pass, the agent had taken pity on him, and after looking at his flight confirmation, he had been allowed to go through without it. He had gotten a new boarding pass at the gate.

By now, my knee was throbbing from all the walking I had done looking for Oscar, and Randy was nowhere in sight. Frantically, I began searching for him; our group was already at the boarding area. Randy and I still had to go through security and get to the gate, and time was growing short. With my bag weighing heavily on my shoulder, I began maneuvering the crutches between people and suitcases until I spotted Randy, who appeared to be in a daze. Although he was looking my direction, he did not see me. It was painful to navigate all the way back across the ticket area to get his attention. Struggling awkwardly on my crutches, we raced towards security and made it to the gate just in time for boarding.

I had knee surgery shortly after returning home from the cruise and was on my way to recovery. To my dismay, the scale had crept up again, and my clothes were shrinking. I couldn't believe that I had gone up two sizes since our wedding day. Most of my life I had been very conscious of my weight. It had been a struggle for me since childhood, and as an adult I had been very diligent about eating healthily and incorporating regular exercise into my life.

Now my days were full of endless work, and I found that I was neglecting my health. With my office at home, the work called to me day and night and left me little time for anything else, except the precious time I spent with my daughter.

CHAPTER 4

WELCOME HOME, BROTHER

N ot long after I recovered from my knee surgery, Randy started having pain in his shoulder. It was no wonder, with all the heavy suitcases and rocks he had been lifting the past few years. With the pain, his moods, temper, and inability to sleep became even worse.

One afternoon we had a group of seniors from a small town north of us out on a shopping trip to our local mall. I was escorting the group, and Randy was the driver. As he was standing outside the bus in the parking lot, a man walked by with a hat displaying the words   "Vietnam Vet Purple Heart." Randy called out, "Welcome home, brother, and thank you for your service."

The man stopped, walked over to where Randy was standing, and shook Randy's outstretched hand. They began talking, and Randy shared with him that he was also a Vietnam veteran. The man asked if Randy was getting any help from the Veterans Administration. Randy told him he had looked into medical benefits but that he made too much money. They continued talking, and the man asked Randy more and more questions, until finally he looked Randy squarely in the eyes, and with a firm but compassionate voice said, "Brother, you need help. It's time you made another visit to the VA."

Randy had the same reaction that most vets in this situation have: he didn't need help. This was the last thing on his mind, especially when it had been so many years since he had left the military, and even more since his days in Vietnam. But the man was relentless in his efforts to help Randy. He had seen the familiar look in Randy's eyes, and was well acquainted with the answers he was hearing as he asked his well-calculated questions.

Before they parted that day, they exchanged telephone numbers. True to his word, this stranger in the parking lot called Randy the next morning and accompanied him to the VA for a meeting with the Veterans Service Officer. His words of introduction were short: "This man needs your help."

With this Purple Heart angel at his side, Randy took the first step to seeking the help that he so desperately needed. Within a week he met with a therapist for a post-traumatic stress disorder evaluation (PTSD) and was also scheduled for a complete physical examination. I had known for quite a while that something was wrong, and I suspected that the dreams for our future were changing. In November 2004 those changes were given a name: Randy was diagnosed with the invisible wounds of PTSD.

Not only was he diagnosed with PTSD, but also diabetes and accompanying complications from exposure to Agent Orange. He was reliving the nightmares of Vietnam. And all of these were repercussions from his two tours in Vietnam more than thirty-five years before. PTSD had begun rising out of nowhere.

Now that Randy was receiving his medical treatment at the Veterans Clinic, he was able to begin the process of dealing with his shoulder. The first thing they did was to address his pain. He was prescribed a narcotic, Vicodin, and immediately had to stop driving. It took several months for the diagnosis, waiting for appointments for examinations, x-rays, and an MRI, but eventually it was determined that he would need surgery to correct a torn rotator cuff.

In the meantime, there was still the pain. As the time lapsed waiting for surgery, the pain grew stronger. With the increased pain, stronger pain medications were prescribed. Randy had now been suffering with his shoulder for over five months; it was understandable that there were many more veterans waiting as well, many with much more severe problems than Randy. So we patiently waited for his surgery to be scheduled.

It was the spring of 2005, a busy time in my life, and for my daughter Andrea. She was now a senior in high school, with all the activities and work of preparing for the next step in her life. This was also the busiest time of the entire year in my travel business. Spring was when all the schools chartered buses for their annual field trips, graduation nights, and music festivals.

Randy was getting worse by the day. He was no longer able to work and had been rated for unemployability by the VA. He had also stopped helping me with even the smallest details of the business. Even when he offered to take care of something, I soon found that I could not count on him to complete the task. He now spent his days sleeping or sitting on the patio gazing out at the golf course, with an occasional comment to a passing golfer. He had begun his therapy for PTSD with the VA, but everything about him was getting worse by the day: his anger, his dark moods, his inability to sleep, and constantly being "on alert" to everything and everyone around him.

★ ★ ★ ★ ★

Early one morning in March 2005, the phone rang. To my surprise it was Fleeta, Randy's mom. It was a surprise because she very rarely called us; Randy normally called her. I was even more surprised when she said, "I forget how to get to your house. I think I'm pretty close though. Could someone come and pick me up?"

"Of course," I replied, confused as to what she was doing here. She lived four hours away and had not been here since our wedding, almost five years before. "I'll get Randy; he'll be right there," I continued.

I woke Randy and told him his mom needed to be picked up. Minutes later, there she was at our doorstep with her suitcase in hand, saying, "I had to leave. I didn't know where else to go. Is it okay that I came here?"

Fleeta was a beautiful woman, tall and erect, confident and beautiful. Her stance was still that of a model, despite the aches and pains that accompany the seventies. We welcomed her into our home with open arms, turning our den into a room for her.

It turned out that Fleeta's husband, Wally, had dementia, which was getting progressively worse. The previous night his verbal abuse had escalated into physical abuse. Fighting off a man twice her size was more than she could endure, but she had finally been able to distract him long enough to grab a few things and leave.

Wally immediately had the bank accounts and credit cards frozen, leaving her nothing but the $42 she had in her purse when she left. She was afraid of him, and struggled with whether, at seventy-two and after thirty-seven years of marriage, to divorce him. And as she spent her days sitting on the couch alone, grieving for the life she had lost and fearing for her future, Randy slept.

Randy's mental status was worsening. He had begun therapy for his PTSD, making his anxiety worse than ever, as the bandages were ripped off his wounds and memories began flowing out like hot lava that had been trapped inside a mountain, suppressed for years and ready to erupt with the fierceness of a volcano.

Adding to his mental state was his ongoing shoulder pain, his constant anger and concern over his mother's situation, along with the unknown factor of what Wally might do. Fleeta was fearful of Wally's explosive temper and his unstable mental condition; the fact that he carried a handgun everywhere terrified her. Randy was now on hyper-alert more than ever, preparing for an unwelcome visitor.

When Fleeta made the decision to proceed with a divorce, Randy began helping her—and dove even deeper into a place that was totally unknown to me. Fleeta had no access to her money, and Randy had not been working for over six months, with only a small disability payment for income. His credit cards were full, putting the bulk of the financial responsibility on me. We didn't discuss his inability to contribute to our expenses; I just did what needed to be done, not wanting to put any further burden on Randy. I was happy to be able to help, and having Fleeta living with us had a miniscule effect on our household expenses.

The three of us were sitting in the attorney's office for Fleeta's free initial consultation. She was advised that they required a $3,000 retainer. Without a moment's hesitation, and not a glance or word in my direction, Randy simply announced, "Debbie will take care of it."

It wasn't a matter of not wanting to help Fleeta, but I was upset with the fact that there was absolutely no conversation with me ahead of time. He had no idea if and how I could do this. He should have known I had been struggling to pay our bills, and that in a few short months I would have to come up with college tuition for Andrea. But he had become lost in his little world, a world that I was no longer part of.

As the pain from his shoulder increased, the current medication was no longer working. We were still waiting to get the date for his surgery set, and

Randy's pain was becoming unbearable once again. The doctor decided on a more powerful pain medication: oxycodone.

Normally Randy was not much of a drinker, with the exception of a beer after a round of golf or an occasional glass of wine or cocktail at a social occasion. Fleeta, however, was accustomed to nightly cocktails before dinner, and Randy soon began joining her in this ritual. This added to the fog that was already surrounding him from the pain medication. Randy's life was now consumed with the divorce proceeding; the rest of his time he spent sleeping.

In the meantime, it was up to me to continue trying to work with the added distraction of our new guest, at the height of my busiest travel season, with taxes to be done, all the while helping my daughter with her college and financial aid applications. This was the first time I had to complete the FAFSA forms, which were the basis for all financial aid for college students. This was an absolute essential task for Andrea's future.

When I finally had the forms completed, I was waiting to receive my pin number in order to submit them. For some reason it did not arrive, so I had to request a new one—and the submission deadline was looming. I told Randy that evening that I was expecting a very important e-mail, so please not to get on my computer. I would not be able to submit the FAFSA and meet the deadline without the information in that email.

The next morning I turned my computer on, expecting to find the e-mail with my pin number so I could submit the FAFSA form before the deadline. Instead I sat staring at my computer in utter disbelief. Not only was the e-mail that I was expecting not in my inbox, there were no e-mails at all. None! Not one! Every one of my e-mail files, old and new, had been deleted.

My entire business was on my computer. Correspondence, contracts, customer confirmations, itineraries, vendor information—everything had been deleted! The anger welled up inside me as I continued gazing at my computer, still thinking I must be imagining this. How could this possibly have happened?

Knowing that there was only one person and one way that this could have been done, I stormed into the kitchen where Randy was having coffee with this mom. "Were you on my computer last night?" He simply stared at me with a blank expression, before finally saying simply, "Yes."

"Did you delete everything on my computer?" I continued. Again, simply, "Yes."

"What part of please stay off my computer—I'm expecting something very important—did you not understand? What on earth were you thinking?" I said with fury in my voice.

"I thought I was helping you."

"How on earth did you think that deleting every file on my computer would be helping me?"

He shrugged his arms, made no comment, and walked away, as his mother looked at me with a solemn face and said, "You have my permission to kill him."

That obviously was not an option. Nor was yelling at him; it would simply fall on deaf ears. So I stood in my fury, anger consuming my entire body. My thoughts were racing as to what to do. I began making phone calls to see if anyone could help me retrieve my information. He had done a complete job—not only deleting the files, but also emptying the trash bin. They were gone. I sat at my desk, staring at my computer, drained and empty.

At that moment I knew that my first priority was to get the FAFSA form submitted. That was my daughter's future. Without financial aid, there would be no college. Andrea had worked far too hard and had too much potential to have this obstacle get in the way.

I began making phone calls and was able to get a new pin number sent and started over completing the FAFSA application. Hours later, when I was finally able to hit the submit button and verify that the application had been received, I breathed a huge sigh of relief. I knew my next task of recovering all my business information would not be easy, but I would put it all back together one step at a time.

After two months Fleeta left for Colorado to stay with Brent and Tweedy. They had been urging her to come, and now that the weather was warmer she thought it would be a nice change, and, as she put it, good to "get out of our hair for a while." Although Brent and Tweedy asked her to stay with them permanently, she decided that she wanted to move to Napa to be near her brother. The divorce proceedings were slowly moving forward, and Wally had been more cooperative than expected.

Fleeta was happy to be close to family and settled into her newfound independence.

★ ★ ★ ★ ★

Randy's shoulder surgery was finally scheduled; it was outpatient surgery at the VA hospital in San Francisco, a four-hour drive from our home. I waited patiently in the waiting room for what I was told would be an hour-long surgery, plus another few hours in the recovery room. Hours went by, and it was now getting close to 10:00 p.m. I was the last one left in the waiting room; it was hours past the time when Randy should've been finished.

Finally a nurse came to tell me that the first thing that had happened was that Randy had fainted while they were putting in his IV before surgery. The surgery had gone well, and they had been able to repair his shoulder, but they had had great difficulty waking him up from the anesthesia. He was now in recovery and everything was fine.

They wanted him to spend the night so they could observe him because of the complications with the anesthesia, but he insisted on going home against medical advice. When I was allowed to see him, I did my best to convince him to stay, but to no avail. So at midnight I loaded him into the car for the four-hour drive back home.

The doctors had told us that his shoulder repair had gone well and that the pain should go away very soon. But it didn't go away, so the doctor continued his pain medication. When the current prescription was no longer doing the job, morphine was prescribed. He also continued his new habit of evening cocktails, even after Fleeta had left. Morphine, mixed with the alcohol and all the other medications that he was now on for his PTSD, plus other health issues, left him surrounded by a dark, gloomy, and angry cloud.

As Randy continued to heal from his shoulder surgery, we received a frantic phone call from Tweedy, Randy's sister-in-law. His brother Brent had been in a horrible motorcycle accident while on duty with the Colorado State Patrol. He was in critical condition with fractured ribs, a punctured lung, shoulder injuries, and a variety of internal injuries. Randy flew out to Colorado to be at his brother's side.

Thankfully, after several surgeries, Brent began recovering from his life-threatening injuries. Tweedy appreciated Randy's help once Brent got home, as he was unable to get out of a chair or out of bed without assistance. While Brent began weaning himself off his pain medication, eventually down to aspirin and Tylenol, Randy continued on morphine.

The weeks without him were actually a pleasant reprieve. The anxiety, anger, and fog created by the pain medication were becoming more and more difficult to deal with. Especially since I worked from home and we were together 24/7. It didn't seem that he cared about me any longer, or about our relationship. I was simply a stranger living in the same house and taking care of his needs. Days would go by without him speaking to me; he would pass by me time after time without uttering a word.

His time in Colorado with Brent and Tweedy seemed to be good therapy for him. He now had a purpose and was needed. He had something to focus on other than himself and didn't spend so much time sleeping. The Randy that we all knew and loved seemed to return as he helped care for his brother.

★ ★ ★ ★ ★

It seemed that I was spending more and more time in my "boo cave," as Fleeta warmly referred to my office. It wasn't until I attended the local Chamber of Commerce barbecue, at which Andrea was being awarded a scholarship, that I realized what a recluse I had become.

At the last minute Randy decided not to join us, saying he wasn't feeling well—something that had become a regular occurrence.

When I arrived, I began seeing people that I knew and had always enjoyed visiting with, whom I hadn't seen for several years. Each one of them greeted me with open arms and smiles. How are you? Where have you been? I haven't seen you for so long! I thought perhaps you had moved.

I asked myself the same question, wondering, where *had* I been? I used to be at all these events and thoroughly enjoyed them. I knew everyone—and everyone knew me. Where had I gone? I had either been locked in my cave, burdened down with work, or overwhelmed with all the things happening in my life.

That night I had a glimpse of what my life used to be, who I used to be, and I missed it. I missed the social interaction, feeling important, and having someone paying attention to me. I missed the smiles, the compliments, and the laughing. I missed all the things that had built me up and affirmed who I was, and that I was okay.

And then I returned home, back to the man I loved who was lost in his own world of medication, pain, and anger. I realized that I felt isolated and lonely. Even when I was surrounded by people, I felt so very much alone.

CHAPTER 5

VIETNAM IN MY BED

And then the nightmares became night terrors. The first time it happened, I had no idea what was going on. I was sleeping peacefully when my dreams were slowly disrupted by a strange sensation. Suddenly, I was struck by fear. In my groggy state, I was aware only of the trembling of the bed. Earthquake? I had been in Eureka, California in 1992 during an earthquake. That morning I had awoken to the same strange sensation.

This time, however, as I became more conscious of my surroundings, I could see that the source of the trembling was coming from the body lying next to me. Randy's body tightening up, then releasing. Every muscle in his body contracting. Then releasing with a series of awkward jerking motions.

This continued until I was fully awake. I lay there quietly, waiting.

Next his legs began rising and lowering, quickly banging on the bed, then quickly rising again, only to lower faster and harder than the time before. Like a jackhammer, both legs in unison, rising and lowering quickly. The faster and harder they moved, the more the bed began to shake. His body began writhing, as if in tremendous pain, and he began moaning in slurred, undetectable words. The words became louder and clearer, until he was shouting in anger.

As the incidents continued, his fists would often begin in the same relentless motion as his legs, punching whatever was in front of him—including me—without pausing between each powerful blow. He would roll over on his side, toward me, his legs kicking at me like shutters in a powerful windstorm.

At the beginning of these episodes, his right hand held onto the bed post in a death grip. This was a habit, or rather a survival technique, that he had learned in Vietnam. Randy explained to me later that no matter where he was sleeping he would always hold onto something with his right hand. This was how he could keep his bearings when startled awake by whatever danger lurked around him. With his right hand firmly attached to whatever was there, and knowing that his weapons were there on his right side, he was always ready to defend himself against whatever might come in the night.

That night in 2004, experiencing Vietnam in my bed, was the first of innumerable nights to come when my peaceful sleep would be disrupted, my own dreams interrupted, as I lay next to a stranger in my bed without moving, in fear of what might come this time. Would his fists start reacting uncontrollably to whatever horrors were going on inside him, rudely awakening me from sleep to dodge his blows? Or tonight, would it be his feet and legs kicking me violently, as he fought against an aggressor in his nightmares?

Perhaps it would be that strange voice, so foreign, coming from his mouth. That mouth that used to utter only kind, gentle words—but was now overtaken by the voice of that stranger lying next to me, spitting out profanity, words I had never heard spoken in his waking hours during all the years I had known him.

And then he began speaking in Vietnamese. Long conversations, his voice filled with fear, screaming in anger. His breathing uneven, irregular, stopping and starting, panting, out of breath. I would find myself mirroring his breathing, my own breath taken over by the power of this stranger, until my chest tightened from lack of oxygen, and I would force myself to breathe.

I would continue to lie quietly, wondering what was going on inside his head. What had happened over thirty-five years ago that kept coming back to haunt him? I lay in fear, not knowing what would be next. When I finally drew up the courage, I'd get out of bed carefully and make my way to a safe distance. Then I would begin the ritual.

"Randy, honey, you're having a nightmare."

Or, "You're hitting me."

Or, "You're kicking me."

Whatever the case was on that particular night. I used gentle words to wake him. "Randy."

"Huh?" he'd reply.

"You were having a nightmare. Do you remember what it was about?"

"No."

"You were kicking me; do you remember?"

"No, are you okay? I'm sorry," he'd say, as he drifted back to sleep.

I would stand there, wide awake, my peaceful night disturbed again. My dreams cut short. If I hadn't been lying there next to him, seeing him with my own eyes, I would have thought he was a stranger. A stranger in my bed.

The nights of sound sleep became few and far between for me, when he lay sleeping in Vietnam. I was always sleeping with one eye open and both ears listening, waiting for the all-too -familiar signs of his battle in the other realm to begin. The signs—his body trembling, the tightening and releasing, his legs moving like jackhammers—were my alarm to wake up and be on alert. Like a guardian angel, I watched over my beloved husband while he was in his other world, speaking a foreign language, shouting obscenities to those in his dreams—strangers to me, enemies to him.

My constant nights of sleep deprivation took a devastating toll on my mind and my body. I lacked energy and focus, my productivity suffered, and my moods were frequently erratic. It took me back to my time as a young mother, when I often felt like a zombie trying to work after many sleepless nights.

When you are a parent with young children and talk of sleepless nights, everyone understands. Everyone is sympathetic. We have compassion for parents of newborns who have endless sleepless nights with babies who've gotten their nights and days mixed up, have colic, or just don't sleep. But eventually it ends, as your children begin to sleep through the night.

But how can you explain your sleepless nights with a stranger in your bed? Who will understand? So you remain silent and try to cope with the growing exhaustion of your sleepless nights. Hoping that it might get better, but fearing that it will *never* end.

As time went on, sleep became more and more difficult for me. It was not only the relentless nightmares; Randy also began roaming the house, crawling in and out of our bed at all hours of the night. The TV was always blaring with the sounds of violence. Sometimes he didn't come to bed at all. Waking up to find no one next to you is a worry as well. *Where is he? Is he okay? Has he had a stroke? A heart attack? Is he in a diabetic coma? Perhaps he is having a nightmare and is sleepwalking?*

So, groggy, I would climb out of bed to go find him to make sure he was okay, to make sure he was safe. There he would be, watching more movies or boxing. Or sometimes he'd just fallen asleep and forgotten to come to bed.

CHAPTER 6

NOT LIKE IN
THE MOVIES

I couldn't believe it was almost time for Andrea to leave for college. I wanted this to be a special time in her life and a wonderful memory for all of us. I wanted that picture-perfect weekend just like you see in the movies. The station wagon overflowing with linens, lamps, and stereos. The entire family along on the trip, helping to get the college-bound student moved into the dorm. Tearful good-byes from the family as they leave the smiling co-ed.

I was the first in my family to go to college. I was so excited to move away, to meet new people, to learn and experience new things. My life at home was wonderful, but I was looking forward to this next chapter. Perhaps it was because my parents had not gone to college—or maybe they hadn't seen the movies—but for whatever reason, they had planned a short trip for the same date as my dorm opening and kick-off events at my new college.

They thought it would be fine for me to wait until they got home, thinking I would still have plenty of time to get moved in before classes started. They just didn't understand all the things going on before that first day of class. Like meeting your roommate and all the other students in the dorm. I was going to a college where I didn't know anyone, and I didn't want to be the last one there.

I had always been quiet and on the shy side, and I was afraid that friendships would already be forming and I might be left out. It would be so much easier to arrive when everyone was just beginning to get acquainted.

I tried to explain it to them but to no avail. I think it was that day, in that moment, that I stepped into my independence and took a stand for what was important to me. I made the decision that I was not going to wait for my parents to come home to take me to college. I had my own car, which I would be taking to college anyway, so there was no reason I couldn't go alone—and I did. As soon as they pulled out of the driveway, I loaded my car and left. I left a note explaining to them why this was so important to me. But I knew they would be mad as I took this first step out into the world on my own.

Alone, my car overflowing with bedding, stereo, and clothes, I arrived at college and began my new life. No tearful good-byes—but many friendly hellos. And a fierce new independence.

Now it was time for Andrea to move away to start her new life; I wanted it to be a happy and positive experience. We began to make plans for her move to St. Mary's College. We decided to drive down the evening before and get a hotel nearby, because Andrea wanted to arrive as soon as the dorms opened up in the morning. There was an orientation and barbeque in the afternoon, which her dad and stepmom would be joining us for.

Andrea had been dating a very nice young man, Randal, for over a year, and she told me that she would like him to join us. I had no problem with that; I had booked a two-bedroom suite, and Randal could sleep in the living room. Randy was still having trouble with his shoulder, so having a strong young man along would be quite helpful. But more importantly, Andrea cared about him a great deal and wanted him to be part of her special day. There was no reason for me to say no to her request.

Not knowing that Andrea had asked me about this, Randy later told me that if Andrea asked to bring Randal I should tell her no, because he did not want him to come along. When I asked what his reason was, he had none. He had just decided that that was the way he wanted it. Randal had never done anything to make either of us dislike him. He was very respectful and polite, came from a wonderful family, and was an excellent student and responsible young man.

I explained to Randy that there was no reason for him not to come, and he would be a big help moving. I added that he would be driving down separately in his Blazer, which would hold more of Andrea's things. Reluctantly Randy went along with the plan for Randal to join us.

When the time came we loaded up Andrea's things, made the four-hour drive to the Bay area, and checked into the hotel. Randy was quite irritable on the drive; I knew he was mad about not getting his way. We had dinner at the hotel restaurant, and I was hoping that food would get him in a better mood—but that didn't happen. We went back up to the room and decided to play cards, something we had done quite often with Andrea and Randal, which we always enjoyed.

We had been playing for a short time, when Randal made a simple comment to Andrea, who was his game partner, "If you have an ace, you better play it now." It was the obvious play to make, so his statement would not have influenced how she played whatsoever.

Randy exploded. He jumped up from the table, pushing his chair back so hard that it crashed into the nearby coffee table, as he threw his cards down on the table with a vengeance and screamed, "I'm not playing with cheaters!"

My mouth fell open. As long as I had known Randy, he had always engaged in table talk. And now, a simple innocent comment and he had to make this ugly scene. Andrea jumped up from the table; tears were streaming down her face as she ran out the door with Randal directly behind her. I sat speechless, my blood boiling. Randy knew how important this weekend was to me, and now he had destroyed it over a stupid card game. I was so angry with him I couldn't speak, as I grabbed my room key and went to find Andrea and Randal.

They were at the end of a deserted hallway, Andrea crumpled on the floor, her face buried in the corner of the wall, crying hysterically, with Randal sitting behind her, gently rubbing her shoulder.

"Why does he have to do that?" she sobbed. "Why does he have to ruin everything?"

I tried to console her. I tried to tell her how sorry I was. She was right. How many times had Randy ruined our good times—for absolutely no reason? When I finally calmed her down, she begged through her sobs, "Mom, I don't want him coming with us tomorrow. I don't want him to ruin everything! I don't want him to do that in front of my dad and Ann! I don't want him to embarrass me in front of my new friends!"

Like a mama bear, I assured my weeping daughter that I would protect her. I left them alone while I went back to the room to talk to Randy. He was furious at me for leaving the room to go console my daughter, furious that I had agreed to let Randal come along, furious that he did not have control. I asked him why he had to make such a big deal over such a petty thing. It was a simple card game, it was supposed to be fun, and now Andrea was sitting in a corner crying her eyes out. With that he kicked a chair over and screamed at me, "Because he was cheating! And I do not tolerate cheaters!"

I looked at him sadly and shook my head. "How many times have you done exactly the same thing? You do that every time we play cards. It's only a game, and now look what you've done."

I was furious with him, but I knew that engaging him further would only make things worse. After giving him a little time to calm down, I gathered all my patience and then quietly said, "I know you don't feel good, so you don't need to get up early and go with us tomorrow morning. With your shoulder, you can't help anyway. You can stay and sleep in. I will be fine without you. So you just rest and hang out here, and I'll come get you tomorrow afternoon on the way home."

He was totally oblivious as to why I was saying that, so he agreed. I suggested that he go into the bedroom to watch TV, so Randal and Andrea could come back into the living room. I reminded him they were still sitting on the floor at the end of the hallway.

I went back out to find them; Randal had finally been able to calm Andrea down. I told her that I had taken care of it, that it would just be the three of us going in the morning, and that I would pick Randy up on my way out of town. As though she hadn't heard me, or wanted reassurance, she reiterated, "I don't want him there!"

I gently replied, my heart in anguish over the night's events, "I know, sweetheart, I've taken care of it. Randy won't be there."

The next morning when the alarm woke me, Randy rolled over and said, "I'm going to help you."

"No," I firmly replied. "You're going to stay here. It's better that way. I'll come back and get you later this afternoon; I requested a late check-out for you."

"But what about the picnic?" he questioned, as though he had no recollection of the previous night's drama.

"Randy, after how you acted last night, Andrea is afraid to have you come to the barbecue. You ruined last night for all of us, and I don't want you to ruin today as well. So sleep in and relax, and I'll be back to get you later on my way home." Surrendering, he closed his eyes and rolled over.

Andrea, Randal, and I got an early start at St. Mary's, moving her into her dorm room. We walked around the beautiful campus and met Andrea's dad and Ann for the barbecue. Together we attended the parents' orientation meeting and welcoming ceremony and had a wonderful day. Just like in the movies, like the happy families taking their first child to college. The day I had dreamed of for myself, and the day I had dreamed of for my daughter.

But despite having had a wonderful day, I could not get the scene from the night before out of my mind. I could see in my daughter's face and hear in her words that things were never going to be the same. Randy had changed. And he had wounded Andrea's heart.

CHAPTER 7

THE PERFECT STORM

The kitchen phone was ringing. I walked quickly from my office to answer it, so it would not wake Randy. It was Fleeta. It was nice that she was now free to call and visit whenever she was inclined, unlike in the days with Wally, when his strong arm of control didn't even allow a phone call to her sons.

"I just returned from the doctor," she said. "She's been running tests on me and wants to meet to go over the results." Then, pausing ever so quickly to draw her breath, "She said that I need to have a family member with me for the appointment."

I froze, knowing her statement had a much deeper meaning. Something was terribly wrong.

"Of course I'll go with you," I said, trying to hide my distress. "And Randy and I will be praying for you. See you Wednesday."

★ ★ ★ ★ ★

Randy did not understand why his mother had chosen to talk to me and not to him. I did my best to explain it was just too difficult to tell your son that

47

there might be something seriously wrong with you. In a mother's eyes, your baby is always your baby—even when he is a grown man.

We arrived at Fleeta's on Wednesday at the designated time to find her pacing on her patio. By the look of the overflowing ashtray, it was obvious that she had spent a long, stressful morning. Fleeta had been smoking since she was fourteen, a habit she and Randy had once shared; he had started at nineteen, while he was in Vietnam. He used to enjoy sitting outside with Fleeta smoking when we went to visit, while I sat inside with Wally.

But thanks to Andrea's encouragement, Randy had given up smoking several years ago. Andrea had looked him in the eyes with the authority of a fifteen-year-old and simply said, "My mom loves you very much, and I love my mom very much. I want you to be around for a long time for my mom, so you need to quit smoking."

He did not say a word in response. However, two days later, he smoked the last of his pack and he was finished. Cold turkey, he quit. Andrea praised him frequently for his efforts. And I was beyond grateful, as I found the smoking distasteful. I never would have considered dating a smoker, much less marrying one, but somehow he had stayed clear of me when smoking until it was too late. By the time I knew, he had already drawn me into his web of love.

When we arrived at the doctor's office, the wait seemed like an eternity. Finally, the doctor called us into her office. She began, "I am very concerned about your test results. I am not sure what the problem is without further tests, but I can tell you that it is very serious. I believe you have cancer, but I'm not certain where it originated and how extensive it may be. You will need to begin more testing. I would like to refer you to an oncologist, but they will not take a referral without a diagnosis. And then, it could take several months to get an appointment . . . they are all so busy."

Randy and Fleeta sat motionless, as I spoke up. "That seems like a very long time to wait. Couldn't waiting that long make a big difference in her outcome?"

"Yes," the doctor replied sadly, "but the oncologists are all so busy, and we just don't have enough of them here in Napa."

"What if we could get her into an oncologist in Redding?" I suggested.

"That would be wonderful. The quicker we find out what's wrong, the better chance that something can be done. Do you know someone?" she asked hopefully.

"Let me make a phone call." All their eyes were upon me as I continued, "I know a wonderful oncologist, and I'll try."

I quickly looked up the number of Dr. Michael Fitzgerald, the angel that had come to me when Aaron had cancer ten years previously. I asked to speak to my oldest friend Mary, an RN in his office, and told her what was going on with Fleeta. Then I waited, and, to my surprise, the voice that came back on my phone was that of Dr. Fitzgerald himself. "Of course I can see Randy's mom, Debbie. How soon she can be here?"

"Tomorrow," I said.

The next day Dr. Fitzgerald was waiting with open arms. After a thorough examination and reviewing the records that we had brought along, he immediately began scheduling more tests for her. The news was not good: Fleeta had stage IV lung cancer, and it had already spread to her bones. Dr. Fitzgerald showed us the film and pointed out how her bones looked like Swiss cheese. He told us she could easily have broken her back simply by lifting a five-pound bag of groceries. There were signs that the cancer had also moved into her brain.

He suggested she begin radiation treatment in hopes of preventing a fracture, which would also help her pain. But any further treatment options would greatly affect her quality of life, without giving her much hope for more time. Fleeta chose quality for her remaining days.

Dr. Fitzgerald asked if we would like to pray with him. Of course, Randy and I answered yes without hesitation. Fleeta, however, remained silent. Dr. Figueroa offered a heartfelt prayer for Fleeta, and when we got to the car, Randy commented on how wonderful it was to have Dr. Fitzgerald pray with us and what a sincere Christian man he was.

Fleeta responded, "I don't really go much for that praying stuff."

★ ★ ★ ★ ★

Under Fleeta's watchful eye, Randy arranged to have her things packed up and moved to Redding. She had not even been in her apartment for three months. Her final home would be with us.

Fleeta's illness brought together all the elements to create the perfect storm: the pain from Randy's shoulder; his self-medicating with alcohol and pain pills; and his estranged brother, Brian, whom he hadn't seen or talked to for more than fourteen years—who came to see his mom and spent two weeks with us.

There were also the divorce proceedings, which had continued slowly. It was critical to get the divorce finalized now that Fleeta's death was looming. Wally had kept Fleeta from her family during their marriage, and she would be damned if he was going to walk away with everything now, leaving nothing to her three sons after the years of neglect.

Fleeta rapidly went downhill after arriving at our house. The morning finally came when she was too weak to walk without support.

That same day hospice had arranged to deliver her hospital bed. We had had quite a discussion about where the bed would go. I wanted it in the living room, where she could be around everyone when the time came that she became too weak to get out of bed. That way I could watch over her while I was working, and when she had visitors there would be more room.

Randy left the house that morning to do errands and go to his support group at the Veterans Clinic. I was pleased to see that he was continuing to get the support that he so desperately needed. I had told him when we brought Fleeta home with us that I was happy to help care for her, but that he would need to step up as well.

He could no longer spend his days sleeping. His mom would require his help and his emotional support as well, so he would need to keep up with his therapy and take his medication. It would be a difficult road ahead, and it would be important for him to be as healthy and prepared as possible. Randy had agreed readily, and now was doing a good job taking care of both his mom and himself. But watching his mom suffer from lung cancer from her many years of smoking gave Randy the need to deal with his stress . . . he began smoking again.

I also needed his help. Not only would Fleeta be staying with us, but we had also opened our home to all those who loved Fleeta and wanted to spend time with her. That meant more cleaning, cooking, laundry, and shopping. I still had my business to run, which was a full-time job in itself. But caring for a loved one during their final days was an all-encompassing job, one I knew if done well would end with no regrets.

After Randy left the house that morning, Fleeta declined rapidly. I knew that for him to come home and see his beloved mother lying in the hospital bed in the middle of the living room would be a difficult sight. I wanted to be able to catch Randy before he came into the house, to do my best to prepare him for the drastic change that had occurred in the last four hours.

Fleeta was worried that it would decrease the value of our house if she died there.

"No, Fleeta," I laughed, "that's only if someone is brutally murdered and leaves their ghost behind. That does not happen when someone dies surrounded by love."

As I said the words, memories were running through my head of another house with a hospital bed in the living room. *This would be the second time for me to have a loved one die in my living room.*

Randy's son, daughter, and their families had come from Colorado and Missouri to say good-bye to the grandmother they had barely known. The living room was full of love and laughter—an attempt to lighten the somber mood that comes with the final farewell of death.

I was sitting next to Fleeta, holding her hand, as she took her last breath. No one noticed that Fleeta had quietly slipped away, until I quietly suggested that the kids go outside for a little while.

Andrea arrived at the house shortly after Fleeta had passed. Before Fleeta moved in with us the previous spring, Andrea had met her only once, on our wedding day five years earlier. But she had become quite fond of her new grandmother, and they had spent many evenings talking and enjoying each other's company. Seeing the hospital bed in the living room with the lifeless body of someone we cared about awakened painful memories in both Andrea and myself, which no one else in the room was aware of. Only the two of us felt the silent bond of the memory we shared in our hearts, of a different hospital bed in our living room.

We waited to make the call to the mortuary until Brent and Tweedy arrived. They had left Colorado as quickly as possible after Randy's call, but missed their final good-byes by less than an hour.

My biggest regret was that Fleeta was not open to hearing about the Lord's gift of salvation. We did not push, but invited, offered, and prayed. Even at the end on her deathbed, when we suggested having our pastor come to visit, she still refused. There is no greater comfort and joy than to hold a loved one during their last breath and hand them into God's loving arms.

There is no greater sadness and sorrow than to hold a loved one's hand during their last breath and know that they have chosen not to invite the Lord into their life and accept his grace and forgiveness.

CHAPTER 8

REMOTE CONTROLLED JACKASS

A month had passed since Fleeta's death, and everything was getting worse. Randy's PTSD was more severe than it had ever been. The overwhelm of the last few months had taken its toll on him. And he now had the new responsibility as executor of Fleeta's estate. He was struggling with the paperwork while grieving the painful loss of his mother. His shoulder pain persisted, as did his use of morphine and alcohol.

Most of the time it looked like a dark cloud surrounded him; days went by without him speaking to me. I just couldn't seem to get through to him no matter how hard I tried. He could walk by me twenty times without even acknowledging my presence. I understood that he was grieving and in pain, and I did my best to provide compassion and understanding, but nothing seemed to work.

This dark cloud went on for weeks. Suddenly, to my amazement, he walked into my office one afternoon and announced, "We need to get away. Find us a trip to Mexico for next week."

"Okay," I said, astounded. After digging to get more details from him about what he had in mind, a few hours later I had the trip set. He only wanted to go for four days, but at least we were getting away. He was in dire need of a change of scenery, something to take his mind off these past few months—and so was I.

The trip was amazing, and exactly what we needed. I had my husband back. We laughed, we played, we talked, we simply relaxed on the beach, letting all our stress and overwhelm be swept away with the outgoing waves of the ocean. I hoped they were being taken far out to sea, never to return.

I fell in love with my husband all over again. He was attentive and charming, and made me feel loved. The man I knew that was deep inside him had come back.

★ ★ ★ ★ ★

Things kept getting better when we returned home from Mexico—until Christmas Eve. I could see the pain in his eyes as my family gathered together around our beautiful, brightly lit tree, covered with sparkling ornaments that each held a special significance for my family. My loved ones surrounded me, as did the music of laughter and joy.

In contrast, Randy had only memories of his mom and of his father who had passed away many years before—voices that were now quiet. I imagined it wasn't just memories, but regrets as well. Randy had shared with me that he had not spent a holiday with his mom since 1965 when he had left for the navy. Did he mourn the time not spent with her?

Alone in his thoughts Randy went unnoticed by everyone but me. I had known the pain of missing a loved one on Christmas, of grieving in utter stillness while everyone else was blind to my aching heart. I was so sorry that Randy had to go through this. My family all cared for him, but nothing replaces the loss of your own family.

A few nights after Christmas we decided to get pizza and a movie and enjoy a nice evening with Andrea and Randal. They would be heading back to school soon, and I cherished every moment I got with them. Andrea had been so busy before Christmas I had not gotten to spend much time with her.

Randy and I had been out doing errands and picking up the movie. When we walked in, it was obvious that Andrea and Randal were already quite involved in a movie. They took a moment to quickly greet us before returning their eyes to the TV. But as soon as Randy walked into the house, he took five steps to the coffee table and grabbed the remote control. Without a word he started switching the channels. Andrea politely said, "Randy, there's only ten minutes left of the movie we're watching. Can we please finish watching it?"

Totally ignoring her, he continued flipping through the channels. I gently said, "Randy, let the kids finish watching their show." I added, "We do have two other TV sets if you want to watch something."

"I'm just checking out what else is on," he replied, eyes firmly fixed on the TV screen as the channels clicked by.

"Yes, but we have two other TVs," I persisted. "Let them finish the show; it's almost over," I pleaded, beginning to get annoyed by his disregard of our requests.

Totally ignoring both of us, he continued flipping through the channels. Andrea, tension beginning to come through in her voice, politely asked again, "Randy, we've been watching this movie for almost two hours; it has ten minutes left—can we please watch the rest of it?" Then, seeing that her words had not stopped the relentless flipping of the channels, she continued, her voice quivering and obviously exasperated.

"I don't get to watch TV at college, and I'd really like just to finish watching this show—it's at the best part." Again, totally ignoring her, he continued flipping, stopping on a boxing match, a death grip on the remote.

I had never heard a foul word come out of Andrea's mouth, not even in her high school years. Andrea had patiently put up with all of Randy's mood swings and unusual behavior for years. But she had finally come to her boiling point and could not restrain herself any longer. She jumped up off the couch and, with fire in her green eyes, looked directly into Randy's cloudy blue eyes and screamed, "You're a jackass!" With that she broke into tears, grabbed her coat from the closet next to the front door, and ran out sobbing hysterically.

Randal quickly grabbed his coat and followed her out the front door. Randy looked at me with his eyes on fire, trying to melt the ice in my eyes.

"How could you let your daughter call me a jackass?" Randy demanded. "How can you just stand there and do nothing? I will not tolerate being disrespected in my own home," he continued.

Now I'm not a mother that defends her child even when she's wrong. Andrea had been good for so long with Randy—so patient, so kind. But we all have our breaking points, and Andrea had reached hers.

"Randy, you were just flat rude and inconsiderate!" I sternly said. "We both asked you politely, and you just kept it up! You could have easily gone into your 'man cave.' But no, you chose to stand there and interrupt them. They were not bothering anyone. They were sitting there very happily watching a show, and you came in for no reason and ruined it!"

At that point he went into a tirade about the fact that he had done nothing wrong. In his opinion he had not done anything on earth that could even be remotely considered rude. His reality of the event was as far away from mine as the Earth is from the moon.

Randy insisted that Andrea be punished, and that I support him under any circumstances. But at nineteen, Andrea was no longer a child—she was a young woman. Was I supposed to wash her mouth out with soap, or perhaps put her over my knee? Had Randy been my child it would have been him being punished. There had been no cause for him to act that way. I explained to him again that I couldn't defend him when he was rude and inconsiderate.

"She didn't need to call you a jackass, but you were sure being one!"

With that, he said he could no longer live under a roof with a woman who did not support him in everything he did. He informed me that I needed to choose between him and my daughter—or he was leaving me.

What Randy didn't realize was that you do not come between a mama bear and her baby. I had missed so much of her life already that a silly incident over a remote control was not going to come between my daughter and me. He went into the bedroom and I went out to get Andrea, fearful that she would get in the car and angrily drive away.

She was in Randal's car, and they were backing out of the driveway to leave. Randal stopped when he saw me and rolled down his window. My eyes went directly to Andrea, who was sobbing and visibly shaking. The full force of bottled up emotions from all the times she had kept quiet were now pouring out of her like lava from a volcano. When the word *jackass* had come out of her mouth, it had released all the hurt and anger she had been holding in.

We talked, and I tried to console her. We talked about how much Randy had changed. I knew that Randy had PTSD, but at that point I knew very little about it. I understood the nightmares, but he had become a real jerk.

I finally convinced Andrea to stay and watch a movie. The movie that they had been watching was long over, with the ending unknown—exactly how I was feeling at this moment about my life. I sent them off to get pizza, assuring them it would be just the three of us.

★ ★ ★ ★ ★

The three of us sat together on the couch eating pineapple and Canadian bacon pizza, watching a comedy. The tears were finally dry but memories fresh, so we did our best to enjoy the show, trying to get our minds off the events of earlier in the evening.

Randy emerged from the bedroom with one shirt on a hanger, walked boldly through the living room where we were sitting, then slowly into the kitchen and out to his truck, slamming the door behind him.

He came back empty-handed, walked back into the bedroom, and again picked up a single item. Back through the living room, through the kitchen again, slamming the door on the way out to his truck, and back again. He took one item at a time—a contrast to his normal method of piling his arms so full of things that it was inevitable he'd end up dropping, and often breaking, something from his overloaded arms. He then took Fleeta's picture off the wall, walked into my office and made a photocopy of it, and then replaced it on the wall.

In a way it was actually quite humorous, watching his procession. It was obvious that Randy was waiting for me to say something, to ask him to stop this silliness. I finally caved in and asked, "So when you leaving?"

"Don't know," he replied

"Where you going?" I quizzed.

"Don't know," he said, matter-of-factly.

"Okay," I replied, and went back to watching the movie. My insides were churning with hurt, anger, and disbelief that this was happening.

Eventually the movie was over. Randal went home and Andrea retreated to her room. Randy was still here. He didn't leave. But he stayed with a vengeance. The dark, angry silence fed the tension, which became unbearable.

The next morning I went in to check on Andrea. She hadn't come out of her room since the night before. When she opened the door, I could see that she was packing her bag.

She said, "Mom, I'm going to stay at Dad's house until I leave for school. I just don't want to be around Randy right now."

That was the last night that she ever slept in her own room, or even at my house.

As I kissed her good-bye, I retreated to my room, overwhelmed by tears and sadness. Randy was still in the house, but with a new level of anger, and a darker, more threatening cloud surrounding him. He was not speaking, just moving throughout the house like a volcano on the verge of eruption. And there I was left in the world of the unknown. Was he leaving? Or was he staying? What was my life going to be like?

For the next two days my heart broke one piece at a time. I was numb. I cried tirelessly and couldn't seem to get out of bed. I didn't know what to do. I didn't know what to say. He continued to walk silently by me, blind to my existence. Each of his cold steps a crushing blow to my heart. Each empty glance shot my way puncturing my heart.

Day three was New Year's Eve. We were invited to a dinner party at a nearby restaurant, but he still had not uttered a word to me. I lay in bed still in a state of mourning. In contrast, Randy had showered and was primping, getting ready to go out on the town without me. He left without a word. Andrea called to check on me, and when she found out that Randy had gone out without me, she said she wanted to come over.

I told her that I was fine and just wanted to be alone. But she insisted on coming over. Randal was with her; they were both dressed up to go to a party. They found me in the bedroom, still not able to move from my bed. I was embarrassed that Randal was seeing me like this. I had always prided myself on being so strong, so capable of handling anything that came into my life. And now, here I was acting like a silly broken woman.

They sat down next to me on the bed, Andrea gently rubbing my arm and quietly trying to console me. They seemed in no hurry whatsoever to get to their party. They just sat next to me, both with a gentle hand on me, wordlessly showing their love and concern. Randal suggested that he go get us all some dinner and we celebrate New Year's together. I was so moved that they would offer to blow off their plans and stay here with me, but I would have nothing of it. I had already done enough to disrupt Andrea's life; she deserved to be happy. I wiped the sadness and tears off my face, and told them how much I appreciated them.

The three of us sat there, broken and confused. How could this man who could be so warm, loving, kind, and generous have this other side to him? This stranger would appear from nowhere, and for no apparent reason he would disrupt our happiness and break our hearts.

Pangs of guilt spread through me over what I had done to my daughter's life with my decision to divorce her father. I had just wanted to be loved, to escape the cold silence that was destroying my essence. And here I was again.

Randy was the first man I had ever dated that Andrea liked. That relationship had started out so well—everything seemed perfect, and it seemed that my dream of happiness had arrived. And then, step by step, the stranger had begun invading our life—and we had no idea where it was coming from. Hadn't my daughter already suffered enough because of my decisions, and God's plan for Aaron? How could I put her in this situation, where she wasn't comfortable in her own home any longer? I cursed myself for the decisions I had made.

My heart was totally broken. I fell into a despair of hurt, anger, and sadness. My bed became my hiding place, where I wished the world would just go away.

Days went by, and Randy was still there, silently torturing me, watching my tears and hopelessness grow each day. He continued to walk by me, showing no concern, not speaking a word, acting as though he could not see me or the pain he was causing me. Why didn't he just leave, let me grieve, and be done with it? But no, he continued to push the knife a little farther into my heart with each moment of his presence, twisting it to inflict a little more pain each time he walked by, showing his cold indifference to my anguish.

And suddenly, as if someone had flipped a switch, he was back. He offered no apologies, no regrets; he just wanted to get on with life. He gave no acknowledgement of the hurt that he caused Andrea, Randal, and me.

We didn't speak of the jackass episode for several years, but when we did, he still viewed himself as the victim and believed he had done nothing wrong.

I was amazed and relieved at Andrea's forgiving spirit. Each time she came home from college she would come to visit, but only for a few hours at a time. She was holding back, keeping her distance, walking on eggshells. What a way to have to live your life . . . and all because of a remote control. And the word *jackass*.

PTSD has a way of taking over your brain without warning. Just like pushing a button on a remote control—suddenly the picture is different. Thoughts and memories from your remote past are triggered, like touching the buttons on a TV remote. Suddenly you are no longer in control of your thoughts, words, and actions. There is a death grip on the remote, and you don't know how to overpower it.

Then, without warning, you turn into a jackass.

CHAPTER 9

NOWHERE TO HIDE

Fleeta had passed away on November 5, 2005; her divorce was finalized just days before her death. That book was closed, but now Randy had his hands full again as executor of Fleeta's estate. This new role and the soon-to-arrive spoils of his inheritance brought an entirely new man into my life. He had a foggy mind and an angry heart, and together they took over our world.

It started when I asked the simple question, "When can you start helping with the household expenses again, and how much can you contribute?" Suddenly this man turned into a little boy who gathered up his toys and said, "Don't touch, they're mine!" This was a complete turnaround from the man who normally asked freely for what he needed from me and gladly shared whatever he had . . . which recently had been nothing.

It was a fair question. His State Disability had run out a few months earlier, and his Veterans Disability was still pending. I had been carrying the financial burden for our household, and I now had the added expense of college for Andrea. I was working as hard as I could and would have taken on a second job, but there were just no extra hours in my day.

But this seemingly innocent question sent Randy into a tirade. I had never seen him act this way before. You would have thought I had asked him to hand over all his riches to me, when I had simply asked for his share for food and shelter.

It was ironic, because Randy had been talking about wanting to "be like my dad," being able to help out his children financially and having something to leave behind for them. I suggested he might want to sit down with a financial advisor or accountant to get some professional help in accomplishing his goals.

He was so angry that he accused me of trying to get his money. Instead of helping me, he went on a spending spree. Every purchase made him feel better . . . for a few days. Then the anger and grief came raging back. He told me he wanted to buy a Harley. I knew he had had a motorcycle in his earlier years, and that lots of men his age had Harleys and loved the freedom that riding brings.

However, those men probably did not have numbness in their arms and legs from neuropathy, high blood pressure, heart problems, and panic attacks. I did not think that those made a good combination with a motorcycle. I loved him and I cared about his safety. I shared that with him, but all he had to say was he didn't care what I thought, he was buying it anyway.

I told Randy, "I hope your next wife enjoys your Harley."

The next day he came home with a new Harley and a helmet for me. I told him I was sorry, he and his Harley could do whatever they wanted, but I would not be riding with him. I cared about my safety, even though I had no control over his.

Later, when I saw him participate in his first and only Honor Guard for a fallen soldier, I understood the draw of the Harley. Watching the funeral procession of a fallen soldier, with over forty veterans on motorcycles, flags blowing in the wind, honoring their brother as they escorted him to his final resting place, brought pride to my heart and tears to my eyes.

Shortly after that he came home one day after a ride, his face white as a sheep; he was clearly shaken up. He announced that he was selling the Harley, with no further explanation. Later he shared only that he had stopped at a red light and couldn't feel his feet. My heart broke for him.

★ ★ ★ ★ ★

On occasion, the old Randy would appear. The generous, loving man that I remembered. With his mother's inheritance and Veterans Disability checks starting to come in, he paid off the credit card bills that had accumulated after his State Disability had run out. He paid off the car and even gave Andrea the amount of money she would have earned at a summer job, in order for her to be able to "shadow" Dr. Figueroa for the summer, supporting her goal of becoming a doctor.

Nevertheless, the distance between us grew. For days on end he would go without speaking to me. Not in anger—I simply became invisible to him until he needed something. Every time he walked by me without speaking, without looking at me, without even acknowledging my existence, it cut me to the core. I knew it was my fault that he was acting this way. It had to be my fault. I had to be doing something wrong to make him behave this way. Maybe if I was better . . . prettier . . . thinner, then he would love me again. He had always told me, "I don't do ugly." I must have become ugly to him.

Randy had changed so much since that first day we met. He no longer cared about his appearance, he was unkempt, and he often went days without showering or shaving. His face was somber, pale, and his blue eyes glazed. His body was here, but what had happened to that man I'd fallen in love with, I wasn't sure. These days not even a small glimpse of him was coming through. The familiar scents of Jack Daniels and Diet Coke grew, and the pain pills continued to be a daily ritual. Randy became even more distant, and the black cloud of anger continued to engulf him.

Ever since Randy had received his inheritance, the topic of money had been off the table for us. Any mention of money, something as simple as reminding him I needed the money for his cell phone bill, would throw him into a place that I didn't want to go—so I avoided it like an angry hornets' nest. I struggled, especially trying to make it on my own financially, working harder than ever. My days and nights were consumed by life in my "boo cave." With Andrea gone it seemed as if I was all alone in the world.

We did not talk anymore. Our dreams of taking off in an RV and working our way across the country, while someone else lived in our house and paid off the mortgage, had seemed like a wonderful plan. We had been ready to go as soon as Andrea graduated from high school. But then Fleeta came and we'd been forced to delay our plans. Then Randy's health problems grew, and the dream disappeared completely.

I didn't know what I was going to do; I was barely making enough money to cover my basic expenses. Working strictly on commissions in an industry where a year's worth of work could be swept away in a hurricane was insanity. I was afraid to ask Randy for anything, not even his share of expenses to live in the house. It just made him angry, and his anger was not a place I wanted to visit if I didn't have to.

I looked for other work options. Each time I found a viable job to go after he would offer to start helping more financially, saying he wanted me at home, and flexible to travel in the RV whenever he was so inclined. So each completed job application would go into the trash, along with his broken promise for added support.

I was in a world of despair. Nothing I did was enough. Not enough income, not enough caring to bring Randy out of his dark hole, not enough anything to keep me from sliding down the deep dark hole with him.

Living 24/7 in that kind of place has the power to overtake you.

★ ★ ★ ★ ★

It was about to swallow me when I heard of a job possibility. A tour company that I did business with in the Bay Area had just lost one of their key employees. I asked Randy what he thought about me contacting them and applying for the position.

Without hesitation he said, "Yeah, great idea."

We actually talked about a plan for our future again and how maybe we could have the life we had dreamed of after all. I immediately wrote a letter, updated my resume, and sent it overnight delivery. I desperately needed a change.

To my surprise, I received a call the same day my letter was received. They wanted me to come for an interview as soon as possible. I wondered if Randy would once again pull the plug on a job opportunity.

I went for the interview and they offered me a job on the spot. We agreed that I would bring my existing business with me, integrating it gradually into the new job. We would discuss the details later, but in the meantime, I would continue operating my company on my own time.

So the decision was made to take the job in Concord, to lease out our house, to "put our life in storage." This was a major life-changing event, but I had to do it. The money was good, but that was secondary. I had to escape. If I did not get away, I knew I could not survive a minute longer with this man who had become a stranger to me.

There was so much to do, and they wanted me to start right away. Randy made no qualms about the fact that he did not want to live in the city—which was exactly how I wanted it. I would get a small apartment in the city and travel back to Redding on weekends. Randy would live in our travel trailer in an RV park in Redding. Our dream was that if we could do this for five years, the house would be paid off and I could retire. We could travel and have the life of our dreams.

Together we drove to Concord to find a place for me to live. As we navigated through the traffic of the city, I realized how foreign this was to me. I had lived in Redding my entire life, with the exception of college, and now at the age of fifty-two I would be moving to a city full of strangers, starting a new job, perhaps even a new life.

I was excited—and scared to death. During my entire career, I had had the independence of running my own company or division without someone sitting next to me, looking over my shoulder. Now I would be working for someone else and have many people looking on, from just steps away.

As we began packing up the house, separating the things that I would take to the apartment, the items for the trailer, and the possessions that would go into storage, it felt like going through a divorce. At that moment I knew I never wanted to be in that situation. As each item was placed on the table, Randy always chose first, and each time he would choose the best, regardless of his need for the item. I knew if it ever came to divorce that he would be ruthless. However, right now, none of that mattered. I just had to get away; I had to escape no matter what the price.

The next Saturday we rented a U-Haul truck and some muscle to help me move to the city. I could not wait for the final boxes to be unloaded and for the truck to leave, to leave me alone in this strange new place. That night, lying in the middle of my bed, I was at peace. There was no stranger lying next to me, thrashing and screaming, disrupting my dreams. By Sunday evening, my new nest was downright comfy. Everything around me felt fresh and new . . . now it was time to renew my spirit as well.

★ ★ ★ ★ ★

Monday morning my new life began, working ten-hour days at my new job, spending my lunch hour in my car working on my travel business. Each night I would put in as many hours as necessary to take care of my personal customers.

We had decided that we did not want the stress of hurrying to get the house ready to lease, so when we listed it with a property management company, we gave ourselves six weeks to get it ready. However, a few days after I started my new job I received a call reporting that they had the perfect tenant—they just needed the house ready in three weeks. Fearful that another renter might not show up when we needed it, we decided to do whatever it would take to get the house ready.

So promptly at 6:00 p.m., after completing my first week of my new life, I headed out for the three-and-a-half-hour drive back to Redding. My mind was going a million miles an hour thinking of all the things that needed to be done to get the house ready for the new tenants. Randy had made his own list before I left: the garage was piled high with his tools, boxes, and boy toys; the shed was filled with yard equipment; his clothes and personal things needed to be sorted and boxed; the yard had to be cleaned up; long-neglected repairs and touch-up work were needed in the house; things had to be hauled to the dump. The things I had moved to the apartment had barely made a dent in what was left in the house. There was plenty for both of us to do.

To my dismay, Randy had done nothing on his list during the entire week I'd been gone. I worked relentlessly throughout the weekend, while he spent his time sleeping and watching TV, assuring me he had plenty of time to get his things taken care of. "I can have it all done in one day," he said with confidence.

When this new plan had come up, Randy had decided not to go on his annual elk-hunting trip to Colorado so he could help me with the move. However, he suddenly changed his mind and decided to go "just for the opening two weeks." He left without doing anything on his list—not even packing a single box of his personal things. I could not imagine how he thought he could get everything done when he returned. He simply shrugged and again told me not to worry.

The next three weekends I made the trip back to Redding, totally exhausted from my long days and nights working my new job plus my business, and now trying to get the house ready.

As I struggled alone trying to deal with all of our belongings, the clock was ticking. So much of this stuff was not worth storing, but it was also too good just to throw away. I made the decision to have a garage sale and try to pare down our things. My parents, both in their late seventies, saw the immense task I was trying to undertake and came to my rescue, working at my side in the blazing heat during the sale.

In the meantime, Randy had finished his elk-hunting trip and called me from Colorado. I was standing in the garage when he called, hot, dirty, exhausted, overwhelmed, betrayed, forgotten, and up to my eyeballs in dirt and junk. He called laughing and happy, informing me that he was finished hunting and now intended to stay and just "hang out" with his brother in Denver for another week.

Listening to his carefree, intoxicated voice, I snapped—all the fury I had been holding inside came out in three small but deadly words: "I hate you!" I screamed into the phone and threw it on the ground, shattering it. Never in my adult life had I said those words to anyone. And the worst part was I meant it. I meant it from the very depths of my soul.

The tears began streaming down my face; my body began shaking uncontrollably as I fell into a heap on the dirty cobweb-covered concrete floor. Despite the 102-degree temperature, I felt as cold as ice. "I hate you" rang through my ears and tore through my heart. "I hate you" . . . words so foreign to this gentle, soft-spoken woman. However, no other words could have described so accurately how I felt at that moment.

I sat in a heap, covered with cobwebs, quivering and sobbing until the tears would come no more. Then the numbness set in. Back in Colorado Randy's reality was that I had had a meltdown over a garage sale. He decided to come home, driving without sleep for the twenty-eight hours, knowing it was time for him to step up and help me. When he arrived home, he soon found that his "one-day" to-do list was not attainable. We had to hire help to finally get everything done in time. We never spoke of those three words, and I never apologized. To apologize would have been a lie.

★ ★ ★ ★ ★

Randy had met a new friend at his VA support group, and he was quite taken with him. When I met John for the first time, he was quite different from Randy's friends from his golf days. John was tattooed, his dark hair pulled back in a ponytail, his head covered by a bandanna. His black leather vest was covered with patches proudly announcing that he had served his country in Vietnam.

Randy was quick to follow in John's footprints, transforming from his Dockers and golf shirts to jeans, chains, and a leather vest proudly displaying the colorful patches revealing his Vietnam War service.

The better acquainted I became with John, the more I enjoyed his warm and generous personality. My first visit to his beautiful 100+-acre ranch showed that he was the exact opposite of Randy in many ways. His ranch was immaculate, not a weed, bit of trash, nor even a cigarette butt anywhere to be found. While Randy was messy and happy in a world of clutter, John was meticulous.

By 10:00 a.m., John could easily be on his second beer. As nice as he was, I was concerned that his alcohol consumption might move Randy even deeper into his own growing drinking habit. John was also battling PTSD and suffering from sleep problems. His solution was to sleep in his "bunker," a tiny room in his detached garage, which was barely large enough to hold his cot. This, he explained to me, was where he felt safe. As I glanced over at his beautiful home, my heart ached for what Vietnam had done to him.

John managed to function well enough to keep up his ranch, care for his adult disabled daughter, and run a profitable business. In one of his meticulously kept barns, a Model T truck was still in operation. He shared with us that it had been his grandfather's, passed down to his father and then to him. When the time came, the Model T would be passed on to John's son.

This sparked the idea in Randy to create the same legacy for his son, and a few weeks later he announced that he had bought a 1947 Ford coupe that he had seen sitting in a field. With John's help, he began restoring the car. Randy was already planning, excited about passing the car on to his son.

Next on Randy's want list was a patio boat. Not just a plain pontoon boat, but a top-of-the-line patio boat. He found just what he was looking for, and soon we were enjoying our weekends on the lake. We loved the solitude of finding a quiet cove to park in, gazing out over the gently rippling water, the moonlight dancing across the lake.

Our times on the boat seemed almost normal, as if PTSD had not invaded our life . . . until it was time to go home, to pull into the boat ramp and load the thirty-two-foot monster onto the trailer. I was scared to death, fearful that I would make a mistake backing the truck and trailer down into the water.

I had watched numerous women bearing the brunt of their men's hostility as they tried to navigate the challenges of a boat ramp. I did not want to be at the receiving end of an explosive outburst by my beloved. If it had only been the two of us at an empty dock, it would have been fine. However, we always encountered impatient boaters who would slip rudely in front of us after we had patiently waited for our turn on the ramp. Or obnoxious campers who would insist on swimming next to the boat ramp, oblivious to the danger to them and their little ones when we were trying to load a thirty-two-foot Sun Tracker patio boat on a windy day.

These events would set Randy's PTSD in motion, destroying the calm serenity that our nights on the lake had provided. Rather than returning home refreshed and happy, we would both be tense and on edge.

Eventually it became too much for Randy to handle. Randy felt renting a boat slip would be much too expensive and too much work. Having to walk down to the boat dock carrying supplies for a weekend was too hard, especially with his painful neuropathy. It all became much more than he was up to both physically and mentally.

The final visit to the lake was filled with obnoxious drunk boaters that circled the small island that was our secret hideaway, their loud music blasting as large waves rocked our boat and disrupted our peace. When we returned to the boat dock the next day, strong gusts of wind challenged Randy's strength and patience and threatened to send us crashing into a nearby boat. The weekend proved to be too much for Randy to handle. He sold the boat.

★ ★ ★ ★ ★

When I accepted the position in the Bay Area, I let them know that I had a few commitments I'd need to complete. One was a cruise that I had planned for my thirty-fifth high school class reunion. I was in charge of all of the arrangements, and it had been challenging to get all the final details ready with my new job. I spent many a long night, after grueling ten-hour days, making sure that each detail was taken care of.

All of my classmates were excited about the reunion. I was excited but also nervous that all the arrangements would come off without a hitch. I really had no reason to be nervous; I had done this hundreds of times. But this just felt different. These were my peers, and I was immediately the shy girl back in high school.

Randy was reluctant to join me on the cruise, but I encouraged him to come; I did not want to be a "solo" when the rest of the group was couples. Mark, my best friend Mary's husband and also a Vietnam Vet, would be going, so he would not be totally among strangers.

Everything went perfectly traveling to the ship. We had a great time throughout the cruise, and Randy was wonderful. He had the perfect sense of when to be at my side and when to let me go "play" with my friends. His old, charming, humorous self came out, and all my classmates enjoyed his wit and fun-loving personality. My husband had returned, and I was ecstatic. He even ditched his Harley gear for the cruise, donned his best golf shirts and shorts, and actually wore his tuxedo for the Captain's Dinner. I was proud to be on his arm, my handsome, charming, well-mannered husband.

★ ★ ★ ★ ★

Everything had gone well. We disembarked the ship in Long Beach and arrived at LAX in plenty of time for our flight back to Redding. But shortly before our departure time an announcement came over the airport PA system that our flight to Redding had been canceled. It was the last flight of the day, and I had forty-two people to get home.

I was told that we needed to get in line for a different flight that was leaving shortly. Evidently, this flight had extra seats and they planned to reroute it to make a stop in Redding. They would take as many passengers as possible, but we weren't all guaranteed a seat. Everyone scrambled to get in line for the limited seats.

I told Randy I wanted everyone in my group to get in front of us, so if we didn't all make the flight I would be there to help make alternate arrangements. We took our place in line behind the rest of my classmates, and I could see that Randy was beginning to tense up and become anxious. He had wanted to be at the front of the line to ensure us a seat.

However, this was my job, to make sure my customers were taken care of first. As everyone waited patiently, a man walked up to the front of the line and interrupted the employee at the desk, screaming his irritation at the top of his lungs, demanding that he get on this flight. The gate agent calmly talked to the man, who continued to yell.

Suddenly, Randy stepped out of line, and, with all my classmates and strangers between the counter and us, began yelling at the angry man to get away from the counter so the rest of us could get on the plane. I was embarrassed beyond words. I firmly told him that the ticket agent was able to take care of it and that his interfering was not helping. But he continued his riotous yelling as the man at the counter turned around to face his attacker.

All eyes were on these two men as they begin hurling vulgarities at each other. My embarrassment turned to fear. I had no idea what might happen next with the volatile potential of Randy's PTSD and the unknown state of mind of the man at the counter.

Another ticket agent stepped in to help deal with the man at the counter. His voice was now inaudible and his back to us. Randy's temper had spiked; he was beet red, with sweat pouring from his brow. He was not going to calm down quickly. I was red hot as well under my calm appearance, but for me it was from the embarrassment of my classmates witnessing this explosion. My stomach was churning with anger.

To my relief there was room on the flight for our entire group, and within hours, we arrived safely in Redding. Later that night when we arrived home Randy let me know that his behavior was very proper; his therapist had told him that he should act on his feelings. He should speak his mind, rather than holding his anger in. I agreed that was important; however, I believed it should be done in a safe and socially acceptable manner. Randy disagreed, saying it was okay to express his anger any way he chose, according to his therapist.

I was livid. I had not met his therapist yet, but it was time. How could I ever be comfortable having him travel with me if this was going to happen again? Traveling and escorting groups was what I did for a living.

★ ★ ★ ★ ★

At my request Randy made an appointment for us to go together to see his therapist. As we discussed the incident, his therapist did not seem to think it was a big deal, but a healthy expression of his emotions.

"Even when it's in front of my customers and it affects my job?" I demanded. "What if the man had reacted physically to Randy? What if he had been someone with a gun? Wouldn't it be better to teach other, more socially acceptable ways to control this anger?"

But my words seem to fall on deaf ears. Since Randy had started his therapy, all I had seen was him getting worse and worse, and now, another part of our life had ended. How could I ever have him travel with me again? How could I risk another scene? I was escorting a golf group to Mexico next month, and I had received permission from the new company to have Randy join me. But there was no way I could risk this happening again. He would have to stay home.

Randy's justification for his behavior was, "You have no idea what it's like to be in a war and fear for your life."

"No, I don't," I solemnly replied. "However, I do know what it's like to be in a different kind of war—the war in which children with cancer are battling for their lives. I know what it's like to live on the floor of an oncology ward and see children missing arms, legs, and eyes lost to the ravages of cancer. Bald heads on young boys and girls from the toxic effect of chemotherapy, parents with faces paralyzed by fear. I may not know what it's like to fear for my own life, but I do know what it feels like to be willing to give up my life for my child. To beg God to let me take on my child's pain, pleading to let me take my child's place. Only to stand helpless, unable to do anything but watch my child suffer and die."

The room fell quiet. Randy, slowly taking in my words, replied in a soft voice, "I didn't know it was like that."

His therapist looked at me with gentle eyes, and with compassion in his voice, said, "You have PTSD as well."

★ ★ ★ ★ ★

I had tried to run away, to hide from the challenges and problems that I had been living with. To do this had taken a great deal of work and effort. Moving out of my home, putting my life in storage, working endless days and nights, with long miles to get home. However, I had felt compelled to go . . . I had to step away from the life that was destroying me.

Then, shortly after I arrived at my new life, my plan was cut short. The entire staff was required to attend a luncheon. One of the owners stood and made a toast, announcing that they would be retiring soon.

Did I hear that correctly? I thought to myself. His wife happened to be sitting next to me. I turned to her and said, "You're retiring?" Without a word, she simply smiled and nodded her head. Questions flew through my mind. Why hadn't they told me? What would happen to the company? I had only been there a month! Now what?

The next morning at the first opportunity I asked the owner who had made the announcement if I could speak with him.

"So you're really retiring?" I asked, hopeful that he would say no, it was just a joke.

"Yes, we are," he replied with a smile.

"Why didn't you tell me when you hired me?" I asked.

"You should have known; we're getting to that age, you know."

No, I hadn't known. They were in their early sixties. Many business owners work far into their seventies, as my father had. They both seemed to love what they were doing and were always traveling with their families.

"What's going to happen to the company?" I continued.

"We are planning to sell it to two of the employees, Curtis and Belinda." My heart stopped. It had not taken me long to realize that these were two people I would never choose to work with. Neither had business management experience, but my biggest problem was their integrity and values. I felt well aligned with the current owners on these things, but had already encountered conflicts with these two potential owners over ethical business standards.

There was absolutely no way that I would be part of a company with these two at the helm. I had signed a six-month lease on my apartment, and my renters had signed a year lease on my house. It appeared that I was stuck—at least for now.

Since I had begun working in the Bay Area, Randy's health had been getting worse. New problems had come up with his heart, and his blood pressure was soaring out of control. He became a constant worry to me, and I was fearful of leaving him alone during the week without my constant oversight of his medication. Somehow I rode out the storm for the remainder of my six-month lease, before giving notice for both my apartment and my job.

I was exhausted, but at least I was sleeping in peace. I was spending ten-hour workdays, using my lunch breaks and endless hours at night to keep my own business going, driving home every weekend, meeting with clients, and doing whatever I could to help Randy. Keeping my business viable was more important now than ever; I would need it to sustain myself when I returned to Redding. I was grateful that I had found out about the retirement before merging my client base into the new company and having nothing to return to Redding with.

When the six months were over, I moved back to Redding, into our thirty-six-foot trailer. I knew I could not survive trying to live and conduct my business from the trailer. Fortunately, my brother offered me space in his office that provided me with a comfortable and quiet place to work and get away from the darkness of living 24/7 with PTSD.

Living in the trailer, sleep became an issue for me again. We were confined to such a small space, with no way for me to escape the gleaming lights, the blaring TV, or the stranger in my bed. However, in some ways life in the RV park was actually easier. No yard to care for, and housecleaning was quick and easy.

From our trailer we could watch people coming and going from the park each day, traveling in their RVs, living their dreams, while it seemed that our dreams continued to be shattered.

Finally, the day came when we could move back into our house. I was home again. My attempt to run away had brought me full circle. There was nowhere to hide from the man I loved and from Post-Traumatic Stress Disorder—Randy's or mine.

CHAPTER 10

A MAN ON
THE EDGE

Randy was at the height of his PTSD treatment. Forty years' worth of suppressed memories had been trickling out, and one of the many changes that happened was his heightened concern for his safety. He became hyper-vigilant. He also seemed to be doing many mysterious "errands" lately. I knew better than to question him.

Then, as quickly as they had begun, they ended. A short-lived affair? Was that why he was no longer interested in me? He had always sworn he would never do that, never do what his father had done to his mother. Besides, between his medication, his state of mind, and the fact that he had totally abandoned his personal hygiene, I believed another woman would be the furthest thing from his mind. Then what could his secret be? I had no clue.

It was a Sunday morning, and he was actually up and ready to go to church with me—a very pleasant surprise. It had been a long time since he had had the initiative to get up and get ready on his own. His attendance had been sporadic over the past few years; between his mental state, migraine headaches, and pain, mornings were not his best time of day. But I was not going to question his eagerness this morning.

I caught a glimpse of him checking himself out in the mirror, turning to each side, looking over his shoulder to view his backside, even giving himself a little pat on the behind. This was something new; I had never noticed him spending so much time in front of the mirror. This man was a constant stream of surprises.

When we arrived at church, part of the family was already there, sitting in "our pew." Randy seemed to be fidgeting and appeared anxious as he tried to get comfortable. My sister and her family arrived and joined us at the far end of the pew. Randy leaned forward, getting my brother-in-law's attention. They exchanged smiles as they both simultaneously patted their sides. What was that? Some type of new secret male greeting?

We were being ushered to the altar at the front of the church for communion when Randy stepped in front of me. As we stood in the aisle waiting our turn, he became distracted and didn't notice they were ready for us to proceed to the altar. I reached my hand up to touch him and get his attention. To my surprise, what I felt was not his soft warm skin—but hard, cold metal.

He moved away from my hand and up to the front of the church. When we returned to our seats, I reached over, touched the firm cool object on his side, and whispered, "What's that?" His face beaming, he said, "It's my CCW!"

"What?" I had no idea what a CCW was.

"You know, concealed weapon—it's a gun," he answered, smiling and patting his side.

I was baffled. I had no idea he owned a handgun—let alone felt the need to have it at church.

As it turned out, the secret errands he'd been running had been purchasing the gun, applying for his California Concealed Weapon permit, and taking the required classes. He had no explanation of why he had not told me about it, or why he suddenly felt compelled to carry a concealed weapon. It was a frightening thing for me, given his current state of mind.

But from that day forward the gun was his constant companion. He carried it on his person everywhere he went, and at night, to my terror, it was in the nightstand beside him. But in time, I became accustomed to his new companion and accepted it as something he needed to feel safe.

★ ★ ★ ★ ★

Shortly after adopting his new companion, Randy came into my office and told me he was not feeling well. This was nothing new; between his migraines and the pain from bilateral neuropathy, feeling bad was a daily occurrence. But when I looked up at him, I could see that this was not one of those common problems. He was flushed, and beads of perspiration were running down his face. He said, "I feel weird."

I sat him down and took his blood pressure. It was high, very high: 218/120.

"Okay, we're going to the clinic," I said. Fortunately, the VA clinic is only five minutes away from our home, and the urgent care doctor was able to see him right away. They began doing tests, fearing that he might be having a heart attack. I stood at his side, not letting him know that fear was engulfing me. I prayed silently that he would be okay.

When the doctor finished reviewing the tests, he stood in front of us. Randy was lying on the gurney, with me standing next to him. The doctor began, "I don't think you're having a heart attack. To me you look like a man on the edge. Are you feeling like you want to hurt yourself?" he quietly asked.

"No," Randy replied.

"Do you feel like you want to hurt someone else?" the doctor continued.

"Yes, I feel like I want to put some hurt on someone."

"Anyone special?" the doctor inquired.

"Nope, just feel like putting some hurt on someone."

I stood like a pillar of stone, horrified. What had happened? Nothing out of the ordinary. We had had a quiet evening watching TV, he had slept pretty well for a change, and now he wanted to hurt someone!

The doctor prescribed some anti-anxiety medication and told Randy to follow up with his primary care physician. The meds didn't seem to work. He continued throughout the day to look as though he were ready to explode. His muscles were visibly tight and contracted, his eyes distant and angry. I was terrified. They sent me home with a man "on the edge," a man who was "feeling like hurting someone."

Randy sat on the couch, his eyes glued to the television with a cold blank stare. I quietly went into my office, closed the door, and emptied my lockbox; passports and birth certificates would be safe in the file cabinet for now. When Randy went outside to smoke, I took the lockbox into the bedroom and carefully put his pistol inside the box and locked it. I slid the lockbox under

Randy's side of the bed and hid the key. The gun and the key would be quickly available should the need arise, but not accessible to the man on the edge.

I did not say a word to Randy about his gun. The next day he came storming out of the bedroom yelling, "Where's my gun?"

I calmly looked at him and said, "I locked it up. It's in the lockbox under your side of the bed."

"Get it out! I need it! What if someone breaks in?"

Still keeping my cool I replied, "The gun and key are in easy reach should the need arise."

"No! I need my gun! Unlock it now! " he screamed at me venomously. His face was bright red as his anger mounted, the veins in his face and neck standing at attention, his muscles tight, ready to attack.

Despite my fear, I gently said, "NO. The doctor said you are a man on the edge, and you said you felt like hurting someone. I am not going to leave a loaded gun at your fingertips. I am afraid. I am not going to unlock it as long as you are feeling this way."

"I would never hurt *YOU*!" he roared.

"Maybe not, but if you hurt anyone it would destroy both our lives," I said firmly.

Randy shot me a look that pierced deeper than a bullet, eyes blazing hot and angry. Defeated for now, he walked away.

Each time we silently passed in the house the look was the same. Each day his only words to me were, "When are you going to give my gun back?" Each day my reply was the same: "When I feel it's safe for you to have it again."

After several weeks, he finally quit asking about his gun on a daily basis. After a month he had calmed down; his anger had subsided. His medication had been adjusted, and his anxiety seemed better controlled. I felt it was safe to return his gun. I unlocked the box and carefully placed the gun back in his nightstand drawer. I didn't say a word to Randy about this.

Another week went by before he asked the familiar question, now in a calmer voice than ever before, "When are you going to give me my gun back?"

"I already did—it's in your nightstand drawer," I said lovingly.

Without a word, he rushed into the bedroom to find his gun exactly where I had told him it would be. When he returned he looked at me, and with sincerity, his voice cracking, he simply said, "Thank you," and walked away.

Randy again began to carry his gun everywhere. Then, after seeing a friend's new pistol, he decided he wanted one just like it. He now had two handguns. He was getting ready for his annual elk-hunting trip to Colorado, and I noticed that both guns were sitting on the kitchen table, along with other things he was packing for his trip.

"Aren't you going to leave one home for me?" I asked, not because I wanted a gun, but because I was curious about his answer.

"Oh, you'll be fine," he said, confidently.

It was interesting to realize that he did not feel safe in our home without a gun, yet he would be leaving me home alone for six weeks and was not the least bit concerned for my safety. I realized that his fears were not really about who might be breaking in, but rather who was still in his head trying to break out. I also realized that I was actually more afraid of having him and those two guns sleeping next to me than the possibility of having a stranger break into my house.

★ ★ ★ ★ ★

Shortly after we moved back into the house, John suggested that Randy put a new engine in his '47 Ford. John had offered to help him with the project and let him keep his car in one of his barns, as well as give him use of all his tools. It was a kind and generous offer and would give Randy a project during the rainy months of winter.

Randy drove the '47 Ford to John's ranch. Then John brought him back home to get his Dodge truck so he could pull the travel trailer to the ranch too. He told me that way he would have a place to take a nap if he got tired, or, if they were working late, he could just spend the night. He also said he would not want to disturb me coming home in the middle of the night.

His explanations made perfect sense to me. When a migraine came on, all he could do was lie down in a dark place until it had passed. And given his sleep habits, the idea of working late into the night was reasonable.

So Randy and John began working on his car. Days went by without him coming home. The days turned into weeks. It was only a forty-minute drive to John's ranch, but he insisted it was too far to come home. Often he would go four or five days without even calling me. When he did bother to call, he would tell me how much fun he was having, and how John, his close friend

Denise, and his daughter were cooking and eating dinner together and how nice it was to be part of a family.

We used to be a family. We used to cook together, and I had loved it. But my daughter never came for dinner when she was in town, thanks to him. I was alone, and he had found a new family. Hearing his words and feeling the happiness in his tone hurt me deeply. He was acting as though he had never before in his life experienced standing in the kitchen cooking with someone.

Cooking with Randy had once been my favorite time of the day. However, he was the one that had stopped wanting to do it. He was the one who was never hungry anymore, or who would sleep through dinner, or who would ignore my invitations to join me after I had made his favorite meal. He would leave me to eat alone.

What had I done to erase those memories from his brain? What had I done that made him not want to come home? What was so bad and repulsive about me that I was not worth driving forty minutes for in two months? It must have been my weight, for one thing. I had gained forty-five pounds since our wedding day. Food was my only companion during these lonely nights and stress-filled days.

★ ★ ★ ★ ★

John's relationship with Denise soon progressed beyond friendship. They were so desperate for privacy that he began each evening to drive forty-five minutes to her home to spend time with her. Randy would stay at the ranch alone—because his wife was not worth the effort to drive home. This had gone on for three months when I received a call from John and his girlfriend, Denise. They put the call on speakerphone and simultaneously began, "You have to get him out of here!"

John began, "Debbie, I'm afraid that he's going to hurt himself or someone else. He is not being safe. I have watched him make some very dangerous mistakes. He is so careless that today he didn't even take time to properly jack up the car he was under. He could have been killed!"

Denise piped in, "Debbie, he is so moody all the time he is making John crazy. John has worked so hard to get better with his PTSD; it's not helping him to be around Randy."

John broke in again, "I offered to help him, but he expects me to work on his car 24/7. I have a business to run, and I want to spend time with my girlfriend. We have no privacy."

"His crap is everywhere!" Denise's voice broke.

John added, "He leaves my tools out in the rain. He never puts anything away. He throws his trash all over on the ground."

I listened as they each took turns emptying out their concerns and frustrations. When they were finally finished, I simply said, "I'm sorry. I will take care of it. He'll be gone today."

What else could I say? I knew every word was true. I sat for a moment contemplating what I was going to say to Randy. The truth was the only option. As I dialed his number and the phone began to ring, fear swept over me about what his reaction would be. I was glad they were at Denise's house so he would not have the opportunity to confront them. Without a doubt, he would be furious that they had called me.

"Hello," said Randy gruffly.

"Randy, I just had a call from John and Denise. It's time for you to come home. You have worn out your welcome at the ranch."

I held my breath waiting for his reaction, but there was none. Only silence, until the click; he had hung up on me. I had no idea what to think. Should I call him back? I was sure he had heard me. So I just waited, knowing that he had a lot to clean up before he headed home.

To my surprise, it was less than an hour before he walked in the door. I could smell him from the moment he walked it. He was filthy dirty, and it was obvious that he had not showered for who knows how long. He had gone unshaven for the duration of his stay. But even through the black grease on his cheeks, his face was red with anger.

I glanced outside and saw that only his truck was there. When I finally got my courage up, I asked him why he had not brought the trailer home.

"It's fine there," he said.

"No, it's not," I replied sternly. "John would like you to move it. And how about your car?"

"It's fine," he replied.

Each day for the next week, I asked him when he was going to get the trailer and his car.

"They're fine," he'd respond.

I was becoming more and more frustrated and angry with him. Each time I replied, "No, they are not fine. John wants them gone." One day I added, "You are being very inconsiderate. John was very generous in all that he did for you. You need to go get your stuff and clean up your mess!"

"It's fine," he said.

After two weeks, Denise called me and asked if I would have Randy come get his stuff. She was very polite and added, "I understand how difficult he is, and what a bad situation it puts you in. We're really sorry that we have to ask you to do this, but we just know it would be impossible to try to talk to Randy ourselves."

I told Randy that I had had another call, and we needed to go and get his stuff. He went into the bedroom. When I went to see what he was doing, my heart stopped and I froze in my steps. He had his pistol strapped on, and he was practicing drawing it. His other pistol was in his left hand.

"What are you doing?" I asked in terror.

"Protection," he answered.

"Protection from what?" I asked.

"John. You never know what he might do."

"Has he ever done anything to make you feel like he would harm you?"

"Nope, but you just never know. He does have a shotgun," Randy replied.

"Well, if you don't feel safe, maybe we should have the sheriff send someone over while you get your things, just to keep everyone safe," I replied, thinking to myself that it was John that would need to be kept safe.

"Nope, I'll be fine. You'll be with me," he said nonchalantly.

We drove to John's in the truck. When we arrived at the ranch Randy punched in the code to open the gate and expressed his surprise that John had not changed it. "Randy," I said, "he's not mad. He just needs his life back."

Randy parked by the trailer and began walking around as though on an inspection. It was easy to see why John was upset. John was meticulous. Randy was like a tornado that had left its debris scattered everywhere—engine parts, tools, and trash were everywhere. Randy was eyeing the area as if he would be able to notice anything missing or changed in the chaos he had created. He did not pick up one item from the barn—not a tool, not a car part, not an empty Diet Coke can.

He simply completed his inspection and said, "Okay, let's go."

"Aren't you going to take your stuff?" I asked, confused.

"I'm taking the car; I'll come back for the rest."

"You're not taking the trailer home today?"

"Nope," he replied.

"Your truck is empty; let's get some of this mess picked up. I'll help you load it up in the truck," I said, hoping to get a positive reaction.

"Nope. It's fine," he said and began walking back to the truck.

When we got to the truck, we could see that John was standing, watching us from his backyard. Randy stopped and took a pose reminiscent of a gunfighter at the O.K. Corral. Feet apart, shoulders squarely facing John, his eyes fixed intently on him. I could see that Randy's hand was in the same position as I had seen earlier in the day, when I had caught him practicing reaching for his gun.

It was obvious that John was simply standing there calmly waiting to talk to us.

"Randy, please get in the truck. I am going over to talk to John."

"Well, be careful. I think it's okay. I don't see his shotgun," Randy said, as he reluctantly got in the truck.

I walked over to John, who put his hand out to greet me. "Thank you, Debbie. I know this is difficult for you, but he was just getting too much for me. He was a danger to himself, and with my PTSD I just couldn't handle it anymore."

I thanked John for all he had done for Randy and told him I would do my best to get him to move the rest of this stuff as soon as possible. I drove away in the empty truck, while Randy drove his car, the trunk of the '47 Ford empty as well. It was six more months before he finally removed the final item from John's barn—the old '47 engine.

★ ★ ★ ★ ★

One of the things that had brought Randy and me together was golf. He was not only an avid golfer, he was a great golfer. Shortly before he moved to Redding, he was a qualifier for the Senior Pro Tour. However, that dream ended when he injured his eye while bowhunting. The golf course was one place where he was truly in his element, at his best, without the ugliness of PTSD.

When Randy's shoulder got bad, he was no longer able to play golf. For several years, his clubs had collected dust in the garage. Eventually he was able to start playing again; however, it became a source of frustration for him. His game had gone downhill, and it seemed he had lost his magic touch. He was still a very good player with an eight handicap, but in his mind, he should still be a scratch player, as he had been when training for the Pro Tour. It was hard for him to adjust to not being quite as good as he had been in his prime.

It became more and more difficult for me to play with him. What used to be something I loved turned into a minefield. I had no aspirations of being a pro or the club champion. I loved the game, and for me it was purely recreational. But lately it seemed that I was not good enough anymore, and he began incessantly criticizing each shot—even my greatest shots, according to him, should have been better. The more he criticized me, the more I lost confidence in even the best parts of my game. He was stealing my fun and love for the game with each word he spoke.

We had joined a traveling golf club that had a monthly tournament at different courses in our area. One of our favorite courses was in the mountains about seventy-five miles north of Redding. We had always looked forward to playing there. But on this occasion Randy had been in a foul mood from the time he woke up that morning. He had had a migraine the night before and had not gotten much sleep.

It was a busy day on the golf course with our tournament and a second tournament right behind us. We were playing with another couple who were also experienced golfers, but the day was quickly becoming a hurry-up-and-wait situation. The course marshal was making his rounds; each time he stopped he told us to "keep up." However, each time he said this we had a group in front of us in plain sight, not yet at a safe distance for any of us to hit.

Course marshals are there to assist players in keeping the play moving and to make sure course etiquette is followed. In my thirty years of playing golf I have always found them to be polite and helpful—even when telling me to speed up my game, which happened frequently when I played with some of my chatty girlfriends.

This marshal was the exception. He very quickly began pushing Randy's buttons. He stopped us again, telling us to "keep up" because there were "real golfers" behind us. Since we were on a short par three, and the group in front of us was still on the green, the marshal's comment pushed Randy over the edge. He jumped up in the marshal's face, screaming at him to get the hell away from us and not to come back. He then threatened to "hurt him" if he saw him again. Being smart enough not to tangle with Randy's fury, the marshal drove away without saying a word.

Randy was visibly trembling from anger, his face tense and burning hot. He turned to me and said, "If he comes back, you have to get between us, because if you don't, someone will be going to the hospital and someone will be going to jail."

So I was expected to jump between two angry men? And do what? Be the one going to the hospital? I was furious that he would even think of putting me in that situation.

Fortunately, the marshal did not return, and Randy began to calm down until we were finishing up on the 18th green. The club president yelled at him and said, "Thanks a lot, Randy. We won't be coming back here. Nice job—you got us black-balled."

This set Randy off again. He felt that our club president should have stood up for him, since the marshal was being a jerk. He said he wanted no more of that BS and we would be quitting the club.

As it turned out, before we left the course that day, more complaints about the marshal were turned in. The course manager apologized and reneged on the ban against our group coming back.

★ ★ ★ ★ ★

The more Randy played, the better he got. Having his game back made a tremendous difference in his mental attitude. He began playing golf regularly and was getting invitations from some of the best players and pros in the area. I was happy that Randy had an outlet that got him out of bed, out of the house, and away from sitting on the patio like a smoking chimney.

At times, however, I felt as if I were getting the leftovers. We rarely played golf together anymore; he encouraged me to play with "the girls." I enjoyed that, but I wanted to do something with him besides sit around the house and listen to him complain about how bad he felt. We had already lost so many of the things that connected us; I wanted to hold on to something—even if he often took my fun out of playing golf. It was still nice to see the pleasure in his face when he made a great golf shot.

He seemed somehow to muster up the energy to go on marathon golf trips with the boys, playing thirty-six holes a day. Then he'd return home and be cranky, complaining for days about how tired he was and how much he hurt. For each day he played, he would take an equal number of days to sleep and recover. I loved to see him happy, so I did my best to take it all in stride.

★ ★ ★ ★ ★

One Sunday morning Randy left early on a golf trip with the boys. We had been invited to a party for Randal's brother, who had just graduated from law school—just one more event for me to choose to go to solo or to stay home alone.

In my younger years I would have chosen to stay home. I was much too shy and self-conscious to go anywhere alone. But today going alone to most social functions was my new life story. I was warmly greeted at the party, and everyone made me feel welcome; however, I still felt alone, especially going home to a dark empty house.

Monday morning came too soon. After grabbing my coffee, I headed into my office, located in the front of the house just ten steps away from my bedroom, giving me a very short commute to work. As I opened the door to my office I stood in the doorway, confused, trying to decipher what I was looking at. The light in the office was dim; the window shades were still drawn. But what in the world was this?

Shattered glass covered the floor, my desk, my worktable, my files; every inch of my office was covered with slivers of glass. I didn't dare step inside with my bare feet; I just gazed at the room. The aluminum mini-blinds were closed tight. I glanced up at the overhead ceiling fan to find the lights were intact. But where had all this glass come from? I withdrew to my bedroom, slipped on some shoes, and went back to investigate further. What a mess!

As I got closer to the window that faces the front of the house, I could see jagged fragments of glass poking out of the mini-blinds. As I slowly pulled the blinds out of the way, my heart stopped. The double pane window had two huge holes, both a good six inches in diameter. I stood paralyzed. The window is only two feet off the ground and large enough for even the biggest person to climb through. The holes were right next to the window latch, making it an easy feat to unlock the window and climb in. How could I not have heard this?

When I re-examined the room, I found two rocks that had ended up on the farthest side of my office. My two dogs and I had been sleeping just steps away, and the dogs had never made a sound. Normally they barked at everything—even the wind. However, they had not made a peep last night. I hadn't woken up either. Was the one margarita I'd had at the party the night before enough to knock me out and deafen me? Alternatively, was I finally just sleeping soundly without Randy next to me?

I was paralyzed as I sat alone, thinking about the "what if's" and "could haves." I needed to have someone put their arms around me and help me feel safe. I would have to settle for Randy's voice to comfort me, so I picked up the phone and called him. That's what husbands are for, right?

The call went straight to his voicemail. With my voice shaking, I left a message telling him what had happened. As I hung up the phone, tears began pouring down my face. Before I had met Randy, my previous house had been burglarized. All my jewelry had been stolen, including both my grandmother's and my great-grandmother's wedding rings, which had been entrusted to me. I remembered how many nights I had lain in my bed thinking about how a stranger had been right there, in my bedroom, going through all my things. I had felt so violated.

I pulled myself together and called the police department to file a report. To my surprise it was only a few minutes before my doorbell rang and an officer was standing there. His first question was, "Do you know anyone who may have done this? Have you had problems with anyone lately?"

"I haven't," I replied with absolute conviction. "However, I have no idea about my husband. I know he just recently called the police about a neighbor across the fairway hitting golf balls at him."

How well I remember that day—especially the look of anger on Randy's face when someone had invaded his space by hitting a golf ball onto our patio, barely missing him. When he came inside to tell me, his face was fiery red, his eyes ablaze with anger, his body tense, every muscle standing at attention ready to fight. Just looking at him scared me. I related that episode to the officer.

When the report on the window was filed and I had finished talking with the neighbors who had gathered in my front yard, I began thinking of what could have happened. As fearful as I was to have been alone, I was thankful that Randy was not at home. The outcome could have been much different. Without a doubt, he would have been awake, or he would have woken up to the sound of the breaking glass. He would have been out the door in a flash, in his underwear with gun in hand.

When I came back inside the house, I saw that I had missed a call from Randy. He left a message: "Thanks! You just ruined my golf game. My PTSD spiked off the charts."

So many things that we used to talk about had been taken off the discussion table. Things I was no longer allowed to talk about with him because they affected his PTSD. Whom was I supposed to talk to? Who was there to help and protect me? So many things were taboo there was nothing left to talk about, unless it was, "Oh, look how cute the dogs are."

I had a full list of projects for work today, but I could do nothing until I took care of the problem at hand. I cleared enough glass away to safely get into my office to call the insurance company and the glass company. I learned it would take several weeks to get the new window. Now what? It had just begun to rain and the wind had picked up, and I had two huge holes in my window. Not to mention I would be alone for the next four nights, the gaping holes an easy target for an intruder.

Thankfully, my brother-in-law offered to come over and board up the window to secure my safety.

By the end of the day, I was spent, work list untouched, feeling totally violated, again. I walked around my block in the rain, looking at each house in the quiet middle-class neighborhood. As I looked at every house, each one had windows facing the street, all untouched. I wondered why? Why my house? Why me? Who did this? Questions that I would never have answers for.

I noticed that I had missed another call from Randy; it had just been thirty minutes after his first call this morning. I had been so busy all day I had not stopped to check my voicemail.

"I'm okay now! The fun has begun!" his jovial, carefree, intoxicated voice announced.

The coldness swept over me, chilling to my bones, I could feel the goose bumps rising up over my entire body. I sat frozen in time, a single tear finding its way down my cheek. What about me?

CHAPTER II

GRIEVING
THE LIVING

One day when I was at the lowest of my low, I confided in Randy. I told him that I didn't really care about my life anymore. I wasn't talking about taking my life, as suicide was not something I would ever even consider as a Christian. I just felt that if I happened to get hit by a truck or be diagnosed with terminal cancer, that would be totally okay with me.

Randy simply stared at me with a blank look and said, "I can't help you." He walked away, leaving me in an even darker place than I had been before sharing my deepest thoughts with him. I lay on my bed, hoping that somehow the mattress would swallow me up and I would simply disappear. I tried willing it to happen. I visualized myself sinking deeper and deeper into the mattress until finally I was totally engulfed in it . . . then simply gone.

But it didn't work. The next day he said again, coldly, "You need to find someone to help you, because I can't." And again he walked away.

Loving and caring for someone with PTSD was so much different from my experience with my ten-year-old son Aaron when he was diagnosed with cancer. When people hear the word *cancer* they understand; most people have been personally touched by cancer. I was immediately surrounded by friends, family, and even total strangers providing prayers, support, and gifts when Aaron was sick. They may not have understood what it meant to have a brainstem glioma, but they all understood the word *cancer*.

In contrast, when you tell someone your husband has PTSD, you're faced with an empty gaze or people telling you there's no such thing. Very few people truly understand what PTSD has done to our soldiers, or the collateral damage to their families. This lack of understanding leaves those of us who are living in this deep dark world of PTSD feeling totally alone.

I knew that I needed help, but taking the steps to get help was difficult for me. That would mean that I was admitting that I was weak and unable to deal with my own life. I had always prided myself on being superwoman—independent, capable of handling anything that was thrown at me. Now I felt like a total, utter failure. Asking for help involved mental health—which was just flat embarrassing.

I'm not sure why I didn't go first to my pastor. Perhaps I thought he wouldn't understand, or that he'd judge me for the thoughts going through my mind. Regardless, a total stranger would be better. Someone trained to deal with whatever it was that was happening to me. So I pulled out the list of preferred providers for my medical insurance and began searching for the right person. I had no idea who the right person might be, but I chose a name, and with my fingers trembling, dialed the phone and made the appointment.

When I arrived at her office, my stomach was churning and my hands were shaking. Where would I start? What would I say? This was all so new to me. I had hired therapists to work with our clients. I had provided training to counselors on dealing with critically ill children and families after my son had passed away. When I was trying to make sense of my first marriage, we had gone to three different marriage counselors. But suddenly this all felt so foreign to me. Sitting in the small, dimly lit waiting room, I felt afraid.

"Hello, you must be Debbie," a warm and welcoming voice called out as the door opened into the next room. "Come in," she invited. I entered the room, which was even smaller than the first, and also dimly lighted. She motioned for me to sit on a small love seat, covered with soft inviting pillows, a box of Kleenex prominently placed on a side table. She sat at a small desk, with her chair pushed away.

As I did a quick once-over of the woman in front of me, my immediate impression was that she had never made it out of the sixties. Her colorful, flowing tie-dyed skirt and too tight paisley shirt assured me that she had been around during the Vietnam era. She spent most of our time together talking about her husband and her travels—nothing remotely connected to or helpful with my problem.

After two more sessions with her, and finally getting to share a little more about my situation, she looked at me square in the face and said, "You are getting nothing out of this marriage. You need to simply divorce him and move on with your life. You also have PTSD. "

There was no explanation of what she meant about me having PTSD, or how I had acquired it, let alone what to do about it. She provided no suggestions or explanations, just the flat statement that I also had PTSD.

So that was it? She was giving me an easy solution, to simply get a divorce. And would that also take care of my PTSD? I realized that I needed to find someone else, someone who had more experience and knowledge about PTSD. I began searching, and this time I dove deeper into qualifications and specialties. I found a psychotherapist who, according to the research, specialized in PTSD.

This time we went as a couple. Well, we *went* as a couple; however, all the time was spent with Randy, his issues, and his totally unrealistic views on pretty much everything. I was having a difficult time trying to deal with this stranger—my husband—whose logic and reason were so very far from mine.

Our appointments for couples therapy were scheduled directly after Randy's support group with his VA therapist, which turned out to be a terrible idea. Randy would leave his group meetings with heightened anxiety and depression from recounting his Vietnam experiences and listening to stories from fellow veterans in his group. Our marriage and my problems were of no concern when his mind was in the horrors of Vietnam.

This, however, was the only appointment time that was available for the therapist. We spent visit after visit learning to communicate, practicing fill-in-the-blank phrases, such as "When a person . . .goes for days without speaking to the person they live with, it can be very hurtful." I felt like a child in school again, with the teacher slapping the back of my hand with a ruler each time I said a word incorrectly.

After six weeks of being taught how to talk, we were no further ahead than when we had started. What good was it to learn to talk to a man who did not want to engage in a conversation, who would go for days on end in total silence?

I was totally frustrated, overcome by the feeling of hopelessness. Were there any answers to my questions? Was there anyone who could help me? My level of depression and anger grew even deeper.

The following week Randy had a conflicting medical appointment and was not able to make our appointment with the therapist. When I arrived alone, I was told that it was his policy not to meet with individuals when he was doing couples counseling. He continued to explain to me that if he met with just me, he would not be able to continue seeing us as a couple.

I told him that was fine. I desperately needed someone right that moment that would focus on me and my needs. As long as Randy was there, I seemed to blend into the wall. He had his support group with the VA and his private one-on-one; I had no one.

So the therapist agreed to proceed with the session. The focus was finally on me. I got to talk without someone jumping in and telling me that I was wrong, that I didn't feel "that way." When I had emptied out what had been building up inside of me, the therapist looked at me and said, "You have Post-Traumatic Stress Disorder" in plain and simple words. He then asked me why I even wanted to try to stay in this marriage.

I told him that it was because of my faith and my commitment. I had already divorced once, and that had devastated my family; I had been the first one in my family to cross that road. As angry and lost as I was at that moment, I knew that the man I had fallen in love with, the man that I had stood with in front of God, my family, and friends and promised to love, honor, and care for in sickness and in health was still inside there somewhere. I was desperately seeking someone to help me find him again.

The therapist looked at me and said, "You know, you're an attractive, intelligent woman. You still have time to enjoy your life; you can easily find a new man. Even though you keep telling me that your religion is keeping you from it, you need to consider yourself and your future. You need to get a divorce and move on."

How could I move on? I was broken. I was depressed. I had no idea who I was any longer, and I had become a stranger to myself. Three professional therapists had now told me I had PTSD—two of them offering the same simple answer: your husband is broken—just throw him away. I loved this man, and I had taken a marriage vow to stick with him in sickness. Did anyone understand that? What would happen if we all decided to leave? What if every one of us that is married to a veteran with the invisible wounds of war decided to leave? What would happen then?

Divorce was not the answer I was seeking. I knew inside that stranger was the man I had fallen in love with, and sometimes a glimpse of him would return. Besides, this was not his fault; this had happened to him while serving our country. He had been a mere boy of nineteen, experiencing horrors that would have rocked the world of a grown man. I wanted to know how to stay, how to live in this world of PTSD, to survive and thrive without losing myself forever.

I did not return to the psychotherapist. I found myself alone again, with nowhere to turn.

Nineteen-year-old Randy in DaNang, Vietnam

★ ★ ★ ★ ★

I continued to struggle. Then Randy finally received notice that his appeal had been approved and he was now rated at 100 disability. This meant that I now qualified for CHAMPVA, a health care program for spouses of disabled veterans through the Veterans Administration.

On my first visit to the clinic to get set-up with my new primary care physician, the nurse asked if I had had trouble with depression in the last two weeks.

I responded, "Yes, I have."

The nurse answered, "Okay, well, CHAMPVA doesn't cover mental health services, sorry." And he walked away.

I made phone call after phone call trying to find someone within the VA that could provide me with the help I so desperately needed. The only option available to me was to have joint counseling with Randy and his personal therapist. This would require my husband's permission. But this was his sacred place. He had developed a rapport with his therapist and felt that he was making progress. To have me invade this relationship was not an option that he was willing to agree to. Again, I was turned away from the help that I desperately needed.

It seemed like overnight I gained almost fifty pounds. I no longer went to the gym or even walked around the block. I was embarrassed to go out in public, to see anyone that "used to know me." I didn't know myself anymore. Depression had set in. I just felt empty; I was no longer able to smell the sweet fragrance of a flower or the rich aroma of a great cup of coffee, to taste a fine Cabernet, or to feel joy and happiness from anything around me.

My world was flat. I felt as if I had been put in prison and the key had been thrown away. I lost my focus and motivation; it took me days to do things that should have taken hours. I was grieving the loss of my husband; he had been replaced by a stranger. So many parts of my marriage were gone, never to return. I also grieved for the dreams for my future that were now dead. It seemed that my road of life had come to a dead end with no detour in sight.

I felt so very much alone. My daughter had moved away to college, the joy of my life now far away, returning home only for short visits. No more nights in her old room, and the ugliness of PTSD taking its toll on her as well.

As I lay in the familiar hiding place of my bed, it came to me that I was *grieving the living*. When my son Aaron died, it was a sad, difficult, and painful time. Many people say that the loss of a child is the worst possible thing that can happen to a parent. But when Aaron died there was closure. I said goodbye; I handed him into God's waiting arms.

As time went on, the constant reminders of the pain diminished; he was always in my heart and mind but not in such a painful way. I did not keep hopeful watch that one day he would return to me. I had unshakable faith that I would be with him again—but in heaven, not on earth. No roller coasters of up and down that come with hope—and disappointment. I was eventually able to begin to heal, so that the pain was no longer there on a daily basis. I was able to move forward with my life, replacing some of the pain with joyful memories of Aaron in my heart.

But when you see the source of your pain every day, it becomes a constant reminder of your loss. He is lying there next to you, so close that you can touch him . . . but you don't dare. You might startle him awake from a nightmare. You might irritate him. He no longer wants to be touched, to be close to you. He has enclosed himself in a block of ice that no chisel can chip away. So you lie next to him, but you might as well be a million miles away.

As you watch him sleep, you long for his touch, for the closeness that used to be a part of who you were together. Those moments that would make the rest of the world go away . . . when it was just the two of you lost in your love for each another. And now, you lie still and ache for that closeness, which you will never have again.

These changes don't just reflect the loss of something, they also carry with them weight, overwhelm, and relentless pain. Not only have you lost a part of yourself, you have received the extra burden of caring for someone else physically, mentally, emotionally, and financially. You look ahead and see things only getting worse, which creates more anger . . . more resentfulness . . . more guilt . . . and more depression.

After my son's death, my grieving was normal behavior. But the effects of my husband's PTSD on me and on our relationship put me into a world that I did not know or understand. He was getting support, surrounded by others in the veteran community who understood what he was going through. I was suffering in silence. No one knew what was happening to me—including me. I hid all of it from the outside world, while I remained totally lost inside the world of PTSD, experiencing a level of anger, depression, fear, and numbness that I had never in my life felt before.

When Aaron died, I don't recall ever feeling as if I had lost my will to live. I felt sadness and I missed him. I felt and continue to feel great pain when I think about how he suffered and wonder what he was thinking throughout his battle with cancer. But I don't recall feeling flat, not being able to smell the roses—at least not the same flat, lifeless feeling that I felt at the height of PTSD invading our life. I did not have the feeling of hopelessness that nothing in my life would ever change. I did not feel that my dreams were gone. Rather I had fear knowing that my life *would* change.

I began to ask myself, "I love him, so is this my destiny? But does it have to be? Is this what he wants for me? I know he loves me, and I know he would like a different life as well. Is it possible for him to move out of his darkness?"

As an outsider looking in, it's easy to say, "He's changed, just get over it." Grieving for someone who is very much alive is quite different than mourning a spouse that has died. There's finality to death. You know without a doubt that they are not coming back. But with PTSD you keep thinking they will be cured. You're hopeful that the person you fell in love with will come back.

And sometimes they do come back, for a moment or day or a week. Not totally back, but just enough to ignite a glimmer of hope that they will come back fully. Then, as suddenly as they came back, they are gone. And the grief starts all over again. Anger replaces hope; how can you possibly move on and finish the work of grieving when this terrible trick continues to be played on you?

How long does it take for acceptance? Can acceptance ever finally come as long as you hold out hope? You begin to fear that hope. The fear begins to overshadow the good times. You become so afraid of being disappointed yet again that, instead of cherishing each and every good and precious moment, you begin to stand back. You don't fully engage in those times; you are afraid to take it all in and enjoy each moment for what it is. You know that as suddenly as it came, it can disappear just as quickly.

I knew that Randy was lost too, in a world I knew nothing about. But his pain was being numbed by morphine and alcohol. His shoulder should have been healed long ago from the surgery; however, there was a pain inside him that was foreign to me just like events in the place where it all began . . . Vietnam.

I needed a GPS to find me in this deep dark place and take me off the road that my life had led me on. I needed to find a detour back to my dreams. I needed to find happiness, joy, and my purpose for being. I needed to reclaim my life. However, I had no idea where to begin. I felt powerless to do anything but stay right where I was.

CHAPTER 12

DEAD END TO DETOURS TO DREAMS

Debbie's Wake-up Sign

I t seemed that my road of life had come to a dead end with no detour in sight, until one morning my wake-up sign appeared. It was Sunday morning, June 6, 2010. Randy and I were driving to church in our normal state of silence, when out of the blue he said, "Debbie's a dead end."

"What did you say?" I wasn't sure that I had heard him correctly, but my immediate reaction was anger at what I thought I had heard.

He nonchalantly responded, "Oh, I was reading the sign," and pointed to a sign on my right that said, "Debbie Lane is a Dead End."

Why on that day, at that time, he decided to read that sign out loud to me, I have no idea. I had driven by that green "Debbie Lane" street sign, with the little yellow "DEAD END" warning attached, almost daily for the past twelve years . . . but those words on that day hit me like a ton of bricks.

Debbie is a Dead End . . . Debbie is a Dead End . . . DEBBIE IS A DEAD END! His voice kept ringing through my ears, the sound of those words making me fighting angry. "NO! I'm not a dead end!" I screamed silently. "I am not a quitter!"

I had faced much worse things in my life than what was happening right now, and I had survived—so I knew I could get through this as well. But at that moment I realized that I had the choice to stay in this dark lonely place or gather my strength and change my life. I made a decision: I was going to *take my life back!*

As we sat in church that morning, I continued to contemplate the sign. I knew that during other difficult times in my life I had been able to make it through because of my faith. I knew that I could not do this on my own. The only way to take my life back from the grip of PTSD was with God's help. I began praying, asking for the strength to begin this journey to reclaim the person I knew was still inside me. I had been living as a stranger, too, totally out of alignment with the essence of who I was. This angry, defeated woman was not me. I was a strong, compassionate, loving, and kind person. I wanted me back.

I also asked God for the ability to move beyond my fear and anger, and to be able to become more compassionate and forgiving. To respect my marriage vows by joyfully loving, honoring, and caring for my husband in his sickness. At the same time to be able to honor and cherish the life that God had given me, by lovingly caring for my own health and happiness. To remember that only by caring for myself would I have the physical and emotional strength to care for all those around me who needed my help and support. I prayed to understand the meaning of the challenges that had been put in front of me and to be able to use these lessons in service to others.

I had lost faith and confidence in myself, and the belief that I had any power or strength to do anything about the uncontrollable events that affected me. I realized that I had been held captive by the invisible bars of fear and self-doubt. If I was going to wage a battle against this stranger, first I needed to know and understand the source of my fear. I needed to know more about this unknown stranger called Post-Traumatic Stress Disorder that had infected our lives, leaving behind two strangers in my bed. Randy had become a stranger to me, and I had become a stranger to myself as well.

My journey began by researching and reading everything I could find on PTSD. The more I learned, the more I was able to understand Randy's behavior and mental anguish. I realized that this was not his fault and that he was trying to get better. He was going to therapy, was attending a support group, and was faithful in taking his medication; however, it would all take time. I was able to feel his pain in my heart and compassion rather than anger towards him. I also learned how I could better support him in his efforts to heal and learn how to better control his anxiety and anger. Slowly I was able to begin forgiving him for all the pain and hurt that he had caused me. I was also able to forgive myself for the sinful thoughts and anger that had consumed me.

I continued to dig deeper, reading every book I could find on PTSD to find out what had happened to me. I learned that spouses are often affected by PTSD, and I began to understand the reason for my depression, anger, anxiety, stress, and physical symptoms. I now realized that I was "mirroring" Randy's behavior, and this was a normal reaction for someone living with a person suffering from PTSD.

But while the effects of PTSD on spouses were acknowledged, limited information and resources were available for spouses on how to deal with the contagious effects of PTSD. There was information about how to help your spouse, but very little on how to help yourself. I found recommendations such as try harder, just get over it, grieve and move on, and deal with your stress. But there were no programs, tools, or steps on exactly how to do this. There was no book or guide to take me by the hand, to help me quickly and easily get to the place that I so desperately needed to go.

I had to take action. I began combing the bookstore again, and this time I came across *The Best Year of Your Life* by Debbie Ford. Yes, it was time to have the best year of my life, so, curious, I picked it up and started reading. I was immediately struck by her words: "When we are waiting for 'one day' to come in order to be happy—to experience joy, fun, passion, or success—we are living in an illusion that deadens our spirits and robs us of our ability to enjoy our lives right now."

Those words described exactly what had happened to me. I knew that I had been living in the hope that "one day" Randy was suddenly going to change back into the man that I had married, that he would be healed from this illness that had infected him. I read further and lit up when I saw these words: "Only by living in reality 100 percent of the time do we have the power to take action, make lasting changes, and become the masters of our lives."

I realized that it was time to accept my new reality. I knew that the Lord was the master of my life, and with his help I could begin to accept the life that hHe had given me, and begin to look for the good in the changes that had happened. My husband had changed, my life had changed, and it was never going to be the same as it was when our love story began. Embracing this thing called change was a very difficult but necessary part of life.

I continued to doubt myself. Did I really have the power to reclaim my life? The years of taking Randy's actions personally had left deep scars. Not feeling love from him had stripped away the love and compassion I had for myself. Blaming myself for what was happening to him and my inability to fix it had left me feeling worthless. Gaining almost fifty pounds at the same time as Randy's loss of interest in an intimate relationship with me had destroyed my self-confidence and left me feeling unattractive and undesirable. My spirit had been crushed.

I knew that I could not control Randy's words or actions. However, I could learn to control my reaction to them. If I could take away the mirror that Randy held, that had so much power over me, maybe I could reclaim my life. What if I held up my own mirror for Randy to see? What if I could show him what love, compassion, understanding, and joy looked like . . . could that make a difference in his life too? It was certainly worth a try.

So I set the intention on that day, June 26, 2010, to begin having the "best year of my life"—to create a year full of gratitude, happiness, health, and forgiveness. A year to begin changing the mirror of PTSD by filling it with happiness, forgiveness, gratitude, and healthy living.

As I set out on this journey, it was not what I had anticipated. I had expected that the "best year of my life" would somehow be without problems. Quite the opposite . . . the year was riddled with challenges, just like the many years that had come before. Numerous trips to the emergency room and a hospital stay for Randy. Another cancer scare that required surgery for me. My entire family in turmoil over my brother's messy divorce, my sister's life-threatening complications during her son's birth, my parents' emerging health issues, and my brother-in-law's arrest and prison sentence. Randy's kids encountering financial and health problems, Andrea and Randal dealing with new careers and a new life as husband and wife in a down economy.

But this was the reality of life. My problems were still here, and so were Randy's. The world was not going to stop while we took a time-out to get better.

As I watched the dreams of people around me crumble, I also saw that solutions were being found. Inner strength was coming out, sacrifices were being made, and life was moving forward. My personal struggles even seemed diminished by the loved ones around me facing their own life challenges.

I realized more than ever that it was time for a change with my own life, time to get on the road to health, happiness, and new dreams. And that no one was going to make that happen but me, with God by my side.

I certainly had the know-how to research and find answers. I had used this gift of being able to uncover resources and find solutions for other people's problems throughout my career. Thousands of people had been helped successfully through my efforts.

I began to read, research, attend classes, search out the experts in each field, and study their work. I studied PTSD more in depth, along with many self-help topics, including self-esteem, stress, anger, grief and loss, sleep, happiness, love, diet, health, fitness, and more. I began testing what I was learning to find solutions that worked for me.

As I dove deeper into the world of PTSD and veterans, I gained a heightened awareness that I was not alone; thousands of other spouses were also suffering in silence just as I had. Many were lost in this lonely world of PTSD and were desperate to get their life back. However, just like me, they had no idea where to begin.

This ignited an idea in me. The years of work that I had done to help myself in business, as well as personally, could be shared with others who were also suffering. I could help them move more quickly to a better place by sharing the tools and steps that I had learned. I drew from my education and work experience creating programs, teaching, and consulting. Creating programs was what I had done my entire career—programs to make people healthier, happier, and more balanced.

I took more classes and did the necessary preparation to become a Board Certified Coach, in order to expand the ways that I could reach out and help spouses of veterans with PTSD. Through coaching I could help spouses find solutions that worked in their lives and support them as they moved forward towards a brighter, healthier, and happier future.

I realized that this is what I had been preparing to do for my entire life. I had been in hibernation, waiting for someone or something to wake me up and tell me my life purpose.

That purpose is you! And my mission today is to assist you in taking *your life back.*

CHAPTER 13

PEACE TODAY, HOPE FOR TOMORROW

Randy and I worked very hard to save our marriage from the perils of PTSD. In order to begin to heal, it was necessary for each of us to be willing do our own work, as well as to work together. As a result, we've been able to create a peaceful daily existence and new hope for our future together.

For Randy it required the desire to get better. He told me that PTSD is like alcohol or drug addiction: you need to want get better, and you have to put in the work and effort on yourself. He did, and he has! In fact, when I look back to where we were at the height of Randy's PTSD explosion, the change has been dramatic. Randy has worked very hard to get where he is today, and he continues to get help from a therapist, go to his support group, and take his medication—all of which are critical.

In addition, he has become cautious with his pain medication use, sought forgiveness from the people he has hurt, and learned to be more patient and present in his reactions to triggers in his life. I have the upmost respect and gratitude for his therapist for his work with Randy, not just for giving me back my husband, but for fostering a kinder, more considerate, and gentler man.

I also give infinite thanks to the Purple Heart Vietnam vet who recognized Randy's pain, took him by the hand, and led him to a place where his healing could begin. Once he walked through that door, it was up to Randy to do the rest. All the actions to get better took courage, determination, and work. Everything he did was on his own initiative. I honor my husband for the work he did to get better.

For example, one Sunday morning on our way to church Randy told me that he needed to talk to Andrea and Randal. My first thought was fearful: *Oh, great, what has he come up with now?* It continued to break my heart every time Andrea came home from school and her time at our house was limited to an uneasy dinner, or an hour here and there. As we were walking out of church, he looked over at them with a face of stone and said, "I need to talk to you."

Their faces mirrored mine, fearful over what he wanted to say. Rather than waiting for a more private place, or sitting down over breakfast, he began right then, on the sidewalk just outside the front door of the church. Randy began pouring out the most heartfelt apology I had ever heard. He explained his PTSD, not to makes excuses but simply as a point of knowledge. He asked for their forgiveness for all the pain he had caused them. He thanked them for hanging in there even though he had been such a jackass. When he finished, the tears were flowing and the hugs close and healing.

I will never know the extent of PTSD's damaging effects on Randy's life prior to our meeting. His three failed marriages, a strained relationship with his children and his brother Brent, and a non-existent relationship with his brother Brian were signs that PTSD may have interfered in his life before we met. Today, he has made amends to all of his

Andrea and Randal in love and engaged

family, and he continues to put a great deal of effort into being a part of his children's, grandchildren's, and brothers' lives. Our family is now whole.

As I share my personal story with others, the same questions continue to be asked:

"Why do you stay?" My answer is that I stay because I can. I now understand that love for him was not enough. I had to learn to love and care for myself so that I did not continue to allow his behavior to destroy me (see the "Eight Steps to Taking Your Life Back" in part 5 for concrete examples of how I did this). I finally realized that I could not look to him to provide a gauge for my personal worth and happiness.

I began to recognize that not all of his words and actions were about me. Most importantly, I remembered that strength, understanding, and compassion were always just a prayer away. And today I also remind myself that I am already the recipient of an amazing, unconditional love, and that any love I receive above this bountiful love from the Lord is a bonus.

Yes, there were times when I thought about divorce, and on more than one occasion, I felt that I just could not go on living in this world of PTSD any longer. I made that phone call for the complimentary consultation. I left knowing that I did have a choice. And my choice was to stay.

"Why would you choose to live the way you do?" My answer is because it works for us. I can remember in the past looking at marriages that were not as I thought they should be and wondering the same thing. There was a time in my life when I would look at married couples who seemed always to be going in separate directions . . . vacations, social events, hobbies, friends, and family. I just couldn't understand . . . that wasn't what marriage was all about. Who would want to be in a marriage like that? Certainly not me. I wanted my husband to be my constant companion, my best friend, and my playmate; what would possibly bring you together if you did nothing together?

"How is your life today?" Really? I have arrived at a happier, more joy-filled place. I am more confident. I am thinner, healthier, and happier. I have learned to deal with my stress and depression. I am sleeping well. My fear has been replaced by a quiet confidence in my abilities and strengths, along with the comfort that I always have someone watching over me to provide for all my needs.

I am now aware that PTSD numbs your emotions to those around you, even those you deeply love. Randy was so wound up in his own world of pain and anger that he was oblivious to what was going on with me. Through knowledge and understanding, I have now found compassion and forgiveness for that time in our life, and have been able to let go of my anger.

I wish I could say that my life is totally wonderful and that I'm happy all the time, but that would not be the truth. I still miss my friend and my lover. I miss the dreams that I had for our future. At times, I am lonely—when we are going our separate ways, and even when he is right next to me. However, there are no guarantees that had I followed the easy path that was suggested I would be happier today. Marriage takes work, love, and commitment. With the Lord's help, I continue to strive to honor my marriage vows, and I have gratitude for the many blessings in my marriage and my life.

Despite his improvements, Randy's PTSD has not gone away: the nightmares, the nighttime vigilance, the problem in crowds, the days of depression, and the lack of intimacy will always be part of our life. His physical problems from the effects of Agent Orange, such as diabetes and neuropathy, will only get worse with time. His pain, migraines, and high blood pressure will be a constant for the rest of his life. Those problems will always be the music that we dance to. We have learned to live a more peaceful existence with the stranger that is part of our life, and we look with hope to the future.

This certainly did not turn out to be the life that I had imagined. But today my life seems almost normal to me—it is our normal. I truly believe that God has designed my life with the pain and challenges that I have encountered for a purpose. I have been provided the knowledge and experience to lead me to where I am today, to fulfill my life's work. I am working diligently on my mission to create a better understanding of how PTSD suffered by our veterans affects their spouses and families—as well as helping spouses to cherish their own needs for health and happiness, so they can have the strength to love, honor, and care for their veteran in sickness.

You see, there have always been wars. And most likely wars will continue until the end of time. And with war comes pain, for those who find themselves in the middle of the war zone, and for those loved ones who continue to support that hero until he or she is safely back at home.

However, today's wars are different and leave a multitude of wounds. For many soldiers the war will never be over. The silent war continues in their minds as a result of post-traumatic stress and traumatic brain injuries. Physical wounds bring relentless pain and disabilities, and the secret evils of chemicals continue to bring innumerable illnesses and difficulties.

Today's soldiers need more help and support from their loved ones than ever before in the history of war. But who will support today's spouses so they can continue to have the strength to hold up our warriors? Again, I wonder, what if we all walked away? What if every spouse of every warrior throughout the ages had walked way? Our warriors' spouses need to be cherished . . . so they can honor and care for our warriors. Helping to fulfill that need has become my passion. Living a life of passion was an essential step in getting my life back.

★ ★ ★ ★ ★

I had not realized how difficult it would be to write my story. I found the anger returning as I recounted the worst years of Randy's PTSD. As I dug deep into my memory and reread my journals in order to share the events of the invasion of PTSD in my life, I found that summoning up my feelings from those years caused me to spiral back down into the deep dark hole of pain and despair. With each chapter, I kept saying I just want to be done. It was reminiscent of my feelings when I was in the depths of my struggle with PTSD; I just wanted it to be over.

But revisiting those memories did more than just recreate pain—it gave me the opportunity to have a much better perspective on how far both Randy and I have come. And it gave me a greater appreciation of what others are going through today.

Since I began helping other spouses, I have heard many tragic stories— stories that make my experience seem like the normal difficulties of a good marriage. Women living in fear that their husbands will be successful in their next suicide attempt. Spouses and children who fear for their lives and are forced to leave because of physical abuse. Flashbacks and PTSD episodes that have led to arrests, court battles, loss of jobs, and even prison. Severe drug and alcohol self-medication by veterans and the collateral damage it causes to families.

In some families, it is not just spouses but also children struggling with the effects of secondary PTSD. Numerous wives tolerate verbal and mental abuse on a daily basis. Thousands of veterans refuse to seek treatment, leaving spouses and children in a world without hope or support. Spouses caring for their wounded warrior with severe physical, mental, and health issues, requiring 100 percent caregiving attention . . . while carrying the entire load of caring for children and a household.

The struggles I faced were minuscule in comparison to the many thousands of spouses that are hurting today and the hundreds of thousands more that will soon be facing the stranger of PTSD when their soldier returns home. If I can help even one family's life to be better, my journey will be worthwhile.

★ ★ ★ ★ ★

In part 5 of this book, you will learn eight essential steps to *taking your life back*. I am honored to share what I have learned to help you create a place of love, understanding, and compassion for your veteran and yourself. There are tools to help you begin to *cherish you* as you learn how to begin accepting your situation; uncovering your power; creating a support system; releasing your anger; learning the power of love, compassion, and forgiveness; overcoming fear; managing stress and overwhelm; designing healthy habits; and enriching your life with passion, happiness, and fun. Your final step will be to set your GPS for your detour to your dreams and a brighter tomorrow.

My health and happiness today is a conscious effort, but much of it has now become a habit. However, sometimes I falter; I forget to use the tools in my box. I don't pay attention to the warning signs; I fall away from my maintenance routine. I find that I'm not perfect.

The difference today is that I have knowledge and understanding. I know what is happening to me, and why. I know how to use my tools to get quickly back on track, to help lift me up and to keep me moving forward on this new road. I have the confidence that there is a brighter future and new dreams ahead.

If I can do this, so can you. I am no different from you. The only difference between you and me is that I have started down the road on a detour to my dreams. Are you ready to join me and take the first step on the road to your dreams—and a brighter tomorrow?

As you begin testing out the tools that you will learn, remember that each love and life is unique. One solution does not work for everyone. Pick your solutions, learn, practice, and master. Repeat as necessary. Change your tools when required.

And remember, sometimes the cake falls anyway, no matter how carefully you follow the recipe.

PART 2

GETTING TO KNOW THE STRANGER: POST-TRAUMATIC STRESS DISORDER

Touch those dusky soldiers, march them from their beds;
Change those dusky soldiers, push them to the edge:
Long-time suffering, see freedom's shore
Deep solemn cliffs echo freedom's roar.

Sounds of love, sounds of hate,
Sounds that set them free;
Sounds of freedom, sounds of fate,
Sounds of liberty!
Release yourself from the past:
Sever the ties to what holds you back.
Place each memory on the fire
One by one, burn all night . . .
Lose yourself in the present.
Disregard recollection and anticipation:
What is "now" is burning bright.

The river of sadness is followin' me;
Like blood on the streets you're stalkin' me.
The river of sadness is gettin' deeper,
The river is blood and you're its keeper.
The river of sadness is drownin' me.
Keeper of the river you've captured me:
I'm all tied up, I'm screamin' now
I can't escape, I don't know how.

from "The Beginning"
by David Saywell

INTRODUCTION

I knew that my husband had changed in many ways. He had post-traumatic stress disorder—but I did not really know what that meant. I had never known anyone with PTSD; at least, that's what I believed at the time Randy was diagnosed. I had no previous knowledge or experience with this strange new diagnosis. Even though I had a minor in psychology and had worked for many years in the health care industry, I didn't recall ever hearing about PTSD, even when I provided recreation therapy consulting to a psychiatric lock-up facility.

I realized that in order to successfully live in this new world, I needed to learn everything I could about what had turned my husband into a stranger. I did, and in part 2, I will share with you the many faces of the stranger that takes over the lives of our veterans.

First, PTSD affects far more than just the mind—mind, body, and spirit all show signs of the trauma of war. We'll begin by exploring the mental, emotional, and physical symptoms common with PTSD. We'll look at the extent to which veterans are affected by PTSD, the numbers of veterans currently diagnosed, the potential for the numbers to grow, and the devastating topic of suicide and PTSD.

Next, we will explore how PTSD affects a veteran's spirituality, looking at both the negative and positive effects of war trauma on spirituality. We'll look at guilt, which has a tremendous impact on many veterans. We'll also discuss the positive relationship between spirituality and health—and how faith can help in the healing process.

Recently PTSD has become a newsworthy topic, and many people are questioning why now—why hasn't this happened in the past? It did, and when we look at PTSD from a historical perspective, we see that PTSD is not something new at all. In fact, there is evidence of the existence of PTSD as far back as early biblical days. We'll look at some of this evidence in this section.

By the end of part 2, you will have gained valuable knowledge about the tragic effects of trauma on the mind, body, and spirit. You will understand how PTSD can turn your veteran into a stranger.

CHAPTER 14 # INTRODUCING THE STRANGER: PTSD

Who is this stranger called PTSD, who has taken over your veteran's mind and body and threatened to destroy your life? How can you start to understand this thing that has invaded your life?

Knowledge is power. The ability to be proactive rather than reactive is essential. In this chapter we'll define PTSD and discuss its symptoms and triggers, how aging veterans are affected, and statistics about the number of veterans affected by PTSD and needing health care.

What is PTSD?

The simple explanation is that PTSD is a normal reaction to an abnormal experience. A more formal definition provided by the National Center for PTSD is:

> **Post-traumatic Stress Disorder (PTSD)** *is an anxiety disorder that can develop after exposure to any event that results in psychological trauma.*

This event may involve the threat of death to oneself or to someone else, or to one's own or someone else's physical, sexual, or psychological integrity, overwhelming the individual's ability to cope.

PTSD does not just happen in combat situations. There are many types of traumatic events that can occur which can cause PTSD such as:

- Being in a war zone, even if not in direct combat.
- Child sexual or physical abuse.
- Terrorist attack.
- Sexual or physical assault.
- Serious accidents, like a car wreck.
- Natural disasters, like a fire, tornado, hurricane, flood, or earthquake.
- Working as firefighters, law enforcement officers, and other emergency personnel.

Most people who go through a trauma have some symptoms at the beginning. However, only some will develop PTSD over time. It isn't clear why some people develop PTSD and others don't.

Some of the reasons as to whether or not you get PTSD can depend on:

- How intense the trauma was or how long it lasted.
- If you were injured or lost someone important to you.
- How close you were to the event.
- How strong your reaction was.
- How much you felt in control of events.
- How much help and support you got after the event.

PTSD has come to the forefront during the past few years, and there is now much more research being conducted in an attempt to answer this question as to why some soldiers get PTSD and others with the same experience don't. New methods are being tested both before, during, and immediately after trauma experiences in an effort to determine if preventive measures are possible to prevent or lessen the effects of war trauma on our military.

There are some conflicting views on the existence of PTSD. Some cite evidence that it was present as far back as biblical times; some deny that it exists at all. For those that claim it does not exist, the spouses of veterans suffering from PTSD in unison will say, "Come live at my house for a week—you will become a believer!"

Symptoms of PTSD

PTSD symptoms usually start soon after the traumatic event, but they may not appear until months or years later. They also may come and go over many years. If the symptoms last longer than four weeks, cause great distress, or interfere with work or home life, your veteran might have PTSD. If they are experiencing some of the symptoms below you should encourage them to seek help.

According to the National Center for PTSD there are four types of symptoms of PTSD. This is an expansion of the three PTSD symptom clusters originally identified in the *4th Edition of the Diagnostic and Statistical Manual of Mental Disorders (DSM-IV)*. The additional symptom included by the National Center for PTSD is feeling numb. These are the four categories of symptoms used for a diagnosis of PTSD:

1. **Reliving the event (also called re-experiencing symptoms).** Memories of the traumatic event can come back at any time. The same fear and horror that was felt when the event happened can be experienced in any of these ways:

    *   Having **nightmares.**
    *   Feeling like you're going through the event again. This is called a **flashback.**
    *   Seeing, hearing, or smelling something that causes you **to relive the event**. This is called a **trigger.** The smell of diesel fuel, the sound of a helicopter, news reports, or hearing a car backfire are examples of triggers.
    *   Having strong feelings of **distress** when reminded of the traumatic event.

- Being **physically responsive**, such as experiencing a surge in your heart rate or sweating, to reminders of the traumatic event.

2. **Avoiding situations that are a reminder of the event.**

- Trying to avoid situations or people that trigger memories of the traumatic event.
- Avoiding talking or thinking about the event.
- Avoiding crowds, because they feel dangerous.
- Avoiding driving if they were in a car accident or their military convoy was bombed.
- Avoiding watching war movies or the news on television.
  - Keeping very busy, becoming a workaholic, or avoiding seeking help because they don't want to think or talk about the event.
- Feeling as though their life may be cut short.

3. **Feeling numb.** It may be hard for them to express their feelings. They may avoid memories. It may be hard to remember or talk about parts of the trauma. For example:

- They may not have positive or loving feelings toward other people and may stay away from relationships.
- They may no longer be interested in activities that they used to enjoy.
- It may be hard for them to experience emotions.

4. **Feeling keyed up (also called *hyperarousal*).** They may be jittery, or always alert and on the lookout for danger, and may experience:

- Having a difficult time falling or staying asleep.
- Feeling more irritable or having outbursts of anger.
- Having difficulty concentrating.
- Feeling constantly "on guard" or like danger is lurking around every corner.

- Being "jumpy" or easily startled.
- Needing to have their back to a wall in a restaurant or waiting room.

A number of physical health problems have also been found to be associated with a diagnosis of PTSD among veterans. These include:

- Chronic pain.
- Sexual dysfunction.
- Obesity.
- Health problems from exposure to hazardous substances.

People with PTSD are also more likely than those without PTSD to experience cardiovascular problems, diabetes, and a wide range of other physical ailments.

PTSD also often develops in people with traumatic brain injury (TBI). TBI occurs from a sudden blow or jolt to the head. It's becoming a growing concern for soldiers coming home from the current conflicts in Afghanistan and Iraq (OEF/OIF), where the main causes are blasts, motor vehicle accidents, and gunshot wounds.

Because TBI is caused by trauma and there is symptom overlap with PTSD, it can be hard to tell what the underlying problem is. However, it's important to be assessed, because people with TBI should not use some medications. And no matter how mild or severe the injury itself was, the effects can be serious.

For more information and resources on TBI and PTSD—symptoms, treatments and diagnosis—visit www.detours2dreams.com.

Aging Veterans and PTSD

PTSD symptoms can occur soon after a traumatic experience, but this is not always the case. While some veterans begin to have PTSD symptoms soon after they return from war, which may last until older age, other veterans don't have PTSD symptoms until later in life. And for others, PTSD symptoms can be high right after their war experience, go down over the years, and then worsen again later in life.

It's a common question as to why, for some veterans, PTSD symptoms show up so many years after they served in combat and begin affecting their lives. There are a number of reasons that symptoms of PTSD may increase with age:

- After retirement from work, symptoms may feel worse, because there is more time to think and fewer distractions from memories.
- Medical problems can increase symptoms.
- Loss of friends, parents, siblings, or spouse can trigger symptoms.
- The aging brain is no longer able to keep symptoms under control.
- The current war scenes on the television may bring back bad memories.
- Alcohol and other substances may have been used in the past to cope with stress. Then if the veteran stops drinking later in life, without another, healthier way of coping, this can make PTSD symptoms seem worse.
- For many aging people it is a time of reflection and a search for meaning in their life. This may entail coming face to face with the horror of their past.

Statistics

Between 1965 and 1975 more than 3 million Americans served in Vietnam. Around 1.5 million American soldiers saw combat, and 58,220 US troops were killed.

The National Vietnam Veterans' Readjustment Study (NVVRS) was mandated in 1983 to investigate PTSD and other postwar psychological problems among Vietnam veterans. Overall the NVVRS found that at the time of the study approximately 830,000 male and female Vietnam theater veterans (26 percent) had symptoms and related functional impairment associated with PTSD.

A re-analysis of the NVVRS data, along with other data from the Matsunage Vietnam Veterans Project (Schnurr, Lunney, Sengupta, and Waelde, 2003) found that, contrary to the initial analysis of the NVVRS data, a large majority of Vietnam veterans struggle with chronic PTSD symptoms, with four out of five reporting recent symptoms when interviewed twenty to twenty-five years after Vietnam.

In response to a request from the Government Accountability Office (GAO), the VA compiled a report enumerating the total number of Operation Enduring Freedom (OEF), Operation Iraqi Freedom (OIF), and Operation New Dawn (OND) veterans who were diagnosed with PTSD by the VA Medical Center (VAMC) and Vet Centers. This report covers health data from October 1, 2001 to June 30, 2012 and contains the following information:

- 1,515,707 veterans have separated from active duty following a deployment.
- 834,463 have obtained health care from the VA.
- 247,243 who obtained VA health care have been diagnosed with PTSD.

These numbers do not include the 2.4 million troops (as of June 30, 2012) who have served or are serving in current conflicts. If we take this 2.4 million and add the 681,244 veterans who have separated from the military and have not obtained health care from the VA, we have 3,081,244 veterans with unknown status in terms of PTSD.

According to an April 17, 2008 news release from the Rand Corporation, one in five military service members who have returned from Iraq and Afghanistan reported symptoms of PTSD or major depression, yet only slightly over half have sought treatment.

Many returning soldiers say that they do not seek treatment for psychological illnesses because of potential peer reaction, and the fear that it may damage their careers. Many also worry about the side effects of medication, or believe that family and friends can provide more help than a mental health professional. But even of those who do seek treatment for PTSD or major depression, only about half receive treatment that researchers consider "minimally adequate" for their illnesses.

Finally, let's not forget another related and tragic statistic: suicide rates among veterans at home. At least 23,000 veterans from the Iraq, Afghanistan, and Libya conflicts have killed themselves since 2008, according to the Veterans Administration, Center for Disease Control, and CBS news. The numbers are continuing to grow each year. The latest study released by the VA Feb. 1, 2013 estimates an average of twenty-two veterans per day commit suicide. In 2012 more soldiers died from suicide than on the battlefield.

Suicide has also taken its toll on Vietnam veterans. In this deadly war, 58,220 soldiers were killed in action. More Vietnam veterans have taken their own lives than there are names on the Vietnam Wall. It is estimated that the number could exceed 100,000.

There is no clear answer as to why this is happening, but PTSD seems to be a common factor.

The long-term consequences for those who do not receive treatment, or are undertreated, create cascading effects for our veterans, such as drug use, suicide, marital problems, and unemployment. And PTSD has a dramatic effect on our veterans, their families, and society as a whole.

It is, therefore, essential that our nation become educated on PTSD, and provide the social support needed for our veterans suffering from the invisible wounds of war, so they can be at ease in reaching out for the help they so desperately need.

CHAPTER 15

THE EFFECTS OF TRAUMA ON SPIRITUALITY

T he experience of war can have both positive and negative effects on a soldier's spirituality. The negative effects can range from simple concerns to spiritual distress, or, at the highest level, spiritual despair, where life has little or no meaning and no hope of resolution.

In this chapter we'll look at a broad range of the effects of trauma on spirituality, from negatives such as guilt and the inability to find meaning in life, to positives such as finding God and its effects on physical and mental well-being.

Spirituality has many different definitions, but for our purposes of discussing the effects of trauma on spirituality, we will be looking at it from a religious point of view. Spirituality is a belief in a power that is greater than ourselves, the place where our deepest values and meanings of life come from, our source for inspiration and orientation.

As we grow and have new experiences, we are constantly reviewing and updating who we are: 1) our self-identity, 2) life purpose, and 3) the meaning we attribute to our existence. These are three very important spiritual functions; whether we think about it or not, we connect with our sense of self, purpose, and meaning every day of our lives. Let's look at PTSD as it relates to these areas.

Negative Effects

When veterans join the military, their view of themselves in the world is now based on their life in the military. When this experience includes war and combat, the trauma of the events can make it difficult for some veterans. "Spiritual injuries" can make it very hard for these veterans to find answers to these three spiritual life issues. They may need support and assistance as they deal with their memories of combat and their view of themselves as the result of their military life.

It's easy to see how this causes the Christian soldier in the midst of war to struggle with his spirituality. On the one hand, he has learned God's fifth commandment in the Bible, directing him with the words "Thou shall not kill." On the other hand, in John 15:13, the Bible says, "Greater love hath no man than this, that he lay down his life for a friend."

What happens to the soldier spiritually when he believes he has failed on both counts—when he has both killed the enemy and failed to prevent the deaths of his fellow soldiers? He is forced to deal with terrible grief and guilt.

Guilt

As Dr. Larry Dewey, MD, says in his book *War and Redemption*, "What they [combat veterans] are most troubled by is guilt over killing, the traumatic grief they suffer for beloved comrades brutally killed and the fear that they may have let their comrades down (guilt and shame) at some crucial point."

Guilt is an emotion that comes with war. It may be perceived or real. *Survivor's guilt* is the feeling that it should have been you that died, not your comrade. In addition, there is the feeling that you could have done more, or that you should still be there helping your friends who are still in danger while you're safe at home.

Real guilt may be experienced over the sin you believe you have truly committed by breaking either man's law or God's law. Perceived guilt is blaming yourself for something that you truly had no control over. But to the soldier, real guilt and perceived guilt feel just the same. They are equally painful.

Often a soldier feels that his or her sin is different from anyone else's. They believe they are unforgivable despite God's promises. Their guilt can be over actions thought to have been against God's laws or over lack of action—in other words, guilt over things that they did or did not do.

Abandoned by God

When bad things happen to good people, the feeling of abandonment by God is understandable. This is especially true when a veteran experiences the horrors of battle. His first thoughts and feelings are often those of anger towards God, questioning why God is not answering his prayers or how he could let such horrible things happen. When his prayers are not answered as he'd like, it's easy to feel that God doesn't care about him or even lose faith that there is a God.

As you might imagine, these feelings of abandonment can also lead to additional problems, especially if the soldier is also battling with PTSD. Dr. Margie Nelson-Pechot explains that this feeling of abandonment brings about negative religious coping skills, and for the veteran already struggling with PTSD, the symptoms can become even more severe. There may also be an increase in depression, anxiety, and stress, and an overall decrease in the veteran's quality of life.

Positive Effects

For some soldiers, war brings a greater connection to God. The trauma of war can actually have a positive effect on their spirituality. For some, their faith is strengthened when they feel God's presence in battle and are brought home safely. They may also find satisfaction in sharing their faith with others, helping them to find comfort in the Lord. They may be able to look with more gratitude on the positive things that have happened during the war experience.

Relationship Between PTSD and Spirituality

Dr. Margie Nelson-Pechot conducted a study concerning the relationship between PTSD and spirituality on Vietnam combat veterans. One of the topics addressed was which aspects of individual spirituality may prevent a soldier from developing PTSD, and which aspects of his spirituality may result in prolonged suffering from symptoms of PTSD.

The result of the study showed that veterans who reported frequent church worship had fewer and less severe PTSD symptoms or no PTSD symptoms. They were also likely to report finding satisfaction and purpose in their lives.

Veterans who reported higher numbers of PTSD symptoms and had more severe symptoms were also likely to report alienation from God and difficulty reconciling their faith with their Vietnam experiences.

These results revealed that overall, veterans' positive experiences of spirituality were associated with better long-term adjustment to combat trauma. The negative components of spirituality were associated with greater long-term distress. Even if these connections are small, growing literature documents the importance of social support for recovery from trauma, including the sense of support from God as a positive source for healing.

How You Can Help

Spiritual pain and suffering can be as real and powerful as physical or emotional pain; recognizing the importance of treating the wounds of the mind, body, and spirit is essential in the PTSD healing process. The Veterans Administration has always recognized that faith is an important healing resource for many veterans, and they estimate that one-fourth of people who seek help for mental health problems go to members of the clergy.

There are many ways we can help our veterans renew or develop the support of a spiritual connection, so vital to their recovery. First, learning about PTSD and how it has affected our veterans and their spirituality is essential. You can gently begin to open up conversations with your veteran; the starting point is to learn what their current feelings are about God in relationship to the war and their trauma. What has made them believe that God has abandoned them?

Next, look at the assumptions about what your veteran felt God should have done when he felt abandoned. Try to get him to consider whether it's still helpful for him to view this in the same way. Is it accurate? Is it productive to hold this view today? How might you help him reframe his thoughts and beliefs?

But the number one tool and quickest, easiest way to begin to redevelop the feelings of spiritual connection with God is through prayer. Prayer can bring about hope, thankfulness, comfort, support, growth, and peace. Prayer can help the veteran become whole again.

Often, roadblocks prevent a veteran from reaching out in prayer. They may feel too guilty or "dirty" to talk to God. They may continue to harbor strong feelings of anger, betrayal, or abandonment in their relationship with God. This barrier can be overcome by providing assurance that this is understandable, that what he's experiencing are normal reactions to trauma.

Hope and help increase as more clergy begin seeing the growing need our veterans have for spiritual healing. As they become more knowledgeable about the specific spiritual needs and wounds of our veterans, they can step up and provide the peace, comfort, and support that our veterans need to heal from the trauma of war.

Sharing this book with your church community and spiritual organizations is a great place to start. VA chaplains, part of the VA health care team, are also available. Another valuable resource for the spiritual community is Family of a Vet's community education packets for church congregations and faith-based organizations.

THE HISTORY OF POST-TRAUMATIC STRESS DISORDER

Today the term PTSD is becoming much more prevalent than in the past. There is a growing awareness of the existence of PTSD—you hear about it on the evening news, see it portrayed in popular television shows, and read about it in numerous news articles. With this new widespread attention, I often hear the question, why now? Why hasn't this been a problem in the past?

If we look back in history, we can find evidence of PTSD as far back as biblical times. Numerous stories in the Bible narrate events of extreme difficulties and trauma, followed by descriptions of behaviors and symptoms that are used today to diagnose PTSD.

One familiar example from the Book of Genesis is the story of Noah, which tells of God's grief as he watched the wickedness of man. The Lord decided to destroy both man and all creatures that he had created. However, Noah found grace in the eyes of the Lord, and God told Noah of his plan to destroy all living things on earth by bringing a flood. God then instructed him to build an ark for himself and his family and to bring two of every living thing on the ark with him.

Noah followed God's commands. The flood came and destroyed every living substance on the face of the earth, with the exception of Noah and those that were with him on the ark.

After the flood, God brought them safely to rest on dry land. Noah planted a vineyard, but when he drank the wine, he became drunk and lay uncovered in his tent. His son found him drunk and naked in his tent.

Is it possible that Noah was traumatized by seeing the destruction of all humankind and the world as he knew it? Could Noah have suffered from survivor's guilt? Was this the reason that he turned to alcohol, a common form of self-medication for PTSD patients, as a means of numbing himself from the pain of seeing the world destroyed?

The book of Job in the Holy Bible shares the extreme suffering, loss of material possessions, grief from the loss of his children, and mental and psychological anguish that Job experienced. It is a heartbreaking story of human trauma. Job talks about his feelings and describes symptoms that are familiar in the diagnosis of PTSD, such as grief, fear, loneliness, frightening dreams, terrifying visions, and the fatigue of sleepless nights—as well as his deep desire to be rid of the pain that was so great death seemed better than life.

Research shows that there is a high degree of similarity between the descriptions of Job's reactions and symptoms of PTSD as described in the most current diagnostic criteria.

Historical medical literature also reveals clinical symptoms very similar to PTSD dating back to the Egyptian civilization. An example of combat-related PTSD can be seen in Homer's great epic *The Iliad*. Written around 730 B.C., it tells the story of a series of horrifying experiences of battle trauma experienced by the ancient Hellenic warriors.

In describing the world of the soldiers in *The Iliad*, Homer pays special tribute to the objects of war and the human condition during extreme situations. We see a glimpse of battle stress and the capacity of humans to resist this trauma. *The Iliad* also tells the story of another tragedy of war: the Trojan women who became war widows who also experienced both physical and mental trauma, illustrating another example of the effects of war on families.

Civil War veterans showed both physical and emotional symptoms from the trauma of battle, which were given the term *soldier's heart* in 1876 by U.S. Civil War physician Dr. Mendez Da Costa. Some of the symptoms included startle responses, hyper-vigilance, chest pain, fatigue, heart arrhythmias, and more.

Shell shock first appeared in the *British Medical Journal* in 1915, and was first thought to be a physical injury from "brain shake." The symptoms included reduced visual fields, loss of taste and smell, and loss of memory. Later it was determined that it was a mental condition, or nervous breakdown, and shell shock was generally seen as a sign of emotional weakness or cowardice.

World War II combat trauma was given the term *combat fatigue* in 1939. It was characterized by symptoms including hypersensitivity to things such as noises, movements, and light. Other symptoms included overactive responses, such as involuntary defensive jerking; easily provoked irritability progressing even to acts of violence; and sleep disturbances, which included battle dreams, nightmares, and inability to fall asleep.

In 1980, as a result of the Vietnam War, PTSD was recognized as a disorder with specific symptoms that could be reliably diagnosed. At that time, the American Psychiatric Association added PTSD to the third addition of the *Diagnostic and Statistical Manual of Mental Disorders (DSM-III)*. Prior to this, many mental health professionals, as well as the general public, had doubted this was a true mental disorder.

In 1993, the World Health Organization recognized PTSD as a separate diagnostic entity in its medical classification list, The International Classification of Diseases and Related Health Problems 10th Revision (ICD-10). The ICD is the international standard diagnostic classification for all general epidemiological purposes, as well as many health management and clinical uses. It codes diseases, signs, symptoms, abnormal findings, complaints, social circumstances, and external causes of injury or diseases, as classified by the World Health Organization. This was an important step in validating the existence of PTSD on a worldwide basis.

In 1994 the American Psychiatric Association's *Diagnostic and Statistical Manual of Mental Disorders – Fourth Edition* (DSM-IV-TR) defined PTSD with three core clusters of symptoms and behaviors: 1) re-experiencing symptoms, 2) avoidance of situations or reminders of the trauma, and 3) hyperarousal.

Today, there are numerous research projects in place to further define, treat, and hopefully prevent PTSD. Much more education than ever before is available for professionals, families, and our communities to help alleviate the stigma that for centuries has overshadowed our heroes' ability to receive needed treatment. Great strides have been made; however, much more will be needed as our soldiers return from the current battlefields.

PART 3

HELPING THE STRANGER: TREATMENTS FOR POST-TRAUMATIC STRESS DISORDER

*There is a time for everything, and a season for every activity under heaven…
a time to kill and a time to heal…a time for war and a time for peace.*

Ecclesiastes 3:1, 3, 8

INTRODUCTION

The trauma of war has taken a great toll on our veterans as they continue to suffer long after they return home from the battlefield. The good news is that there is a growing amount of help to treat PTSD, giving hope for anyone suffering from or living with the disease.

In part 3 we will look at how military indoctrination affects our soldiers' minds, and how this can cause both positive and negative effects when our soldiers return home. We will then look at how therapy can begin to turn around the harmful effects of military indoctrination on a soldier who has faced war trauma and returned home without learning how to re-integrate into *normal life*.

Today treatments for PTSD encompass a wide range of options, from traditional psychotherapy and medication to a growing number of complementary and alternative treatments, including ancient practices and new technologies. These treatments range from resilience training to equine therapy, from yoga to a variety of mind/body techniques. We will take a comprehensive look at one mind/body technique that is showing great promise in helping to control many of the symptoms of PTSD: Emotional Freedom Techniques (EFT), also referred to as Tapping.

At the conclusion of part 3, you will recognize that there is hope for a better life while living with PTSD. The variety of treatments available today shows tremendous promise and welcome results in treating the trauma of war.

CHAPTER 17

COUNTERACTING MILITARY INDOCTRINATION

n this chapter we will focus on the effects of military *indoctrination* and what PTSD treatment is striving to accomplish with our veterans.

Many people don't have a true picture of exactly what happens during military indoctrination, the first phase of training for those entering the military—or the reason for it. We have all seen plenty of television shows and movies about the drill sergeant yelling at the new soldier to drop and give him fifty. But that doesn't begin to give us a true or complete picture of what goes on.

I believe it's important to have a clear understanding of the purpose and importance of military indoctrination for the soldier going into combat, as well as how that indoctrination continues to affect our veterans once they return home. This knowledge will also help us to understand what treatments are attempting to accomplish as we move into the next two chapters on traditional and complementary/alternative treatments.

I was honored to interview Dr. Chet Sunde, a clinical psychologist who treats veterans with PTSD. Dr. Sunde also has eight years of military service training as an infantry officer. In our interview, which forms the basis for this chapter, he describes the indoctrination process, the ramifications of learning to neglect oneself for the higher good, and what treatment must attempt to accomplish.

The Indoctrination Process

Dr. Sunde, can you give us an overview of what military indoctrination is, why it is necessary, and the problems that it causes once our veterans are safe at home?

Yes, this is a very important piece in the overall understanding of PTSD. The initial psychological preparation of soldiers during training is referred to as *indoctrination*. Indoctrination is the process of inculcating ideas, attitudes, or fundamentals. It is often distinguished from education by the fact that the indoctrinated person is expected not to question or critically examine the doctrine they have learned. The term is closely linked to socialization, but in common discourse, *indoctrination* is often associated with negative connotations, while *socialization* refers to cultural or educational learning.

The first thing they do is send people off to basic training. The whole idea of basic training is to erase as much as possible of Mom and Dad's rules and start instilling Uncle Sam's rules. Uncle Sam's rules all have to do with the mission—whatever the mission is, as determined and interpreted by the President all the way down through a variety of different people. If you're a new recruit or a private in the military, it's the interpretation of the person directly over you that counts the most.

The purpose of all basic training is to prepare a person for going to war. It doesn't matter if he's going to be a cook or anything else. The purpose of basic training is to instill certain discipline and change the rules they live by so that if they're needed in a dangerous place they'll go there.

And what does Uncle Sam have to say about a person's survival? That you have to fight unless we tell you otherwise. So to break it down a little bit . . . food, that's a basic need that will trigger this part of the brain to start getting really noisy. But imagine one of these vets in basic training saying, Excuse me, Sarge, I'm really hungry. What does Uncle Sam have to say to that? Too bad, suck it up, drive on. What if I'm thirsty? We'll tell you when you will eat; we'll tell you when you will drink. I'm really tired, Sarge. Suck it up and drive on.

It's all the same. Ignore your survival.

That's the first rule. Your survival isn't important any more. We'll decide whether you survive or not. We will decide what you really need or not. We'll decide, if you are afraid, whether you will fight or flee. Of course, in most cases going into another country and facing people who may want to kill you does not go along with survival. So you are being trained to ignore and detach the logical self-aware part, the intellect, from this part.

When there's anxiety and irritability because you're feeling, I'm scared and I need to get away from a threat, or I'm hungry and I need food, or I'm thirsty and need to drink, or tired and I need to go to bed—ignore that. Don't even pay attention to that. That creates a major change for most people in the rules and relationship to their survival instinct.

And how about their emotions? What do you think Uncle Sam has to say about a sad recruit? I miss my mom. Suck it up and drive on. Happy? They don't care. Guilty? You feel guilty about something you were told you need to do? Maybe killing somebody or something else? Too bad. Suck it up and ignore it.

The only emotion that comes close to being acceptable would be anger. Because we can use anger to make you go fight. Anger with irritability is a great combination for war. But it's not really even your anger. A true emotion has to do with what *you* care about.

People in Iraq, Afghanistan, and Vietnam, in most cases have not done anything to the individual soldier—so the soldier doesn't actually have his own anger at them in most cases. Training has to do with this: anger is okay if it's anger that Uncle Sam says is okay. Let's go kill the gook. Let's go kill the hadji. They will make a person into somebody to focus our anger. But it isn't your anger. You're angry because we told you that you couldn't sleep. There's no respect there; you ignore that, you suck it up. So the rules become very self-neglectful, abusive even.

How about the intellect? What does Uncle Sam have to say to a soldier about their ideas? Learn what we teach you, and if you start doing that really well, you'll advance, you'll make more rank, you'll get a little more leeway. But really, it comes down to, now you can make decisions as long as those decisions are based on the general rules that we've already established. So do it our way.

Let's consider the consequences of an attentive versus neglectful relationship with oneself. All relationships can be characterized in one of three ways or a combination:

1. **Healthy and attentive.** An attentive relationship means I pay attention, I'm aware of the other, and then, if there's a problem, I move to help fix that in a positive way. An attentive mother who hears her baby cry will go see what's wrong. It's a healthy relationship.

2. **Neglectful.** Neglect means I don't pay any attention. I ignore you, I ignore it. A parent might notice, Oh yeah, the baby, I forgot to feed it. Well, I'll get to it later. Neglect means either I don't pay any attention at all, or when I do, I don't act to do anything about it. It's an unhealthy relationship.

3. **Abusive.** The unhealthiest is abusive. That means, Oh, I pay attention, I see you, and I hurt you. I hurt you physically, emotionally, or verbally. I attack, I put you down, and I criticize you.

All relationships fall into these three categories. And Uncle Sam teaches people to be neglectful—ignore your hunger, ignore that you're tired, ignore that you're scared, and ignore your emotions. If they pop up, if they break through, and if it isn't Uncle Sam's time, now the abuse comes. Drop and give me thirty for saying you're tired or hungry.

You are now living under the FIDO rule: **F**orget **I**t **D**rive **O**n.

This is ingrained; it's all training. It starts with basic training, which has to do with discipline, controlling, suppressing, and ignoring.

But there's a purpose for this training, and it's not all bad.

The Purpose of Indoctrination

You cannot take a person who has a healthy relationship with themselves and just uproot them from high school or at any other time in their life, then put them in a combat zone and think they're going to be able to fight the mission and be successful—or even survive. Without doing this training, a person can't survive. If they tune in too much, and if they respond too much to their basic natural instincts or their basic natural emotions, they're not going to be able to be in a combat zone. They'll die, and the people that depend on them will die. So there's a good reason for the training.

The problem is what we do once Uncle Sam is done using the person. Vietnam is, of course, the classic example. Once your time is up, drive on. Good to see you, so long, go back home, and go on with your life as if nothing has happened.

Just being in the military with these rules, without ever being in a combat zone, has some helpful aspects. You can come out of the military and you can work really hard and get things done, because you often neglect yourself in order to get that mission done, whatever it is. But if a person doesn't change that once out, their life isn't going to be balanced and healthy. Their relationships aren't going to be as good if they're approaching everything from that attitude.

Now, if you've exposed somebody to combat, it's going to be much worse, because they've been in real life-and-death situations. They've been trained, and they've experienced noises and smells and situations that cause their survival part to say, Danger, we're going to die, we've got to react, we've got to do something—"fight-or-flight" right now!

They're used to ignoring that awareness of it, so it just kind of takes over. Training is about "act without thinking" in a life-and-death situation over and over and over again. So now they come back home, and the sound of a helicopter, for a Vietnam vet for example, triggers the automatic response in them.

Relating Symptoms of PTSD to the Treatment

Let's now look at the symptoms of PTSD and how treatment can help. A soldier's intellectual part is taught just to focus on the external mission and problem at hand, whatever that might be. So when a vet comes home and hears loud noises, or if certain sounds or smells trigger the **fight-or-flight**, it's as if it's life or death. Vets have been trained to fight in response to these stimuli, so most of them go into attack or fight mode. That's a problem; that's why PTSD is an anxiety disorder—because anxiety is a constant issue. Irritability and anxiety are the biggest symptoms they all have.

The next symptom is their **emotions**. We've put them in a situation in which we've taught them to completely ignore their emotions. But that doesn't make them go away, it just suppresses them. That's not a healthy way to live your life. It's healthy for combat but not healthy for living your life once you return home.

Once they've been put in a combat zone, they've seen things; they've seen their friends die, and they've seen ugly things that would cause normal responses of healthy anger, healthy sadness, or even healthy guilt if they've actually done something wrong. But they've been taught to suppress that.

So treatment is about learning to attend to the unmanaged anxiety caused by fight-or-flight and/or suppressed emotions—learning to tune in to the body's natural survival instinct and manage it, to breathe and relax, saying to himself, I'm not in danger. If we're literally not in danger, if our life literally isn't being threatened, we really shouldn't have much anxiety. Anxiety is for survival, and even in a civilized place, this is the only function of anxiety. Anxiety isn't something we should get rid of, it's an attention getter. But if it goes beyond that initial attention, now we're staying in a mode as if we're in threat—but we're not, so now it becomes dysfunctional.

The most important thing during treatment is the change in their relationship with themselves. They need to start developing attentive reactions; for example, they might tell themselves, When my emotions come up, I won't call myself weak. If I were to cry about something, it's not because of weakness.

It's how to tune into themselves, pay attention to their body, pay attention to their emotions, and learn to calm down their fight-or-flight response, because it's being triggered over things when there's really no survival issue going on.

It's difficult for somebody who's been programmed to have an unhealthy relationship with himself, then put into a very unhealthy environment, then *not* later re-programmed or retrained. But that's all treatment is, retraining them in many ways to do the very opposite of what they were trained to do to go off to war.

Dr. Sunde, as a spouse, I believe it's essential that we encourage our veterans to get treatment. One surprise benefit I've noticed with my own husband is that through therapy, not only have his PTSD symptoms been better, but he's also a better person overall. He now has traits that he didn't have before—great traits. I've read articles that say this is being seen in many different vets going through PTSD therapy. Can you tell me why?

I would suspect that it's allowing them access to their heart, their emotions. When they first start to tune into that, they may feel the relief of no longer avoiding suppressed emotions. Emotion is at the heart of the matter, figuratively and literally; it's what we care about.

The fact that somebody has PTSD is a good sign for their overall health potential, because that means they care about something beyond themselves. When they start to get the anxiety out of the way and process some of the suppressed emotions, they can now have access to sharing their emotional life with the people they care about, which is a good thing and allows for the positive in their lives.

It's all about that attachment drive at the heart of the thing. Somebody who doesn't care about others doesn't have access; it exists, but it's a rare thing. There are people who really have no emotional attachment. And that's what we call a sociopath. They will not have PTSD, because there is nothing to suppress.

The full transcript of my interview with Dr. Sunde, in which he provides details of his psychology model for treatment of PTSD, is available on my website at www.detours2dreams.com.

CHAPTER 18

TRADITIONAL TREATMENTS

A growing number of treatment options are available for PTSD today. They include traditional talk therapy and drug therapy, as well as numerous complementary and alternative therapies that are showing good results in managing the symptoms of PTSD. In this chapter we'll discuss traditional treatments; alternative treatments will be covered in chapter 19. Often a combination of treatment options is required to fully respond to the various symptoms of PTSD.

The information presented in this section is not a recommendation or endorsement of any particular treatment; it is meant only to provide you with awareness and education about some of the available options, to help you support your vet. Of course, each veteran needs to work with his or her medical and mental health team to establish a plan of treatment that best meets their individual needs for physical, mental, and spiritual healing.

In this section we'll look at the following traditional therapies most commonly used by the VA for PTSD treatment: cognitive behavioral therapy (CBT), including cognitive therapy (CT), cognitive processing therapy (CPT), and exposure therapy (ET); mindfulness-based cognitive therapy

(MBCT); group therapy; brief psychodynamic psychotherapy; family therapy; and medication.

Cognitive Behavioral Therapy (CBT)

Cognitive behavioral therapy is a psychotherapeutic approach to healing based on a combination of basic behavioral and cognitive principles and research, of which several have been found to be effective in treating PTSD.

In *cognitive therapy (CT)*, a type of CBT, the therapist helps the client understand and change how they think about their trauma and its aftermath. The goal is to understand how certain thoughts about the trauma cause stress and make their symptoms worse.

Cognitive processing therapy (CPT) gives the client a new way to handle these distressing thoughts and gain an understanding of these events. By using the skills learned in this therapy, he can learn why recovery from traumatic events has been hard for him. The way we think and look at things directly affects how we feel and act, and CPT helps a patient learn how going through a trauma changed the way he or she looks at the world, themselves, and others.

In *exposure therapy (ET)*, the goal is for the client to have less fear about his memories. It's based on the idea that people learn to fear thoughts, feelings, and situations that remind them of a past traumatic event. *Prolonged exposure (PE)* is a particular exposure therapy that works well for many people who've experienced trauma. Its four main parts are: education, breathing, real world practice, and talking through the trauma.

Mindfulness Based Cognitive Therapy (MBCT)

Mindfulness Based Cognitive Therapy (MBCT) is a way of thinking and focusing that can help a person become more aware of his present experiences. Mindfulness can be as simple as noticing the taste of a mint on your tongue, or things you do every day without thinking about them, like brushing your teeth in the morning. Mindfulness involves paying attention to the feelings and sensations of these experiences.

Mindfulness practice can help veterans develop more compassion toward themselves and others. They may be less likely to sit in judgment of their thoughts, feelings, and actions, and may become less critical of themselves. Using mindfulness to become more aware and gentle in response to their trauma reactions is an important step in recovery.

Research has also shown mindfulness to be helpful with other anxiety problems, avoidance, and hyperarousal.

Group Therapy

Many people want to talk about their trauma with others who have had similar experiences. In group therapy, the veteran can talk with a group of people who also have been through a trauma and who have PTSD. Sharing his story with others may help him feel more comfortable talking about his trauma, which can help him cope with his symptoms, memories, and other parts of his life.

Group therapy helps veterans build relationships with others who understand what they've been through. The veteran learns to deal with emotions such as shame, guilt, anger, rage, and fear. Sharing with the group also can help them build self-confidence and trust. They learn to focus on their present life, rather than feeling overwhelmed by the past.

Brief Psychodynamic Psychotherapy

In this type of therapy, the veteran learns ways of dealing with emotional conflicts caused by his trauma. This therapy helps him understand how his past affects the way he feels now.

Using this therapy, the therapist can help the veteran:

- Identify what triggers his stressful memories and other symptoms.
- Find ways to cope with intense feelings about the past.
- Become more aware of his thoughts and feelings, so he can change his reactions to them.
- Raise his self-esteem.

Family Therapy

PTSD can affect the whole family. Your kids may not understand why your veteran gets angry sometimes, or why they're under so much stress. Families may feel scared, guilty, or even angry about the veteran's condition.

In family therapy, each person can express how the veteran's behavior affects him, as well as his fears and concerns. The veteran can talk about his or her PTSD symptoms and what triggers them. Family members can discuss important issues related to their veteran's treatment and recovery, such as how the veteran is likely to react to treatment, how soon it will work, and how much improvement can be expected. By doing this, families will be better prepared to help their veteran.

Many families have found it beneficial for the veteran to have individual therapy for their PTSD symptoms and family therapy to help them with family relationships

Medication

While studies suggest that cognitive behavioral therapies have greater effects in improving PTSD symptoms than medications, some people prefer medications. They may also benefit from receiving medications in addition to psychotherapy and other types of treatments, as medications can be used to address the biological basis for PTSD symptoms and consequently benefit psychological and social symptoms.

A number of biological changes have been associated with PTSD, and medications can be used to modify the resulting PTSD symptoms. However, Vietnam era and other veterans whose PTSD symptoms have been present for many years present a special challenge. Studies have shown that long-term PTSD is more resistant to the effects of medication in treating symptoms.

The main biological disturbances found in PTSD are the impaired regulation of the naturally occurring stress hormones in the body and increased sensitivity of the stress and anxiety circuits in the brain. Researchers have found differences in both brain structures and brain circuits that process threatening input between patients with PTSD and those without.

Medications prescribed for treating PTSD symptoms act upon neurotransmitters related to the fear and anxiety circuitry of the brain. Most of the time, medication does not eliminate symptoms, but it can reduce symptoms when used as part of an overall patient treatment plan. A number of medications can be helpful for specific PTSD symptoms, including nightmares, suicide prevention, anxiety panic attacks, insomnia, depression, and hyperarousal symptoms.

This is meant only to be a brief overview for the purpose of bringing awareness to the fact that medication is available for treatment of PTSD, as well as variety of accompanying symptoms. Medications do not work the same for everyone. It is essential that each PTSD patient work closely with his medical and mental health team to make the best decisions for himself. Careful consideration should be given to the veteran's medical condition, and the side effects of the drugs should be fully understood, as well as drug tolerance and possible drug interactions.

As with all types of treatments, there are common roadblocks to the effective use of medication. These barriers include:

- The fear of side effects, including sexual side effects.
- Believing that taking medication is a sign of "weakness."
- Concern of becoming addicted to medications.
- Not taking medication properly, forgetting dosages, using only when symptoms get severe.
- Self-medicating with alcohol or drugs along with prescribed medications.

Medication can be a valuable part of a veteran's overall treatment plan. Ongoing work in the area of PTSD gives us hope to be able to have early intervention in the course of PTSD using a combination of psychotherapy and medication that would prevent or lessen the effects of trauma on the brain. It is important that all members of the veteran's care team work together to create a plan that is best suited to the veteran's specific needs.

Visit my website, www.detours2dreams.com, for the most current information on treatments and medications for PTSD.

CHAPTER 19

COMPLEMENTARY AND ALTERNATIVE TREATMENTS

There is a growing awareness not just in the United States, but also worldwide, of the tragic, lifelong effects of PTSD on military and their families. Along with this awareness comes a growing interest in the benefits of using complementary and alternative treatments for PTSD.

The medical community, private organizations, and the military are testing multiple approaches to deal with the growing problem of PTSD in our military and among our veterans. Many of these treatments have been in use for thousands of years, while others are using the most advanced new technology and tools.

Some military hospitals, installations, and practitioners who had previously used strictly traditional treatments for PTSD are beginning to open the doors to alternative therapies for their patients. Gregg Zoroya reported in *USA Today* that "the Pentagon is seeking new ways to treat troops suffering from combat stress or brain damage by researching such alternative methods as acupuncture, meditation, yoga, and the use of animals as therapy."

This new theme is "a big departure for our cautious culture," Dr. S. Ward Casscells, the Pentagon's assistant secretary for health affairs, told

USA Today. Casscells said he pushed hard for the new research, because "we are struggling with post-traumatic stress disorder (PTSD) as we are with suicide, and we are increasingly willing to take a hard look at even soft therapies."

The military is also beginning to use new technologies such as virtual reality, biofeedback programs, and phone apps to deal with PTSD symptoms. Telehealth and web-based information and technology are appealing and familiar to the younger generation, and it is hoped that this will bring about more openness to seeking treatment.

The VA has even created The PTSD Coach, a free app to help veterans learn about and manage symptoms that commonly occur after trauma. Some of the features include information on PTSD, treatments, tools for screening and tracking symptoms, convenient and easy-to-use skills to help handle stress symptoms, and direct links to support and help.

Some veterans are reluctant to have the stigma of mental health care or are concerned about the side effects of prescription medication; they're searching for alternatives to deal with their symptoms of PTSD. With the growing number of cases of PTSD, it's crucial to look at each and every option that may provide help for our veterans.

Some of the complementary and alternative treatments currently being used to treat PTSD and reporting positive results include Resilience Training; animal therapy; art, music, drama, and recreation therapy; mind/body techniques, including EMDR, biofeedback, hypnosis, Reiki, and Eastern medicine; and energy psychology, in which a primary therapy is the Emotional Freedom Techniques (EFT). Let's take a brief look at each of these.

Resilience Training

Resilience Training involves psychology tools to help the patient adapt well in the face of adversity and trauma, and to maintain alertness and composure in high-pressure situations. Its results enable the patient to develop a mindset to meet challenges and overcome obstacles that block success, including moving from seeing the glass half-empty to seeing the glass half-full. Resilience traits can be learned by training and practice.

Animal Therapy

The use of Equine (horse) Therapy has been successful for many years in the recovery from physical and mental impairment, including depression, trauma, and a variety of physical conditions and disabilities. Many organizations are successfully using Equine Therapy to assist veterans suffering from PTSD.

Specially trained service dogs are now also being used to assist veterans suffering from PTSD to integrate back into society. These dogs are able to help jolt a veteran back from a flashback, dial 911 on the phone, and even sense a panic attack before it starts. The dogs also provide emotional comfort, optimism, and self-awareness.

Art, Music, Dance, and Recreational Therapy

Art therapy is a powerful medium for expressing creativity, but it also has healing properties, having emerged in the 1930s as a viable form of treatment for mental disorders. Art, music, and dance therapy create a safe way to express and deal with feelings without having to speak. Recreation Therapy, which takes advantage of these and other creative arts, is used to enhance or regain mental and physical functioning, focus on abilities, regain independence, and improve overall quality of life.

Mind/Body Techniques

Complementary and alternative medicine now encompasses a broad range of healing techniques that include the following:

EMDR

Eye movement desensitization and reprocessing (EMDR) is another type of therapy for PTSD. Like other kinds of counseling, it can help change how the veteran reacts to memories of his or her trauma.

In this therapy, while thinking of or talking about their memories, the veteran focuses on other stimuli, like eye movements, hand taps, and sounds. For example, the therapist will move his or her hand near the patient's face, and he or she will follow this movement with their eyes.

Experts are still learning how EMDR works, but studies have shown that it may help patients have fewer PTSD symptoms.

Biofeedback

Biofeedback involves using a machine, at first, to see bodily functions that are normally unconscious and occur involuntarily, such as heart rate and temperature. As patients using biofeedback observe how their body reacts to stress, they learn to control their reactions, and eventually they can perform the techniques to control their reactions without using a machine. Studies suggest that biofeedback, among other forms of relaxation training, may be an effective treatment for some people with PTSD.

Hypnosis

Hypnosis induces a deep state of relaxation, which may help people with PTSD feel safer and less anxious, decrease intrusive thoughts, and become involved in daily activities again. Hypnosis is usually used in conjunction with psychotherapy and requires a trained, licensed hypnotherapist.

Reiki

Reiki is a type of energy healing used for relaxation, stress management, pain, and inner healing. The Reiki practitioner's hands either lightly touch the patient's body or are held slightly over it, allowing energy to flow through areas most in need of healing. The practitioner helps to transfer this positive, healing energy, thought to come from the Universe, to the recipient. There is no scientific evidence to confirm the effectiveness of Reiki.

Eastern Medicine

Eastern medicine being used to treat the symptoms of PTSD includes yoga, meditation, acupuncture, and herbal remedies. Yoga is used for stress reduction and relaxation. Transcendental Meditation is shown to reduce symptoms such as anxiety, depression, family problems, alcohol use, and insomnia, and to increase calmness. Acupuncture is used to ease pain and depression. Herbal remedies are used to provide relief from symptoms such as stress and anxiety, and to promote better sleep.

Energy Psychology: Emotional Freedom Techniques (EFT)

In the field of "energy psychology," which addresses the relationship of the body's energy systems to emotion, cognition, behavior, and health, is a practice called Emotional Freedom Techniques (EFT), or "tapping," which is finding great promise in helping with symptoms of PTSD.

EFT is unique because it combines Eastern wisdom about acupressure, or "meridian points" in our bodies, with traditional Western psychotherapy.

I had the pleasure of interviewing Dr. Dawson Church, the founder of the Veterans Stress Project. Dr. Church shared with me that he first began working with veterans when he became intrigued by reports coming in from therapists who had begun using EFT to treat PTSD in veterans returning from Iraq in 2003. They were showing such good results that eventually he did a pilot study, which was published in a peer-reviewed psychology journal.

The study showed that levels of PTSD dropped dramatically when veterans received the EFT training. That led to a second pilot study of a group of veterans and their spouses who were suffering from PTSD. It showed that both family members and veterans improved after a weeklong of intensive EFT. That in turn led to a full-fledged randomized control trial, published in a psychiatry journal, which showed the same thing: EFT worked reliably.

The numbers were startling: 86 percent of the veterans who had clinical PTSD entering the study walked out without clinical PTSD after six one-hour sessions. In another study Dr. Church conducted, participants demonstrated a 24-percent decrease in cortisol levels after an hour of EFT. The second group received an hour of talk therapy, while a third group received no treatment. These two groups showed no real change in cortisol levels.

Dr. Church stated that there is no other therapy that can do this right now. Inspired by these results, he started the Veterans Stress Project, which now reaches over 3,000 veterans with free sessions of EFT.

Below is the text of our interview:

Dr. Church, how many practitioners are using EFT for veterans with PTSD?

In the Veterans Stress Project, we have about 250 practitioners from the United States, Switzerland, England, Germany, France, Canada, and Mexico. It is estimated that 10 million people worldwide have used tapping to alleviate problems such as depression, anxiety, and insomnia, as well as severe PTSD, physical pain, and even illness.

Tapping on certain points on the body sends signals directly to the stress centers of the mid-brain not mediated by the frontal lobes (the thinking part, active in talk therapy). And because EFT simultaneously accesses stress on physical and emotional levels, EFT gives you the best of both worlds, body and mind, like getting a massage during a psychotherapy session.

Are any therapists that work with the VA using EFT at this time?

The VA does not approve it, but many VA therapists have heard of it and some openly offer EFT with PTSD treatment; others fly under the radar as it's being used. So it is being used in the VA, but it is not officially recognized.

Is there any move to try to change that?

Yes, I have been working with a group of about fifteen congressional representatives to knock politely but persistently on the door of the Secretary of Veterans Affairs. We have made several appeals to him and we will be making more. We will just keep on going until we get into the VA. This type of therapy is there, and it has been proven, and yet is unavailable to veterans and their spouses who are suffering so terribly.

Do you think that EFT can actually eliminate the need for drugs and traditional therapy with veterans?

No. I do not believe that EFT will eliminate the need for drugs or therapy, because EFT works best within the context of good medical and mental health care. Some veterans have very difficult mental health issues. They may have depression, anxiety, PTSD; they may suffer from phobias or have hostility issues. With that toxic mix of psychological mental health issues, you need a good licensed mental health practitioner. You can't just think you'll use EFT and it will all go away. We have all these things available, but none of them replaces the other one. So I would say to make use of the best care possible, from whatever source it comes.

Many vets are very reluctant to get treatment, especially a treatment that's not very well known. What would you tell the spouses to help encourage their veteran to try EFT?

I think you can encourage a veteran to get treatment. They may or may not go, but the spouses can certainly use it themselves. So whether or not your partner is working on himself or herself, it's important for all of us to work on ourselves. What we found in this study with veterans and spouses, which I described to you earlier, is that those who were mutually reinforcing got the most out of it. In other words, the veteran desired to change, and the spouse reinforced that desire. We had two motivated, mutually supportive people, and they got great results. If the spouse is dragging the veteran kicking and screaming to treatment, then you don't have a motivated person. It might work, but not as well.

How can someone get involved with the Veterans Stress Project and learn about EFT?

The first step is to visit our website at www.stressproject.org. We have therapists and coaches eagerly waiting for that call for help. The website is also packed with information about EFT, as well as a free manual that you can download. The second step is encouraging practitioners and coaches to be trained in EFT, so they are able to offer it directly to veterans and their spouses.

Dr. Church, is there anything else that you would like to add?

Yes, veterans and their families need to prepare for PTSD. It's important for spouses to watch for the signs and become familiar with the symptoms. PTSD gets worse because of something called *neuroplasticity*, where our brains change over time based on the stimuli they receive. People often are symptom free when they get back from deployment, and then a year or two, ten, or even thirty years later, they start to show symptoms of PTSD.

So if a spouse is aware of the symptoms of PTSD, he or she can be on the lookout for them, and if noticed, encourage their partner to get treatment. There is help at the VA and other places to get early diagnosis. The main thing is to start the work early and don't wait for it to run its course.

We get calls from spouses who say it has been forty years since Vietnam and their husband is getting worse—why is that? PTSD is a progressive condition and tends to get worse over time. So early intervention is important. Don't wait a year, three years, or five years until you get full-blown symptoms. Jump in and get the treatment now.

Yes, Dr. Church, that is such an important point. My husband is one of those whose PTSD came up over thirty-five years after the fact, and we had absolutely no idea what was going on. That's the primary reason I decided to get involved with what I'm doing: if people recognize it from the beginning, they can get treatment early on. One final question: with some types of talk therapy, it seems that many veterans get worse because they're dragging up all those memories. Is that the case with EFT?

That is what we call *retraumatization*, when you relive the traumatizing event. With EFT several pieces of research show just the opposite: you do relive the traumatizing event, but EFT uses stimulation of acupressure points to send the body a soothing signal. It tells your physical body that even though I am having this horrible memory, I don't have to go through the stress response. Once you break this condition response loop in the body one time, it seems to stay broken. So we find that retraumatization is a real danger in regular therapy, but all the research on EFT shows just the opposite.

★ ★ ★ ★ ★

During the year prior to speaking with Dr. Dawson, I had become familiar with Tapping (EFT) and the many things it's being used for, from better focus at work, to weight loss, to headaches. After my interview with Dr. Church, I began talking to Randy about this strange thing called "tapping" and suggested that he might want to try it for his pain. Randy was a good sport about reading the material and watching the videos, and although skeptical, agreed to sign up for the research program.

We took the trip to Santa Rosa to meet the practitioner that would be working with him, and to take a blood test for his cortisol levels at the beginning of the study. Dr. Church explained that tapping on specific meridian points has a positive effect on cortisol levels. Cortisol, known as the "stress hormone," is integral to our body's "fight-or-flight" response. But however useful in short bursts, releasing cortisol too frequently, as happens with chronic stress, may have serious impact on physical, mental, and emotional health.

The morning he was to begin his tapping sessions, Randy confided in me that he wasn't sure he wanted to go through with it. He was uncomfortable saying all that "silly stuff." I had just completed six weeks of tapping with another practitioner and had had amazing results. So I encouraged Randy just to try it this once and see how it went. I reminded him that it would all be by phone and totally private.

Reluctantly he followed through with his session—and became a believer. He began tapping as many as six or seven times a day for his pain, his migraines, and other symptoms—and it was working. He tapped on motivation and energy to clean the kitchen on my birthday, and it worked. He sat in church and tapped on his migraine, and found relief. Randy faithfully completed all ten sessions with his EFT practitioner.

At the completion of Randy's ten EFT sessions, I had the opportunity to review his results with Dr. Church. Before starting the sessions, Randy's PTSD symptoms were assessed using the PCL-M (PTSD Checklist Military), a self-assessment tool used by the military to score PTSD severity. The assessment rates seventeen areas of problems and complaints, and uses a scoring system of 1-5, with 1 indicating no problem at all and 5 indicating extreme symptoms. The lowest possible score is 17, and the highest, 85.

Dr. Church shared that before beginning the EFT sessions Randy had scored 72 on the PCL-M, which shows a very high severity of symptoms. After the ten sessions of EFT, Randy scored 30 on the PCL-M—a significant improvement in his symptoms.

So Randy has found a new tool to use in conjunction with his medication and his talk therapy. A free tool, with no equipment required, which he can use anywhere, anytime.

Tapping may not be for everyone; however, I'd like to emphasize that there are tools that can help you find a "neutral emotional state," the ultimate place to be for optimal health and wellness. Some of these tools may seem very "woo-woo," and yes, I used to think the same way. But what if you could find relief from some of your symptoms with a silly thing like tapping, or yoga, or mindfulness, or meditation? It wouldn't hurt to try, and it just might work for you.

PART 4

LIVING WITH
THE STRANGER

*With new insight you have the added wisdom
and power to change your approach rather than
seeking to change your partner.*

★ ★ ★ ★ ★

*We mistakenly assume that if our partners love us they
will react and behave in certain ways — the ways we react
and behave when we love someone.*

★ ★ ★ ★ ★

*When men and women are able to respect and accept
their differences, then love has a chance to blossom.*

★ ★ ★ ★ ★

*The same ideas that enrich a healthy relationship
will also assist couples in overcoming more
challenging problems.*

Dr. John Gray

INTRODUCTION

Life with a veteran suffering from PTSD requires the same abilities needed for any successful relationship. Both require the ability to respect, empathize, and feel compassion for each other. The willingness to compromise, to give and take in the relationship, is essential for peaceful co-existence. And it's important to have sufficient interest, care, and concern to become familiar with the unique qualities, characteristics, and special needs of your partner. Even having a basic understanding of the differences between men and women can provide valuable insight.

But while PTSD brings on the same issues and challenges of a typical relationship, it involves much more. In part 4 we will discuss some of the leading causes of discord in a relationship: communication, money, sex and intimacy, and infidelity—and why PTSD can intensify the struggle in each of these areas (including some of the biological reasons). You'll also find tools and suggestions to help you proactively deal with issues that might arise in these areas.

PTSD also brings unique symptoms and behaviors to a relationship. We'll look at how these can interfere with the peace within a relationship—so much so that the spouse is walking on eggshells most of the time. Having knowledge and understanding of how you can assist your veteran in terms of symptoms, triggers, and support during therapy can be invaluable in both your veteran's healing process and maintaining harmony in your home.

CHAPTER 20

WHAT'S PTSD AND WHAT'S JUST BEING A MAN?

One evening during a spouse support group meeting I was leading, one of the women who had been quietly listening as others shared their stories of living with a veteran with PTSD announced, "It sounds like we're all living with the same man!"

Another woman thoughtfully said, "So, Debbie, what's PTSD, and what's just being a man?"

"That's a great question, and I know exactly where to find the answer. Shall we make that our topic for next week?"

The women agreed, anxious to hear the answer to this question.

When I got home that evening, I searched for a book that I had read many times during my dating years, especially when I was trying to figure out what was going on with *that guy*. I found it safely tucked away on the top shelf of my bookcase.

I realized that I hadn't read it since I met Randy. I hadn't felt the need for it in the beginning, because I understood him perfectly—or so I thought. And by the time PTSD had totally invaded our life, I didn't want to know about a man from Mars. I desperately needed to know about my husband, whose mind had returned to Vietnam.

As I read the title of John Gray's #1 *New York Times* bestseller *Men are from Mars, Women are from Venus: The Classic Guide to Understanding the Opposite Sex*, it made perfect sense to me. In order to better understand our spouses' PTSD behavior, we needed to first remember the basic differences between men and women—and to be reminded about what constitutes normal male behavior.

Dr. John Gray, the author of this most famous relationship book ever published, with years of successfully helping millions of couples and extensive knowledge of the effects of combat on our veterans, graciously accepted my invitation for a personal interview to help answer these questions. Following is our interview:

Dr. Gray, can you explain what is "just being a man" and what behavior goes beyond that with different PTSD symptoms?

I think that is a great distinction to make and a good question, because the PTSD response is often going to be an exaggerated male response. And because it can be so exaggerated, even when it's just an expanded normal male response, you think, Oh my gosh, this is unsolvable.

Dr. Gray, one of the things you talk a lot about in Men are from Mars, Women are from Venus *is the male retreating into "the cave." I know from my own experience, as well from other spouses, that this is a very common behavior for veterans with PTSD. Could you give us some insight into this behavior from the standpoint of what is normal male behavior?*

Men process stress differently from women. So when a man withdraws into his "cave," which is the way men primarily cope with stress, a woman can easily misinterpret it. A woman might be thinking he doesn't love me, he doesn't care about me, or I must have done something bad.

For a woman to suddenly build a wall around her heart and to completely shut down takes many years of feeling ignored and neglected. Gradual resentment begins building up and building up. It is sort of swept under the rug until she can tolerate it no longer, and then suddenly there is just, okay, I'm finished here. It takes a woman a long time to get to that place of "I don't care."

But with a man, it's actually his first defensive reaction. It's as if suddenly there's a huge wall up around his heart—and then just as suddenly the wall is gone. And when the wall goes up, a woman can easily misinterpret it to have the same meaning it would have if the woman's wall goes up. For a woman, it's a gradual process of slowly letting that wall down and rebuilding trust and finding forgiveness for things where she felt resentful.

For a man, simply dealing with stress, which is not about her at all, can activate a whole wall around his heart, and that phenomenon is called shutting down. It's literally an automatic reaction, such as when somebody hits your knee and you have an automatic reflex.

When a man is in danger, he survives by his blood flowing to the back part of the brain, which causes faster reaction time. That's not the part of the brain that's able to hear another point of view, that's able to be patient, that's able to be empathetic, that's able to be understanding. So when a man becomes stressed or in danger, or perceives himself to be in danger, all of the relationship skills that bring men and women together are basically gone, and he's in fight-or-flight mode.

When you're with someone that you love, you don't want to fight them and you don't want to leave them, so you're in a state of confusion. You have to realize that historically men have been in danger, and the way they process danger is by being quiet and not talking. So when a man is feeling danger, and his cortisol levels are rising, he needs to quiet his mind.

The worst thing he can do is talk to the person with whom he's feeling defensive or whom he's threatened by. Men have adapted this way for thousands and thousands of years. It is a time to be quiet and focus on what he can do, what the solution is. This is why when women tend to be upset, men want to interrupt and solve the problem. What's the solution? If we can, in a sense, kill or get rid of the problem, then we can be at ease and peaceful again.

So if there are lions, tigers, bears, and bombs dropping, it's a high level of stress. If it's to the extent that a man feels powerless to solve the problem, he will experience a greater emotional reaction. In times of great danger, he will have a very, very strong reaction. If it's moderate danger, he has less of a reaction; if it's just moderate stress, he has no reaction.

The difference between men and women is that under moderate stress, women have eight times the emotional reaction that a man has. Then, if she's actually upset with him, let's double that. The way he misinterprets that is that she is really, really upset with him. That triggers a feeling of threat inside him. He feels that she's looking at him like a lion, tiger, or bear, when in her mind, she's actually just saying, "You forgot to empty the trash," or, "I forgot to run this errand. I need help; I'm stressed out about this." It's just moderate life problems.

His brain misinterprets it, and he becomes defensive if he doesn't recognize that women have a different emotional reaction to things. As soon as a man becomes defensive, you need to stop communication. This is the biggest problem between men and women.

When a woman is feeling threatened, there's a strong emotional reaction. Something that would help calm her is to talk about what she's feeling, to talk about her experience, to talk about what's happening inside of her. Because of her experience in needing to talk things through, she thinks that if he's experiencing stress, she should go to him and ask, "What's the matter? What are you feeling? Why are you saying that?" Or tell him, "Don't talk to me that way."

These questions and comments can increase the emotional intensity of his reaction. The ideal thing to do at those times when his upset is increasing is to stop conversation. Arguing is the worst thing you can do at that moment. You just have to go slow and say *time-out.*

Understand that the way he processes stress is that he calms down by forgetting about whatever his problem is. Whatever the threat is, he needs to withdraw. He needs to relax by doing something that is not endangering him, that is not threatening him in any way. That is called "cave time." So he pulls into his cave and does anything that will distract his attention from the problems that he is facing in his life. The distraction could be a TV show, sporting event, reading a book, listening to music, a form of meditation, easy exercise. These are all distractions.

Dr. Gray, what are some examples of exaggerated "cave behavior" that might be exhibited by veterans with PTSD?

He could drink, take drugs, or drive his motorcycle or his car fast. These are ways that men actually *withdraw* from the stresses in their life—by creating another danger where they feel in control. This feeling is created by stimulating the brain chemical dopamine. Dopamine needs to function in the brain to give the alertness and the energy for faster reaction time and pleasure. Danger is a super dopamine stimulator.

But when a person is in combat or in danger for a long time, he's getting high levels of dopamine stimulation all the time. That has the effect of what's called *down regulating dopamine receptor sights*. This is desensitizing dopamine receptor sights so that normal stimulation doesn't produce the effect a person seeks. He then looks for super stimulation to get the effect.

This "drug addict" now becomes bored and flat. Life is boring, life is not motivating, and life has no purpose. There is no motivation because the receptor sights have been in a sense *down regulated* by excess stimulation. So he looks for things to get that dopamine stimulated. Most soldiers have a gene that converts alcohol into dopamine. If they're not going with alcohol, they tend to go with high sugar, which also stimulates dopamine.

Another dynamic that goes along with PTSD is that when a man or a woman has been in danger consistently for a period of time, it literally has the effect on his or her brain as if he were taking an ADD drug, cocaine, or methamphetamines—all super dopamine stimulators.

The other big one is Internet pornography. Men need to be taught that doing Internet pornography is just like taking cocaine; there's no difference. The same part of the brain lights up your *down regulating receptor sights*—you're just finding another combat situation.

Like combat, pornography stimulates high levels of dopamine. So does anything you do sexually that you wouldn't want to tell your minister or priest about. If you wouldn't want your mother to find out, you wouldn't want your children to know, you wouldn't want to be found out by anyone—that becomes illicit sex.

Many soldiers want to do these things because they're immoral according to what our society's morals are. If everybody accepted them, they wouldn't be such dopamine stimulators. Anything you don't want to be caught at or that creates danger stimulates high levels of dopamine.

We see so many soldiers coming back and committing suicide because they're depressed, they're not motivated, their life has no purpose. That's the brain chemical dopamine; one of the common symptoms when you don't have enough dopamine is wanting to kill yourself. They've just flattened out their dopamine receptor sights by being in combat and danger. They give up.

[Note: Veterans' and loved ones' confidential crisis hotline: 1-800-273-8255]

Dr. Gray, is there anything that can help these veterans to return to normal?

Yes. They have to *up regulate* those dopamine receptor sights so the smile on their wife's face is enough to make them happy. So that just being together in normal conversation is stimulating and gives them energy and motivation. So that it doesn't have to become an extreme emergency to be motivated, nor does it have to be a drug or super stimulant to motivate them, to give them pleasure in their brain.

Their brains have changed. Veterans' brains come back different and this is measurable. The back part of the brain, which has to do with automatic reaction, has grown. The front part of the brain, which has to do with communication, empathy, understanding, and creativity, shrinks. But it will grow back. What you use will grow. The key thing to finding balance again is these dopamine receptor sights, which flatten out—that's what addictions do to you.

Combat and addiction do the same thing to you. You begin depending upon excess stimulation to feel pleasure. The normal stimulation doesn't give you pleasure and, therefore, doesn't motivate you. So it's just a vicious cycle; it gets worse and worse.

You come back from combat and you drink lots of caffeine. Or you go and lift weights. That produces excess challenge, which also stimulates dopamine. So we're not just going to lift some heavy weights, we're going to really push it. And what happens is a drug-like experience.

All of these intense experiences cause one to lose the ability to have a normal healthy relationship. The brain has to be changed back, and it takes time to get back to normal, just as when you go off any drug addiction. But the process of coming back from combat is the same.

Going off the drug in this case means to put yourself in a situation where you're not seeking out excess stimulation to feel better. You actually have to go through the process of feeling bored, which can produce a great deal of anxiety. You have to back off from excess stimulation and at the same time fortify your body with extra nutrients, which are massively depleted by being in combat. Often soldiers have no awareness of this, or why they feel boredom, flatness, and lack of purpose. This often creates a feeling of needing to get back into combat for some order, and to find a sense of purpose, which produces dopamine.

So veterans need to have jobs, they need to feel successful, and they need to know they are going to go through a down period of boredom. During that period, they have to use all the willpower they can to minimize depending upon excess stimulation and addictive stimulation in order for the receptor sights to *up regulate* again, so they can come back into normal life. These are some of the dynamics that many of our soldiers are just not aware of.

Thoughts of suicide occur when there is a dopamine deficiency in the brain, so we have lots of suicide. We have many soldiers who aren't even considered suicides because they die in motorcycle accidents. That's an easy way to die with dignity for many people; the way they perceive it, it looked like an accident, but really, they killed themselves. At the same time, it also can just be the truth that riding a motorcycle fast is like a drug: it's dangerous, and, therefore, it stimulates high levels of dopamine.

If we become aware of what is bad for us and know what our options are, then we can start making choices that are good for us. A man can produce huge amounts of dopamine being in a men's support group with a leader to facilitate the conversation. He can produce huge amounts of dopamine by taking L-Tyrosine, MSM, vitamin C, grape seed extract—these very basic things—and doing something productive.

Having a job is the number one stimulator of healthy dopamine levels. However, even with a job, one has to recognize that in the beginning it may be quite boring.

Dr. Gray, do you have some final thoughts to leave us with?

We go through such elaborate preparation to prepare young men to go into battle—all kinds of extreme training. Yet we have no elaborate, extreme training on how to leave battle. The consequence of that is unemployment, homelessness, drug addiction, and much higher levels of suicide, divorce, and addiction. All of those things are the proven outcome of the lack of support we provide our veterans when they come home. Just as we've put them through extreme training to prepare them for going into battle, we need to bring them into extreme training to bring them back into a healthy normal life.

CHAPTER 21

HOW YOU CAN HELP

The number one thing we can do to help our veterans with PTSD is to understand that we cannot change, control, or cure them. There are, however, many things we can do to support our veterans, to encourage them, and to create a peaceful existence. It is important to understand that your veteran's behaviors are not always about you. Being able to recognize and respond appropriately to both normal male responses and PTSD behaviors is vital.

Our experts, Dr. John Gray and Dr. Chet Sunde, provide their insight to help us better understand PTSD behaviors and how we can best respond to our veterans. Again, these discussions assume the vet is a male, but many answers can be applied to both genders.

Suggestions from Dr. Gray

Dr. Gray, what suggestions can you offer to our spouses to create a more peaceful existence when living with PTSD?

It is important that spouses understand that the veteran with PTSD needs to be able to "face the danger" in a calm place. What people have to do after a trauma is leave it, find safety, feel secure, and get into a good routine. But it's important to understand that, once the veteran is feeling good, once he's feeling relaxed, then those unresolved feelings will start to come up. That's why PTSD seems to show up out of nowhere.

It's paradoxical because, if the veteran starts feeling better, he says, "I don't want to go there," but that's the only time he *can* go there that will have a lasting beneficial effect. Once he's feeling calm and safe, that's the time to talk about what happened, when he's in present time remembering the past and the danger is over.

Once he feels safe and he feels that the listener understands and is not being threatened by what he's saying, then he can talk about those feelings that are coming up.

However, when the feelings come up, they don't always just say, "Hi, I'm experiencing my unresolved feelings of being in danger." They come up as an exaggerated response to his partner's criticism, or his partner's complaining, or his partner's dissatisfaction with him, or his partner's look of disapproval.

Spouses have to realize that even the slightest hint of disapproval can be misinterpreted quite easily as rejection and criticism to a man who is experiencing PTSD, and that can set him off. It's like when a man withdraws and pulls away—that's easily misinterpreted by a woman as he doesn't love you, rather than that he's actually doing something very important for himself. His stress level has just been activated because he's feeling rejected in some way; whether she intends it or not, it doesn't matter—he's feeling rejected in some way.

It's just like the reaction you might have if you were alone in the dark and heard a little noise—you might feel danger, and you would have a much stronger reaction than if you were in the sunshine having fun with your family and heard a noise. We need to be aware of this hair-trigger reaction to things.

When men feel they're in danger, their testosterone levels increase and their dopamine levels increase. Testosterone levels increase to give them faster reaction time to solve the problem—to fight or flee. In a situation with a spouse, they don't want to fight her and they don't want to flee her.

So they go into a state that is very unfamiliar to men: feeling powerless to do anything about the situation. They can't run, they can't attack—so what do they do?

There is a mechanism in a man's body that, when he feels powerless to solve a problem, causes his testosterone to convert into estrogen. Estrogen makes him more submissive—that's the reason it's there. If a man is in a dangerous situation with another alpha male and he's about to be killed, he realizes he's powerless to solve this problem and he can't get away. His testosterone levels have to be reduced very quickly so that he is not motivated to continue the fight. His testosterone will convert through an enzyme called aromatase. Aromatase is produced when a man experiences high cortisol levels. As his testosterone is converted into estrogen, it makes him not want to continue to fight.

However, it will flood his brain with emotion. If men are not trained to *not* talk when those emotions happen, they will go back to fighting and arguing. That's where the ugly part of men comes out. They can be fighting and become cool, collected, present, and able to make the best decisions. But if their brain is flooded with emotion while they're fighting, they will not make the best decisions. They will do everything wrong and make a mess of things. This is the shutting-down reaction, which occurs in relationships when couples argue at a time when a man is experiencing this.

This happens because, at the moment of danger, when a man's testosterone shifts into estrogen, he stops caring. It's a moment where he has to distance himself from any feelings. This is his way of protecting her and himself from making a stupid mistake: he stops caring.

However, if she continues to promote a conversation, or if anyone continues to poke at him in that state, then he will feel those strong emotions, react, and make a big mistake. This is when fighting is not healthy.

Unfortunately, once a man comes back from combat, fighting is one of the things that happen. Men become very argumentative, yell, and scream—and they can actually become addicted to that. They promote fights because it stimulates high levels of dopamine.

Once you're feeling good, safe, and secure, then talk about the experiences that he doesn't usually want to talk about. That's the time to do it. It helps to integrate that past experience into present times so the brain can let go of it.

Otherwise, there's a part of the brain that thinks it's still in combat, still in danger, and he reacts inappropriately.

★ ★ ★ ★ ★

Dr. Gray's explanation certainly makes it clear why so many spouses often feel the necessity of walking on eggshells around their veteran. Now we can understand the science behind it and the importance of dealing with these times appropriately.

If your veteran has not acknowledged that he may be experiencing symptoms of PTSD, and has not sought help or begun treatment, starting that conversation when he is feeling good, safe, and secure would be a good time.

The VA's *Coaching into Care* program works by telephone with spouses and families to help you find the right words to begin talking to your vet about seeking help with his readjustment, while still respecting his right to make decisions. You can find information at www.coachingintocare.com.

Dr. Gray's Tips for Supporting Your Veteran's Appropriate "Cave Time"

- Don't disapprove of his need for withdrawing with punishing behaviors through words, tone of voice, looking wounded, or pushing him away physically or sexually when he comes back.
- Don't try to help him solve his problems by offering solutions. Unsolicited advice makes a man feel that that you do not believe that he can do it on his own.
- Do practice patience and trust that he will figure it out on his own or ask for help when he is ready. Make his feelings more important than perfection. Ask what he needs . . . a hug, to vent, help with something, or to be left alone.
- Don't try to nurture him by asking questions about his feelings, such as: What did I do? Are you mad at me?

- Do not give up things that you want to do in order to be with your veteran when he doesn't want to be with you. Again, go and do things that make you happy.

More great information from Dr. Gray can be found in *Men are from Mars, Women are from Venus: The Classic Guide to Understanding the Opposite Sex.*

Suggestions from Dr. Sunde

Once our veteran begins treatment, there are additional things that are important for us to be aware of in order to provide support, which Dr. Sunde shares in the following interview:

Dr. Sunde, I've noticed that many spouses find that when their veteran first starts therapy for his PTSD, his symptoms, anxiety, and moods seem to get much worse. Is that typical?

Yes, it's very typical. First, it's the anxiety of being in therapy. They are used to ignoring and avoiding their thoughts and feelings. Now, here they are coming to some stranger, and a group of strangers. That's anxiety provoking all by itself—but then we're also going to talk about those things they're trying not to remember.

When the anxiety is up, I teach skills to tune into it and bring it down. He learns, when the emotions are there, to share inside himself, if nowhere else, or with me one-on-one, or in our group session. All emotions need to be acknowledged and felt; they pass and become less intense over time.

Dr. Sunde, can you give some suggestions about how a spouse can support her vet as he's going through this initial part of therapy?

Ideally, the spouse would have this information in advance. Then it's working together. The spouse is someone who can help the vet do what I do in a therapy session, which is to become a biofeedback mechanism.

The vets are trained, and even beyond their training, their only coping skill has been to avoid. They do their best to avoid even seeing it in themselves. So the spouse can be a biofeedback mechanism. Now obviously the spouses need to have an okay about this so the vet doesn't feel like he's being attacked or overly scrutinized. The spouse can simply say, "Honey, look at your leg; you're anxious. What does the doc say to do about it to relax? Is there anything I can do to help you relax? Do you need your space?"

For these guys, at first and ongoing, they need to pull into the cave, so to speak. Go to a place where it is quiet, with less stimulus. But I tell them, "This is what you've done all your life, so that by itself isn't going to help you."

We don't say to the spouse it's okay for him to always go away and not interact with you or society. At first we just don't want their anxiety and irritability to get too high. We want to recognize it and manage it, and that may mean going somewhere else, then coming back—that's what we're trying to get him to do.

Essentially, the spouse can help them to see the anxiety, because at first they don't notice it. If they don't notice when it's at a 50 percent level, then when something new comes along, like some driver cuts in front of them, if they're already pretty tense and anxious and irritable, it doesn't take much to trigger what looks like rage. It's not rage though—it's fight-or-flight. Often the vet will say afterwards, "Oh, I'm sorry, honey," or, "Yeah, I know that shouldn't really bother me. I overreacted to that. I was a real jerk about that."

That's a sign that it wasn't anger. Anger is about something you care about—you'd still be angry. You'd say, "Well, yeah, of course I was angry about that because they hurt you (or someone else)."

You can help them become aware, give them the space to breathe, and relax. I teach everybody to breathe and relax your body. That's the only thing to do to manage anxiety. Awareness and bringing the anxiety down is what's necessary.

Do you have any final words of wisdom for the spouses that are trying to understand and support their veterans?

Breathe, relax, and take care of *you*. The more spouses have self-awareness along these lines, the better. What they need to know is that all we can try to control is ourselves. You cannot force somebody else. That's why the veteran's motivation is such a big issue. If somebody comes here and thinks that I am going to cure them or fix them, there is no way. That is not possible.

It's a 50/50 effort. I can help a person, but they have to do the work. A family member needs to recognize that they can't fix their vet; they have to take care of themselves first, and then give the vet space. Work with them, but don't ignore your own emotions. Just because a person has PTSD doesn't give them the right to intimidate or neglect you. You're not going to help them to learn how to be attentive to themselves if you are not attentive to yourself.

Learning To Cope With Your Spouse's PTSD Triggers

It may seem that all of our veterans' PTSD symptoms *just happen* for no reason. However, there are actually internal and external things that can trigger PTSD responses. These triggers can be external things and situations that happen around the vet. They can also be internal, such as memories and certain feelings that come up inside him or her. A trigger is anything that brings about the symptoms of PTSD.

Some triggers are common to many veterans, and some may be unique to your partner. Understanding what triggers are, becoming familiar with your partner's triggers, and developing coping strategies to help your veteran avoid or deal with these triggers is an important way you can help support him.

Triggers may include a scene on television; reading about an event in a book or the newspaper; seeing people that remind a vet of his or her trauma; a specific place; the anniversary of an event; certain smells, words, phrases, or situations; sounds; and feelings.

Common triggers are the sound of a helicopter or loud noises, such as gunshots, fireworks, a car backfiring, or a door slamming. Smells such as diesel, smoke, blood, and explosives are typical triggers for vets. Situations may be those such as crowded places filled with strangers, rooms with no windows, or places where you can't see outside.

Many triggers are specific to your vet and his particular experiences and memories. Talk to your vet about his personal triggers. Let him know that you want to be able to better understand the things that can bring on his symptoms so you can help and support him better. He may not be aware of all of his triggers or might not want to talk about them. In this case, it is helpful for you to begin paying special attention to when your veteran's PTSD symptoms come up. Observe what is happening around him that may be serving as a trigger. Take note, and consider ways that these triggers may be avoided or dealt with in the future.

Coping Strategies for Common Triggers

- Always choose a table at restaurants that allows your veteran to face the door.
- Pay attention to any changes in your surroundings that can quickly trigger your vet: noise levels increasing, a room becoming more crowded or chaotic.
- Learn to recognize small changes in your vet's demeanor, such as facial expressions, nervous gestures, and signs of agitation, which may alert you to a potential problem.
- Keep a watchful, loving eye on your vet, and help your spouse to easily escape if the situation is becoming difficult for him. Suggesting that he step outside for some fresh air or change what he's doing may be all that it takes to calm him down.
- Help your veteran to totally remove himself from the triggers, if necessary.
- Make a plan ahead of time to provide a safe and loving exit from social situations if the need arises.
- Do not become angry or make your veteran feel guilty if he needs to escape from a situation that is causing him anxiety.
- Totally avoid potential situations that may trigger PTSD symptoms when possible.
- Continue to attend events and activities that are important to you, even if it is not comfortable for your veteran to join you. Let him know that you understand and support his decision. Without guilt or anger, let him know that you appreciate his supporting your need to attend without him.

The Language of PTSD

By this point in your life, you have probably learned that there are different communication styles, and that men and women communicate differently. When PTSD enters the picture, a completely new element to the art of communication enters with it. Let's go over some of the key skills that you will need to practice for successful communication with your veteran:

Allowing Silence—For however long it takes.
- Allowing silence gives your vet time to think things out and process, rather than acting out too quickly.
- Remember that not talking is sometimes just being quiet.
- The best thing to do during a PTSD blowup is just to stop talking. You haven't lost; you are just smart enough to know that right now the best defense is just to stop engaging.
- Control your urge to *chase by talking* when your vet withdraws, shuts down, or pulls away.

Active Listening—Even when it annoys him. PTSD changes the brain, and often thoughts are distorted or jumbled up. Sometimes your veteran may not realize that he is talking aloud while processing his thoughts.
- Repeat what you thought was said using your own words. Then ask, "Is that what you said?" Let him know that you just want to be sure that you understand/heard correctly/got it right.
- Often times he doesn't really mean what he says. Not intentionally, but the words just don't come out the way he intends. When this happens don't criticize, just assure him that you are trying to be sure that you understand.

Short, Clear Communication—The fewer details you provide, the better. When talking to a man with PTSD, forget the fluff, the details, the why. Give him simply the facts. Give him the when and the where. If he wants more, he will ask. For example: Please pick the kids up from school at 3:00 pm today.

Patience—Tell your veteran the same thing as many times as it takes. PTSD can cause memory problems, so be patient when he forgets things.

- Be polite and gentle when reminding him about things that he has forgotten.
- Put his appointments on your calendar.
- Write him loving "Honey Do" lists and post-it reminders.

Asking for What You Need—In a healthy relationship both partners are free to ask for what they want and need, and both have permission to say no if they want. As women, we tend to believe that our needs should be anticipated and his support automatically offered. Men don't simply offer—they need to be asked. So we need to become comfortable communicating our needs to our spouse.

The PTSD Game Rules—Calling a Time-Out

At some point when things are going smoothly and there is no conflict (which may be a very rare moment in a PTSD relationship) discuss how to handle times when emotions begin to escalate. It is important that you both feel comfortable calling a time-out, and you are *playing by the same rules*. Here are two basics you might want to add to your personal rules:

- Verbally say time-out and use the T-sign, as it is used in sporting events. Your veteran may not hear you say time-out, but when the T-sign is held prominently in front of his face and you are no longer talking, eventually he will get the message.
- Immediately call a time-out if you are being disrespected or feel threatened, either verbally or physically. Go somewhere that you feel safe, and stay as long as necessary for your partner to cool down.

No-Talk Rule—There may be some topics that trigger your veteran's PTSD that you may want to mutually decide to avoid talking about. Things that might be appropriate to have a no-talk rule for may include your job, problems surrounding your extended family that don't directly affect your veteran, or perhaps an event from the past that needs to be let go.

At one point, everything was off the table for me to talk to my husband about. All problems seemed to cause too much stress for him to handle.

This created a great feeling of isolation and abandonment for me. So be sure that you create a personal support system for yourself of friends, family, and professionals with and from whom you can share, vent, whine, and receive the positive strokes you need.

★ ★ ★ ★ ★

My final word—possibly the two most important things required to live successfully with your veteran's PTSD—is to let go of the past and take care of yourself. We must accept the fact that our spouse has changed. He will never be the same as before he went to war. We therefore need to take the time to grieve the passing of the person who once was, and to embrace and find new ways to love the person he is today.

CHAPTER 22

PTSD AND MONEY

oney is a common problem in all relationships, even more so for today's veterans. According to the Bureau of Labor Statistics numbers released December 7, 2012, unemployment rate fell to a four-year low of 7.7 percent. But there is a marked difference between the unemployment rate of the population at large and for a specific demographic of individuals roughly between the ages of 18-30. For veterans, this usually means individuals who served in the Iraq or Afghanistan wars.

Among these veterans, the unemployment rate was 10 percent, the highest rate of unemployment of any service period. For female veterans of these wars, the unemployment rate was a sky-high 12.9 percent. For young veterans, transitioning between military and civilian life adds to the stress of facing unemployment well into their post-service years.

When a veteran is suffering from PTSD, additional factors compound the problem. The veteran may have difficulty keeping a job because of trouble concentrating, sleep disorders, authority issues, and work-related triggers. Or he may be totally disabled and unable to work. If the veteran requires full-time care, his spouse may not be able to work outside the home, placing additional strain on their finances.

Spouses of veterans with PTSD and other wounds of war face tremendous challenges today. It is easy to become overwhelmed when taking over most of the family and household responsibilities, as well as the added burden of financial worries.

I had the pleasure of interviewing Barbara Stanny, author, speaker, and a leading authority on women and money. Barbara's mission is to help women take charge of their money and take control of their life. Here are some of the insights she shares with us:

Barbara, overspending is a common behavior for veterans with PTSD as a means to feel better. Many of these veterans also believe that their life is going to be cut short, so they have little concern for the future. For spouses who are trying to keep the family afloat financially, as well as protect their future, what recommendations can you give us?

What you are dealing with is a real mental/emotional dysfunction. The problem is not about money. If you only address it as money, you will never solve the problem. My mentor told me *with overspending, you can never get enough of what you don't really need.* So I think that keeping it about money perpetuates the dysfunction.

That said, there are things you need to do to protect yourself financially as a wife or family member. But keep in mind, it's not about the money; it's about the trauma and the pain and the emotional angst that the spending will cover. I just want to put that disclaimer in there.

It's a basic truth: problems with money are never about money They say the number one thing couples argue about is money—but here, too, the problem is not money. Money is only a symptom of something deeper, always.

So when you make it about money, you don't ever get to the symptoms. Even if you clear up the spending issues, it will show up somewhere else, like overeating, porn, drinking, or in some other way. Like others, veterans will continue to do something to try to make the pain go away. They need to numb. So it is a real mental health issue with veterans, and they need to get treatment for these symptoms.

Several things need to happen. First, the spouse needs to protect herself financially. I think every spouse should do this before her mate goes to war—to make sure she truly has money in her own name, to protect herself and her family financially. I would advise every woman to do that, and to seek help from a financial planner.

Part of the problem is that oftentimes we women feel so uneducated, so ignorant about money that it's hard for us to have an informed conversation. But the wife needs to educate herself financially. She needs to get up to speed—that's the first thing.

And of course, that's probably the last thing she wants to do, because money is easy to ignore until you can't ignore it anymore. Most women don't get serious about money until they hit a crisis. And certainly having a husband with PTSD is a crisis. But while it's hard to focus on learning about money when you're in a crisis, that's the first thing she needs to do.

Here are some resources I recommend:

There's a wonderful international financial planning group called Garrett Planning Network (www.garrettplanningnetwork.com). Sheryl Garrett started this; she wanted to help make competent, objective financial advice accessible to all people. This is a network of hourly-based, fee-only financial planners. I highly recommend finding a few people in your area, interviewing at least three, and making an appointment. Use them to look at your financial situation, to educate you, and to help you deal with a strategy and a plan to have this conversation with your husband. (Sheryl Garrett, CFP, co-authored *A Family's Guide to the Military for Dummies* and wrote the *Personal Finance Workbook for Dummies*).

There's also a great resource for people in debt. The National Federation of Credit Counselors (www.nfcc.org) is a nonprofit organization that offers free or low-cost service. If you need help getting out of debt, they will work with you, help you create a plan, negotiate with your creditors, all of that. Beware of "debt consolidators" who charge a high fee and promise to get you out of debt. Don't walk, run away from them.

Next, I will give you three steps on how to get smarter about money. It's not that complicated, and it doesn't take a lot of time to learn. It doesn't take a lot of money to create financial security. What it takes is small steps consistently taken.

Let me start by sharing my personal story. I grew up in a wealthy family. My father was the *R* in H&R Block. The only thing he ever told me about money was *don't worry*, so I didn't. I married a man who was a compulsive gambler and he lost a fortune of *my money*. I was terrified. Anything to do with finances, my eyes would glaze over and my brain would fog up.

I'm going to share what I did to get smart. If you do these three steps for at least three months, preferably six months, you will be amazed at the difference:

1. Every day read something about money, even if it's only a minute or two, or just the headlines of the business section of the newspaper. Getting smart or smarter about money is simply familiarizing yourself with the jargon and the current trends. If you're standing in line at the grocery store, instead of picking up *People* magazine, pick up *Money* magazine and read it. Before you go to bed at night, read one paragraph of a financial book. I'll recommend a couple that I really like. Of course, I love my book *Prince Charming Isn't Coming: How Women Get Smart about Money*.

    Some other really great basic books are *Personal Finance for Dummies* by Eric Tyson and Liz Weston's newly released book *The 10 Commandments of Money & Surviving & Thriving in the New Economy*. Liz is the most read financial columnist on the internet today and writes for MSN. She has a talent for making the most complicated financial matters easy to understand (asklizweston. com). So everyday read something about money, even if it's just for a minute or two.

2. Next, every week, have a conversation about money, preferably with someone that knows more than you do. I think we women do not talk about money. We'll moan and groan about it, and we'll complain. But when's the last time you sat down with a friend or a colleague and said, "What are you doing in this economy? How are you investing? Where are you putting your money? The interest rates are so low, where's a good place to park my money? How did you get smart about money? What did you do?"

    One of the things women are doing more and more now is study groups and book clubs around money books. This is a great way to learn because we women are so relationship oriented. I would go to classes . . . anytime anything was free that had to do with money, I would go. Of course, they were trying to sell you something, but it didn't matter, and I would always learn something. I would also ask the teacher if I could pick his or her brain.

I was a journalist and I was hired for a freelance project to interview women who were smart with money. Those interviews changed my life. I saw how willing these women were to talk about money, how much they enjoyed talking about it. These were all women who were smart, and I realized all women need to do this more often.

I offer free monthly *Money Monday* calls; you can call in and ask questions about money. We have this great community of women and that's what we do for an hour and a half, we talk about money. We talk about issues, we talk about problems, people pipe in, and they give you suggestions. All the details, as well as many other resources, can be found on my website www.barbarastanny.com.

3. Every month save some money. Automatically have money transferred from your payroll checks or your checking account to a savings account. Not just in the joint account, but in an account under your own name. Because what you don't see, you don't miss. You would be surprised how quickly this adds up. It's very easy to set up automatic savings. I would rather see someone start small, like $10 or $25 a month, and then work up, because saving is a habit.

So if you do these three steps—every day read about money, every week talk about money, and every month save money—you will be amazed at how much you know in three to six months.

It's very important in protecting yourself and your family that you become educated about money, because it is important that you participate in financial decisions. Financial decisions need to be made based on knowledge, not fear, ignorance, or habit, which is how most of us make our financial decisions.

I think knowledge is the most important tool you can give to spouses. Because what is being asked is that a woman step up to the plate and into her power to have tough conversations with her husband.

That is the key. I have said in all of my books: this book is not about money. And I think the reason women have so much trouble understanding money is not because money is so complicated, it's because we are afraid of our power. We are afraid of rocking the boat. We are afraid of deviating from our normal behavior, which is often dependent. We are so afraid of working with each other, especially with a traumatized husband.

You need to be fierce, like a mama bear, fierce for your children, for your family, for yourself. That's why the knowledge of finances gives you the confidence to do this. And that's why I would love to see women getting help. I would love to see women who are dealing with husbands with PTSD, who are dealing with financial challenges, coming together to support each other. I think when we try to do this alone, it is really difficult. It's really important that we get support from our peers, from our girlfriends, from other women in our boat, that we get support from mental health counselors, that we get support from financial professionals.

CHAPTER 23

SEX, INTIMACY, AND PTSD

I n most marriages sex and intimacy are a key factor in the gauging of happiness and satisfaction. That is how it should be; it is God's plan for us. As the Bible says:

> *For this reason a man will leave his father and mother*
> *and be united to his wife, and they will become one flesh.*
> Genesis 2:24

Sex is a sacred, beautiful gift, the deepest level of intimacy that you and your spouse share. But when PTSD enters a marriage, things can change dramatically, leading to distance, separation, and sexual dissatisfaction. In this chapter we'll look at the problems associated with PTSD and sex and intimacy, as well as possible solutions.

Sexual dissatisfaction, if ignored, can create numerous problems in the marriage: emotional disconnection, resentment, rejection, infidelity, pornography, and even sexual addiction. It is therefore essential for both spouses to understand each other's needs and the effects of PTSD on sex and intimacy. Such understanding will allow a relationship to be built on love, intimacy, giving, compromise, boundaries, comfort zones, and selflessness.

The topic of sexual problems in veterans is not commonly discussed publicly. However, it is creating numerous problems and concerns for our veterans and their spouses, including for males decreased sexual desire, premature ejaculation, and erectile dysfunction.

Not a great deal of research has yet been conducted on this topic; however, what has been done shows alarming results. According to Matthew Tull, PhD, studies on sexual dysfunction among Vietnam veterans with PTSD showed rates of sexual dysfunction as high as 80 percent. A researcher at the Veterans Affairs Pacific Islands Health Care System in Honolulu, Hawaii looked at rates of sexual dysfunction among fifty-three male OEF/OIF veterans, all of whom were receiving treatment for PTSD. Of the fifty-three veterans in the study, only six did *not* have sexual dysfunction. That calculates to almost 90 percent experiencing some form of sexual dysfunction.

Feast or Famine

Many wives of veterans describe their sex lives as "feast or famine." Either extreme takes its toll on marriages and the partners involved.

A number of contributing factors can cause *famine*, in which there is little or no sex and intimacy. Some men may suffer from one problem and others from multiple issues. These issues can include:

- Medication side effects. Many of the drugs prescribed for the multitude of PTSD symptoms can make it physically impossible to have sex.
- Anxiety.
- Feelings of disconnect and attachment from loved ones.
- Anger and irritability.
- Survivor guilt. Some vets do not feel deserving of having pleasure.
- Sexual avoidance. Because PTSD has left them numb, some vets no longer have any mental or physical desire for sex.
- Avoiding activities that may lead to the expectation of sex. This includes the most innocent intimate behavior, such as holding hands while sitting close together.

- Keeping the relationship nonsexual as a means of accepting their sexual frustration. Eventually their sexual interest is diminished.
- Separation of sex from love and emotion.
- Upset and embarrassment at being unable to perform. This causes some vets to avoid it altogether, rather than put themselves in such a situation.
- Fear of being out of control during the moments of ecstasy. They are afraid to lose control even for a few seconds. There is also fear regarding what they might do or say. Intrusive thoughts and memories of their trauma resurfacing is also a fear. And there may be fear about their ability to control aggressive behavior caused by their trauma.
- Physical wounds and scars. Seeing these wounds may bring up memories of their trauma, creating pain and anger. Having you see their scars may cause embarrassment and fear that they are no longer physically attractive to you, or that you will be turned off by their wounds.
- Diminished interest in activities that the veteran previously enjoyed, including sex.
- Lack of importance. Many vets struggle with the life issues surrounding their war trauma and PTSD. Sex seems unimportant in comparison.
- Lack of energy and being too tired due to sleep problems.
- Emotional numbness. When their mind is not interested, it is impossible for their body to react.
- Physical problems such as tension, headaches, and gastrointestinal problems.
- Drinking and drug use, which affects sexual performance and desire.

On the opposite side of famine is the *feast*. The far end of the spectrum on the feast side is sexual addiction. The veteran is using sex as his drug of choice. He never seems to have enough of the sexual high, and is constantly wanting and needing more. This leads to problems of turning to porn, having abnormal desires, and extramarital affairs. Dr. John Gray discussed some of the biological reasons for this behavior in chapter 20.

This dark side of the veteran's struggles with PTSD can make life difficult for his wife. He can quickly turn from yelling and displeasure at her to wanting sex—referred to by many women as "sex on demand." It is often not even "make-up sex." The vet goes directly from verbal assault to insisting on having sex at that very moment.

When the veteran suffering from PTSD has an affair, it may not be because he has fallen out of love with his wife. Affairs often happen because the veteran wants to see if he can experience *those* feelings again. He may not be willing or ready to accept the sexual numbness that has overtaken him due to PTSD. This is especially true if he is still in denial over the possibility of having PTSD.

Most women have the need for intimacy and loving actions before sex. Now comes a separation of sex from love and emotion. The veteran may also have controlling issues during sex, wanting to control each part of the event. These behaviors create a vicious cycle, and without intervention, can quickly destroy a marriage as neither husband nor wife have their needs met.

A Woman's Perspective

The effects felt by a woman related to her veteran's problems with sex and intimacy can be crushing to both her self-esteem and her heart. She can believe that her husband's lack of interest in an intimate relationship, or inability to perform sexually, is her fault. She may believe that he no longer finds her sexually attractive or that she is unable to satisfy him.

Other behaviors by the veteran, such as emotional numbing, anger, withdrawal, yelling, name-calling, depression, explosions, drinking, self-pity, self-hatred, and drug use can make it difficult for the wife to maintain the desire for intimacy and a sexual relationship with her husband. Emotional disconnect, lost feelings of love, resentment, pornography, and rejection can lead to infidelity by the wife, as well as the husband.

The loss of the intimacy and their sexual relationship can create strong feelings of grief as a woman mourns the loss of a very important part of her relationship. So much of their relationship has already been lost due to the effects of PTSD, and now the loss of intimacy adds to this great sense of grief.

It is much easier to accept the fact that the sexual part of the relationship is gone when you can see the physical wounds and read the side effects of medication. However, the loss of all forms of intimacy is hard to explain, much less accept. It is difficult not to take it very personally and to feel the inadequacy, pain, and loss when he no longer wants to sit next to her on the couch, go for a walk, go on a date, or simply hold hands.

Other common effects on women can include depression, weight gain as a way to punish themselves or their husbands, avoidance, and feelings of failure. Women may also become emotionally numb, angry, withdrawn, and depressed. In addition to food, alcohol and drugs may also be used to dull the pain of rejection.

When sex does happen, many women feel that *he's not even there.* There seems to be a total emotional disconnect and no longer the intimacy that was once shared. To some it may feel like they're having sex with a total stranger. This can cause numerous other feelings of discomfort, even fear, to rise up in a woman.

God's plan is for sex and intimacy to be enjoyable to both partners. Neither should be disrespected nor degraded. When there is sexual discontent, it should not be ignored, as it can lead to greater problems. The mutual benefits gained from sex will be lost, including:

- Physical release of tension.
- Communicating affection and love.
- Reduction of isolation and loneliness.
- The most important means of human physical and emotional gratification.
- Appreciation of themselves and their partners.
- A means of being emotionally close.
- Feeling cherished and valued as a person.
- Warmth and security.

These feelings of loss can create resentment and anger if you believe your spouse could be doing more. Do you feel as though you're getting the leftovers? Do you see the effort and energy that your spouse gives to other things and other people, leaving little or none left for you? Are you making it a priority to plan and set time aside in your life to spend with your spouse in a stress-free, rested environment? For both husband and wife stress, overwork, and anger can take the mental desire out of having a sexual relationship.

And what about the woman's role in all this? Spouses can ask themselves these questions: Are you guilty of complacency? Has fear of rejection or the numbness simply made you stop trying? Have you decided that it is okay to become lazy and not put forth any effort?

Because eventually there will be nothing to feel but emptiness. You will become two numb strangers going through life together, without caring about any sense of warmth between you, blind to the needs of the other—one partner thinking it is a perfect marriage, when to the other it is hardly bearable. Is this where you want to be at the end of your love story?

When God gave us the precious gift of intimacy, he also provided guidance as to how we should honor and protect the sacred treasure:

> *But since there is so much immorality, each man should have his own wife and each woman her own husband. The husband should fulfill his marital duty to his wife, and likewise the wife to her husband. The wife's body does not belong to her alone but also to her husband. In the same way, the husband's body does not belong to him alone but also to his wife. Do not deprive each other except by mutual consent and for a time, so that you may devote yourselves to prayer. Then come together again so that Satan will not tempt you because of your lack of control.*
>
> 1 Corinthians 725

Temptation and Guilt

God instructs us not to deprive our partner of sex. There is a big difference between not being able to give and not being willing to give.

Are you being selfish in your giving by placing your needs above the needs of your spouse?

What is the cost to your relationship and to your spouse by withholding God's gift of pleasure from him?

Are you allowing resentment to grow in your spouse because he believes you are withholding love and affection?

Are you becoming resentful because you are not communicating your need for affection to your spouse?

Is it possible that your spouse will be tempted to look elsewhere for intimacy?

Caring for your spouse and caring for yourself can be difficult to balance. Because we are human, we can be faced with temptation, which may seem impossible to resist. God provides this promise in times of temptation:

No temptation has seized you except what is common to man. And God is faithful; he will not let you be tempted beyond what you can bear. But when you are tempted, he will also provide a way out so that you can stand up under it.
1 Corinthians 10:13

At times of temptation, it is especially important to remember God's promise and call upon him for strength. Infidelity can crush a marriage beyond repair.

It is also important to keep in mind that this precious gift of sexual intimacy should be given lovingly, without bringing pain, shame, or harm to your spouse. It's important to keep the physical, emotional, and spiritual well-being of your partner in mind. Sex should be a place of joy and peace, honoring boundaries and comfort zones.

In this same way, husbands ought to love their wives as their own bodies. He who loves his wife loves himself.
Ephesians 5:28

If guilt is one of the factors getting in your way of a satisfying intimate relationship, it is time to look at forgiveness—forgiving yourself for the past and forgiving your spouse for things they have done to hurt you. It may be difficult for us to believe that God truly has forgiven us. Ask God to help you feel his forgiveness within your heart and to allow you to move forward in peace and joy.

Solutions

Enjoying a more fulfilling intimate relationship despite the effects of PTSD is possible. It requires time, work, and effort. But when a couple works together to give each other the necessary support, change is possible, and renewing this aspect of your relationship is well worth the effort. Things can be done both individually and as a couple to help strengthen the intimacy in your relationship.

Of course, sex and intimacy are problems that most of us would prefer to keep inside the privacy of our bedrooms. However, not reaching out to sources available to help is denying yourself and your spouse the enjoyment of one of God's greatest gifts to us.

Encouraging your veteran to have an open and honest conversation with his doctor is an important step. Remind him that although he may feel embarrassed, it is not his fault, and many other veterans with PTSD have similar problems. The physician, working together with the pharmacist, may be able to offer ideas for changing medications or the timing of drugs for the least impact on sexual performance.

For some men drugs for erectile dysfunction may be an option. However, even with the help of drugs such as Viagra, Levitra, and Cialis to treat the physical effects of erectile dysfunction, if a man doesn't experience sexual arousal, these drugs do not work. And the ED drugs are also not advised when taking medications such as alpha-blockers and nitrate medications.

It is crucial for the veteran to work with the psychotherapist about his concerns and problems regarding sexual performance and intimacy. A therapist may be able to work on some of the PTSD symptoms causing problems with the psychological aspect of sex and intimacy.

Change begins by expanding your communication, learning to compromise, and recognizing and honoring comfort zones and boundaries. Meeting with a marriage counselor can be very helpful in working through a variety of these problems. Many pastors provide free or low-cost marriage counseling.

For some couples there will be no option but to live in a sexless marriage. But this does not mean that intimacy should disappear. These couples will need to work even harder to form new areas of connection and intimacy. Other couples will need to work with the problems that are unique to them and come up with solutions for a satisfying intimate life for both of them.

Remember that intimacy has many aspects, the physical being just one part. Other things brought you together as well. Emotional intimacy, such as warm and loving words and actions, can bring the romantic part of your relationship back.

How can you begin to bring that spark back into your own marriage?

The intellectual part of your relationship is what first connected you and brought you together. Do you remember how you used to connect, how you could communicate without even talking? What can you do to renew that intimacy?

Do you remember your spiritual intimacy, the common values, beliefs, and essence of who you are that brought you together? In this troubled time of fighting to keep your relationship healthy and well, can you call upon your spiritual oneness to guide you and help you?

In relationships struggling with PTSD, it is common for many parts of the previous relationship to be lost. You look at your spouse and feel as though he is a stranger. It is important to look back and remember what made you fall in love with him, look at who he is today, and find new things to appreciate and love about him.

Learn new ways to create intimacy outside of sex. Remember those special glances that used to melt your heart? The slight brush of his hand that sent your heart rushing? The special connection that you felt when your eyes met from across a room? Those feelings and moments shared between the two of you? Bring those back to life.

If your veteran is afraid of moments of intimacy because in the past it led to sex, he may fear that you still hold those expectations. Talk to him. Let him know you understand. Let him know that it is about your love for him, and tell him the reasons you love and appreciate him. You are not looking for anything except having your heart filled with love and warmth.

Self-esteem can be a problem for both the man and the woman. Make an effort to build up your spouse in loving ways. Compliment him, let him know he is still attractive and desirable. Create new and special loving gestures that work for you today, to replace what you have lost.

Another source of support is from the Lord. All of these changes take work and commitment to your marriage. Reach to the Lord for daily strength and support to help you honor your marriage vows and bring a renewed love back into your life.

Each couple and marriage is different. The combination of problems that you are dealing with due to your veteran's PTSD is also unique. But sex and intimacy in a marriage are much too important to simply ignore, hoping that things will change on their own. Nothing will change until both partners take action. Working together will provide an opportunity to grow closer and create a deeper relationship than you ever thought possible.

CHAPTER 24

THE REALITY OF A FUTURE WITH PTSD

U p to this point this book has provided you with a great deal of information about PTSD: what it is; its history; treatment options; and its effects on spirituality, dealing with money, sex and intimacy, and relationships.

But the question everyone wants to know is, can PTSD be cured? There is a growing interest in research to see if PTSD can be prevented or the effects lessened by early intervention.

I asked Dr. Sunde if he thought it was possible to 100 percent cure or train people how to deal with their PTSD symptoms and to be symptom free. Here's his response:

Yes, I think it is, although I've only worked with two or three vets that I would say came in meeting full criteria for PTSD and left not really meeting the criteria. I wouldn't say symptom free, but the symptoms weren't controlling them anymore, and many of the symptoms had gone away.

Both of these were Iraq vets. One wasn't even out of the military yet. The military sent him to me before he was even discharged. We were able to catch it very early, and they were moderate symptoms.

So it's relative to how severe the symptoms are, how long they've been there, and how motivated the person is. Most of my cases are Vietnam vets. The Iraq and Afghanistan guys are slower to come in, because they think that because they're getting back, everything will now be fine. It often takes a number of years before they really recognize that just being back and out of the military hasn't made their life okay.

So in my work with Vietnam veterans, we're talking about men whose symptoms have been unrecognized—and unmanaged. I don't know that I've had a Vietnam vet that I would say no longer has PTSD. But I have seen huge changes in how well they manage it and how much lower their symptoms are.

The key to the future is for your veteran to have the motivation and support to be able to seek treatment, and to stay with it. The loving, compassionate support that you are able to provide will make a tremendous difference, not only in your veteran's future, but also in your own future. Together you can learn to control PTSD in your life, rather than letting your life be defined by PTSD.

★ ★ ★ ★ ★

In the meantime, it is important to deal with the reality of your future and living with your veteran's PTSD. It is generally accepted throughout the medical community that PTSD cannot be cured—it's something that you and your veteran will always have to live with.

That is not to say that PTSD can't be controlled. It is possible to learn how to live with the symptoms and triggers that are part of PTSD. But you have learned about many innovative new treatments in this book, as well as treatments from ancient times that can help alleviate the symptoms of PTSD. Many people claim their treatments are curing PTSD. And our greatest hope for the future is that those claims will prove to be true.

The tools we've shared can help you create a "new normal" that works for you. By using these tools and the information provided here, you and your veteran will be able to create a life specifically designed around what works for you in creating your new normal.

In the final section of this book, "Secondary Stress Disorder: 8 Steps to Taking Your Life Back," you will learn how to care for your own health and happiness, which will enable you to be a strong and compassionate support for your veteran.

PART 5

SECONDARY
STRESS DISORDER:
8 STEPS TO TAKING YOUR
LIFE BACK FROM THE
CONTAGIOUS EFFECTS
OF THE STRANGER

The Beginning

I walk along the great bank of a lake.
The sides crumble and tumble, I cannot fall.
I cannot follow them to the mirror.
The hand on the other side. . . Waiting.

If the lake is a mirror, can a mirror be a lake
into which you plunge?
The surface, a barrier or division
Separating us from a world so close, yet of
which we know so little.

It's like that.
Experiences travel obliviously by.
Their lessons smile at us, and we fail to acknowledge
their kind offer.
Challenge the mirror and expose yourself to
how it really is.

It might not be like that.

David Saywell

INTRODUCTION

It is common for spouses living in the world of PTSD to wonder, what is happening to me? Am I going crazy? Why am I so angry? I've been sad before, but never depressed for days and weeks on end! Why do I feel like my life is hopeless?

In parts 2, 3, and 4 we learned about our veteran's PTSD and how we can help him. Now it's time to look at another part of post-traumatic stress disorder: the contagious effects of our veteran's PTSD *on us*. It's called *secondary traumatic stress*, and information about this aspect is vital for loved ones and spouses caring for a veteran with PTSD. In part 5 we'll look carefully at this disease and discuss the eight steps to taking our lives back!

[**Author's Note:** The information in this introduction, especially "What is Secondary Traumatic Stress?," "The Vicious Cycle of PTSD in Marriage," and "Overcoming Denial," is based largely on an article that appeared in an April 2007 in the *Croatian Medical Journal*, "Secondary Traumatization of Wives of War Veterans with Post-traumatic Stress Disorder," by Tanja Frančišković, Aleksandra Stevanović, Ilijana Jelušić, Branka Roganović, Miro Klarić, and Jasna Grković. The article is referenced and excerpted by permission of the *Croatian Medical Journal*, Vol. 48, No. 2., pp. 177 – 184.]

What is Secondary Traumatic Stress?

According to the Croatia study, "Secondary traumatic stress is a natural emotional reaction to the traumatic experience of a significant other. It is the stress caused by providing help, or wishing to help and offering emotional support to a traumatized person." It's almost identical to PTSD, except the exposure to the trauma is indirect: it happens through close contact with the victim of the trauma. Other terms for secondary traumatic stress include *compassion fatigue*, *vicarious trauma*, and *secondary post-traumatic stress disorder*.

Symptoms of secondary traumatic stress that are the same or similar to those present in PTSD include "nightmares about the person who was traumatized, insomnia, loss of interest in things that used to be enjoyable, irritability, chronic fatigue, changes in self-perception, and changes in the perception of one's own life."

Living with and/or caring for a veteran with PTSD can have negative effects not only on spouses, but also on *all* those with close contact: mothers, fathers, friends, siblings, grandparents, aunts, uncles, and, worst of all, children. This is because it can cause you to begin *mirroring* their behaviors and moods. Their triggers become your triggers; you share their moods, their anxiety; and you become numb, just like them.

The study states, "The exposure to stress caused by the veteran's PTSD symptoms or other psychiatric and health conditions, combined with the lack of social and emotional support and the increased demands upon the family, creates an increased risk for specific mental problems related to living and caring for a veteran with PTSD." And the irony is that the same family that is affected by the veteran's difficulties in everyday life "is also expected to provide nearly all the support that the veteran needs."

The family "witnesses his sleepless nights, restless dreams, absent mindedness," and anxiety as they try to avoid upsetting him." The family quickly learns how to *walk on eggshells. "*The veteran's low frustration threshold, lack of patience with his wife and children, inability to fulfill his previous family role, and verbal and physical aggressiveness all influence the relationship with the spouse, children, parents, and family members and friends."

A number of studies support the reality that veterans' PTSD symptoms can negatively affect marriages and family relations. One previous study shows that "close and long-term contact with an emotionally disturbed person can cause chronic stress, which in time leads to various emotional problems, including depression, anxiety, problems with concentration, emotional exhaustion, pain syndromes, and sleeping problems."

How Does it Happen?

When your partner first arrives in your life, he is new and fresh. His laughter is contagious, his smile infectious. Soon you find yourself drawn into his alluring spell. As you gaze into the mirror of his love, his reflection creates a new image for you. You begin to shine in the rays of his love. Eventually you become one . . . each of your images reflecting back the good of each other.

Then it happens. It may be sudden, from the moment he walks in the door returning from the ravages of war. Or it can creep up quietly, like a stranger in the night. His shadowy existence, inside, hiding, lurking, allowing you to see just a small glimpse at a time . . . until finally the pieces all come together and there, lying in bed next to you, is a stranger.

This stranger becomes a new and different influence in your life. As his presence begins taking over your world, you succumb to his power. Soon you begin to be infected by his potent moods—but this is different from the man you fell in love with. This infection is not laughter and joy. This stranger infects you with his pain. The pain of trauma, anger, and guilt.

As your infection grows, it spreads and engulfs your life with the overwhelm of caring for this stranger. You have sleepless nights and stress-filled days.

One day you look in the mirror and you don't recognize the face looking back at you. This infection has taken over you and your life. You have become a stranger to yourself. And you don't like that stranger you see in the mirror!

You want to scream out, "What happened to me? I want my life back!"

But where do you begin?

How do you break that mirror so that the ravages of PTSD do not continue to consume you?

How do you move from the dead end that seems to be blocking your hopes and dreams?

How do you fight the infection that has been growing inside you since PTSD invaded your life?

How do you stop the pain?

How do you heal your wounds?

How do you protect yourself from being infected again?

The Vicious Cycle of PTSD in Marriage

Before PTSD, husband and wife commonly share the responsibilities of their life. In active service military families, one spouse may have been carrying the burden while waiting for their loved one to return home from war. When he comes home, they have the expectation that the load will once again be shared. But when PTSD enters the picture things change. It is expected that the wife will provide the greatest support to her husband. This is especially true of a veteran's wife's role. The wife holds this expectation herself, as does the husband, the rest of the family, and our society.

Veterans' wives are also responsible for maintaining balance in the family, compensating or covering up for the husband's lack of emotional engagement with other members in the family, especially with their children. They assume a large part of the emotional, practical, and financial responsibilities for the family.

The Croatia study describes this vicious cycle this way:

- The wife's overfunctioning is her way to avoid conflict by making fewer demands on her partner.
- "The overfunctioning wife enables her husband to underfunction, who in turn increases his demands on his wife."
- "Overfunctioning and full care of a household, plus an ill husband, may create feelings of resentment and exhaustion for the overburdened wife."
- "This increases stress and vulnerability for depression and leads to the loss of identity for the wife."
- This ends up in a vicious cycle (see chart to the right):

It is easy to become lost in this new world of caregiving and PTSD. Your identity has been stolen; you feel trapped in this prison. The face

Vicious Cycle of PTSD in Marriage

 Husband & Wife Share
Responsibilities

PTSD ENTERS

In Order to
Avoid Conflict
Wife Begins to
OVER-function

 Wife Asks LESS of Her HUSBAND

Which Leads To
OVER-functioning WIFE
AND
UNDER-functioning HUSBAND

 HUSBAND INCREASES Demands on Wife

OVER-functioning WIFE Now with
FULL CARE OF
HOUSEHOLD & CARING FOR
ILL HUSBAND

 WIFE Becomes RESENTFUL & EXHAUSTED

Which Increases the STRESS and
VULNERABILITY
for DEPRESSION

Which Leads to the WIFE Losing Her Identity

you see in the mirror and the feelings you're feeling are unexpected and foreign to you. They are the feelings of a stranger. Your life has spun out of control.

This happened to me. That is exactly how I felt. I knew better, but I was caught in the vicious cycle of PTSD. As a recreation therapist, I knew that it was not healthy to do more for my husband than he truly needed. In adapting activities for people with special needs, the number one rule was to adapt the minimum amount necessary for the participant to have success. In my work with the aging population, the number one rule in determining the level of care was the lowest level available to meet their needs. You never wanted to provide more care than they needed and have them stop doing things for themselves.

But that was exactly what I was doing to avoid conflict with my husband. And the result was *caregiver overwhelm.*

Overcoming Denial

Once I understood that what was happening to me was secondary traumatic stress, things began to make sense. For a long time I had thought I was all alone, that no one else understood or was going through the same horrible ordeal that had overtaken me. But during my research, I found that spouses of war veterans throughout the world are being affected by their loved ones' PTSD, just as I was. The only problem was: they didn't want to admit it.

In the Croatian study, research was conducted in Croatia on fifty-six wives of war veterans diagnosed with PTSD and receiving treatment. Of these, thirty-two of the wives had six or more symptoms of secondary traumatic stress. Twenty-two women met the diagnostic criteria for secondary traumatic stress. Only three women had no symptoms. Of those in the study:

- 70% reported emotional disturbances.
- 63% reported avoidance of thoughts and feelings.
- 56% reported periods of rage and annoyance.

Twenty-two women met the full standard for PTSD themselves. Two-thirds, or about thirty-seven, of these women felt they needed professional psychological help. *Only four sought help.*

Good News

There is hope! Life can change for you. Life can get better. You have the strength within you, and the support and tools are available to get your life and your dreams back! Perhaps even a better life than you ever could have hoped for or imagined.

I have been there too. Did you see yourself in my story? Did you say, "I have felt that pain as well; I feel that anger; I feel that loneliness"?

I learned how to heal and grow and find not just the old me, but a new and improved me. My husband also found his way back, and he is a better person today.

I broke the mirror, and so can you! In this next section I will show you how, step by step, to take a detour from the path you're on back to the road to your dreams. You will learn to treat your pain, heal your wounds, build your immunity, and create a brighter future. Are you willing to do the work and make the decision to join me?

I searched for answers and was relentless until I found them. I tried numerous tools. I searched out experts in every field to learn from, to help me and to help you.

And I discovered eight steps to take you from where you are to where you want to be.

8 Steps to Taking Your Life Back

This isn't a quick fix—it's a hard journey. But the hardest part is making the decision to take that first step. I've done the legwork for you; in the pages to follow, you will find the information, tools, and resources you need to get your life back.

But be warned: you can't stop then! This is a continuous journey of learning, practice, and putting into action what you have learned—then repeating. As things change, you may need to adjust and pick different tools. Only by your continued diligence will you stay strong and protect yourself from slipping back into the infectious world of PTSD.

But the work and the journey will be worthwhile. You will be able to live a life of love, honor, and caring for your veteran, as well as cherishing your own health and happiness. You will reap the rewards of a fulfilling, happy, and healthy life.

Here are the steps we'll look at in detail in this section:

1. Knowledge, understanding, and acceptance about the stranger called Post-Traumatic Stress Disorder form the first crucial step to taking your life back. Educating yourself not only about the invisible wounds of PTSD but also the physical illnesses and problems that your veteran may have gives you power to better control your reactions to the situation.

2. Step 2 is about learning how to reclaim ourselves and finding the power to shield ourselves from the detrimental, so-called "mirror," effects of our spouse's PTSD. Finding our spiritual strength, reclaiming our self-esteem, examining the choices that will support us in breaking free of the contagious effects of our veteran's PTSD, and uncovering our essence are topics we'll explore in this step.

3. Assessing current needs and finding support will be our emphasis in step 3. We will look at how well you are currently utilizing your existing support system, as well as identify additional resources for support.

4. Fear, pain, and anger can paralyze us, making it impossible to move forward. When we are able to release these feelings it frees us to become more loving, forgiving, and compassionate. We'll talk about how to do this in step 4.

5. Overwhelm and stress are common problems. Exploring tools to relieve and overcome these problems—step 5—is essential to being able to handle all aspects of our life and health. We all can benefit from having tools at our fingertips to use daily to keep these problems at bay.

6. A successful long-term life with a veteran suffering from PTSD requires our ability to build up our resistance in order to protect ourselves from

the ongoing effects of the illness. In order to provide the best care for our family and our veteran we must start by cherishing ourselves and providing great self-care and attention through healthful eating, sleeping, and exercise practices, step 6.

7. Creating the spark in our life gives us a reason to get up each morning. Something to look forward to, to bring us joy, to give our life meaning . . . the often neglected but much needed link to make our life full and complete. In step 7 we'll look at fun, happiness, and passion as ways to find this meaning and joy.

8. The final step is putting it all together into a unique life designed just for you! Step 8 is creating your GPS—Goals, Plan, and Support—to take you from the dead-end road where you were stuck back on track toward your dreams.

CHAPTER 25

STEP 1: KNOWLEDGE, UNDERSTANDING, AND ACCEPTANCE

Knowledge is power.
Francis Bacon

I t is undeniable that knowledge is a very powerful tool. However, I believe that the first step to getting your life back from the ravages of your veteran's PTSD must go beyond simple knowledge. This first step of the program requires not only knowledge, but also understanding and acceptance. Without all three in place, knowledge has little value and does not provide you with the strength required to move forward.

We gain knowledge through education, training, and becoming well-informed on a particular topic. With PTSD, we need to become thoroughly acquainted with all aspects of the subject—PTSD and other problems can look very different when reading about them in a book from seeing them in action in our own lives.

Next we need to understand how to apply the knowledge we've learned in the context of our own lives.

And finally, we need to be able to decide if we accept or believe that what we have learned is true and correct for our veteran. It would do little good to learn about PTSD, have a full understanding, and yet fail to accept the reality that our veteran has PTSD.

Gaining Knowledge

There is a great difference between knowing and understanding. You can know a lot about something and not really understand.
Charles F. Kettering

In Parts II and III we focused on what PTSD is, its symptoms and its treatments. But your wounded warrior may have other physical and mental illnesses in addition to his PTSD. Traumatic brain injuries, physical injuries, loss of limbs, blindness, hearing loss, and health issues from exposure to harmful chemicals are just a few of the conditions that your veteran may be dealing with. In order for you to assure the best care possible for him, and be prepared to advocate on behalf of your veteran, it is important that you become educated on each of these problems._

Knowing the facts about all of the physical, mental, and emotional problems that your veteran is dealing with will make you better equipped to help him. Having a thorough knowledge of what to expect in the future—how the changes caused by PTSD may affect your veteran's life and your own life—will help you begin to create a support system and design your future based on these changes. This will allow you to take a proactive role in your future and take control of the things that are within your power.

Use the questions below to begin gathering and learning what you'll need to know about your veteran's medical issues. If your veteran has more than one problem, it will be helpful to complete these questions for each diagnosis.

What You Need To Know

1. What is the diagnosis, and what might have caused it?
2. What are the typical symptoms?
3. Is there an inter-relationship between any of the problems?
4. What are the treatment options, risks, and side effects?
5. What changes can be expected, both immediately and long-term?
   - Physical
   - Mental
   - Emotional
   - Spiritual
   - Lifestyle
6. How will these changes progress over time? Will they go away? Get better? Get worse?
7. How might these changes affect you?
   - Your family?
   - Your finances?
   - Your social life?
   - Your physical and emotional relationship?
8. What additional services may be needed?
9. Who will be involved in your veteran's care team?
10. What skills will you need to learn to care for your veteran?
11. What financial support is available?
12. Will your support system include emotional and practical matters?

Understanding and Applying What You've Learned

Understanding is the first step to acceptance,
and only with acceptance can there be recovery.
J.K. Rowling

Learning about your veteran's medical and emotional problems, as well as the changes that lie ahead in your life as a result of these, can put you in a state of confusion. You may be experiencing a roller coaster of emotions. You may feel as though you have lost all control and have no choices as to the direction of your life. So if you're going to get through this, it's crucial that you fully *understand* your veteran's problems and have realistic expectations—about today and the future. This will help direct the course of your life.

In order to take the information that we learn and begin the process of true understanding, we need to fully embrace the facts not only with our minds, but also with our hearts and our senses. Notice what kind of mental picture has been created based on everything you've learned. Are you putting a negative or positive spin on your situation?

Other questions you can also ask yourself to check whether you understand what you've learned include: Do you recognize the action steps that need to be taken? Are you able to objectively look at what you have learned and question what you don't understand? Have you made the decision to just cope with these changes? Or are you ready to learn how to thrive in this new life? Do you understand that life is a constant series of changes and transitions and your veteran's medical and emotional problems are simply one of the many things in your life that you will be faced with?

Try to be as honest as possible as you reflect on these questions. Then I recommend that you write down the answers to the next set of questions, which will help you take concrete steps to gaining control of your situation.

Your Plan of Action for Gaining Control of Your Situation

1. What do you need to learn more about?
2. What resources are available to you?
3. Who can help you understand what this all means?
4. How might your life change as your veteran's problems get worse?
5. How might your life change as your veteran's problems get better?
6. What can you do now to prepare for the next step?
7. Are you enjoying each good day?
8. What will never change?
9. What are you missing by waiting for _____ (fill in the blank) to happen?

10. Are you living in 100 percent reality of your veteran's condition?
11. What is holding you back from accepting your new reality?

Finding Acceptance

Along with becoming educated and applying your new knowledge to your veteran's problems, it is also essential that you're able to come to a place of acceptance. For many of us this can be the most difficult step.

Acceptance does not always come easily because it involves change. And change brings up all kinds of emotions and reactions, including fear. The unknown makes us uncomfortable. Even thinking about change can be uncomfortable because we are creatures of habit.

I'll show you what I mean. Let's do an exercise to demonstrate how we are all creatures of habit and, because of that, naturally uncomfortable experiencing what's new and different.

Exercise

Start by sitting with your arms down next to your body, but not on the armrest of your chair. Now I want you to simply fold your arms. Notice how you have them folded, which arm is on top? Did you fold your right arm over the left or did you fold your left arm over the right? Notice how comfortably and naturally your arms automatically folded, and how good that feels.

Now unfold your arms. Fold them again, but this time fold your arms in the opposite way. For example, if your left arm is on top, swap it so that your right arm is on the top. Rest with your arms that way for a moment. How does this new way of folding your arms feel? Most likely, it feels uncomfortable or awkward. You might have the urge to unfold your arms and fold them back the normal way—whatever *your normal* is.

This simple exercise points out that change is uncomfortable for all of us. We are, after all, creatures of habit, so it's natural to want to stay with what is comfortable and familiar. Change feels difficult and unwanted, so we try to resist it, even when we don't want to. That's why it's important that we have complete knowledge of the changes happening to our veterans and understand why these changes are happening.

Change also involves loss. Aspects of our relationship and our dreams can disappear. We are not ready for these changes and we don't want them. We liked our veteran the way he was. We liked our life the way it was. So we try to stay comfortable by pretending that things are just the way they were—again, resisting the changes with all our might.

Overcoming Grief

When the change involves the loss of something significant, it can be much more difficult to come to a place of acceptance. Common feelings that occur before coming to a place of acceptance are denial, anger, bargaining, regret, and sadness—all normal stages of loss and grief. We're all different, and we move through these stages in different orders, intensity, and timeframes. But they're all common experiences on the path to acceptance.

Denial is generally the first stage in the grief process. A part of us cannot accept the change that has happened. In the case of our veteran it may be especially difficult to accept invisible wounds like PTSD.

Anger is the next stage. We may be angry at our veteran, we may be angry at God. We ask the question, "Why me? Why now when my life has just begun?"

In the next stages, bargaining and regret, we begin trying to come to terms with what has happened. We may try bargaining with God, hoping that we can change our veteran's outcome. We may feel regret and guilt about things that we could have or should have done differently.

Sadness is actually the sign that we're near the end of the grieving process. Sadness is a healthy emotion; it means we are now feeling the loss, and by feeling the loss we are able to come to terms with it. We may want to move through this stage very quickly, because it is painful. But in order to heal this stage, it is very important that we be patient.

Acceptance is the final stage in the cycle of grief. When we have reached acceptance we know that our healing is complete. We are now able to incorporate the changes that we have faced with our veteran's PTSD into our daily life. We are now able to create our "new normal."

Have You Reached Acceptance?

Can you answer YES *to* these five questions?

1. I fully understand my spouse's condition, the treatments, and the expected progression.
2. I accept the changes that have happened to my veteran.
3. I accept that my veteran has changed and will never, ever be the same as he was before the trauma or illness.
4. I accept the changes in my life caused by the trauma my veteran has experienced.
5. I am hopeful when I consider the future, despite the changes that have occurred in my life.

Helpful Tools to Acceptance

- One way to help move towards acceptance is to change the way you look at your veteran's problems. You can reframe your thoughts by looking at what positive things can come from this. It may be quite difficult at first to find anything positive about your veteran suffering, but dig deep to find even a small positive thing. As hard as it may be, look for a benefit or a positive aspect and try to find opportunities for growth.
- If it is difficult for you to reframe your thinking in a positive way, then simply notice the changes that are happening, and do not put

a label on them in terms of being good or bad. Simply be aware of these changes.

- It is important to stay present and avoid the urge to physically or mentally run away and hide from the changes that are happening.

- Having confidence in your ability to get through these changes will help you with acceptance. Look back at a previous experience in your life when you were forced to make a change. Perhaps it was the loss of a job, a relationship, a health problem, or a loved one. Think about the tools and the ability that you had to get through what at that time seemed to be the worst experience of your life. Remember that if you did it once, you are capable of doing it again.

- Adjust your view by resisting considering yourself a victim. One strategy to move beyond feeling like a victim is to look at others in similar situations to yours. No matter how bad your situation feels, you will find others who are much worse off than you are. Looking at what they are dealing with, you will see that you are not the only one struggling.

- Relax and be flexible. Understand that your veteran has changed, and, no matter how much you resist, you have no control over what has happened. It is normal to have difficulty facing change. We often want to ignore it, hoping it will go away. Try to honestly face your feelings about your veteran's problems.

★ ★ ★ ★ ★

The first step towards any change is always the hardest. As you finish reading this first step, you may not yet be at a point of acceptance. But don't worry—that's perfectly normal. Continue to use the tools outlined here to help you. Learning and having a complete understanding of what to expect both today and in the future is an important beginning.

The next seven steps will continue to prepare and move you forward into your new life, away from the ravages of PTSD.

Action Step

What one step do you need to take immediately to gain more knowledge or understanding about your veteran's PTSD?

1. _____

CHAPTER 26

STEP 2: UNCOVERING YOUR POWER

*Inaction breeds doubt and fear. Action breeds confidence and courage. If you
want to conquer fear, do not sit home and think about it. Go out and get busy.*
Dale Carnegie

We have discussed how living in the world of PTSD can cause us to lose our identity, our confidence, our self-esteem, our dreams, and ourselves—leaving us feeling out of alignment with the essence of who we are, powerless to change. So how do we reclaim ourselves? By uncovering our power! Finding the power within us gives us the strength to shield ourselves from the mirror effects of our veteran's PTSD.

In part 1, I shared my story about how this happened to me. The vicious cycle of PTSD in my marriage stole not only my identity, but also my belief that I had the strength or the ability to do anything differently. I was left feeling alone and helpless. I became numb to everything and everyone around me. My self-esteem plummeted.

Then, as I began reaching out to other spouses, I realized that this was common among those caring for a veteran with PTSD. I had to find a way back to myself—and the purpose of this chapter is to share with you how I did this.

In step 2, we'll first look at the importance of connecting (or reconnecting) with our spiritual strength. Then we'll explore how to reclaim our self-esteem, with some expert advice from Dr. Joe Rubino, internationally acclaimed self-esteem expert.

Next we'll look at the kind of choices we can make to support healing and break free of the stranger's mirror. We'll also explore how uncovering our essence is critical to reclaiming ourselves—and how reestablishing our values supports this.

Finding Spiritual Strength

People often talk about religion and spirituality as an important part of their life. However, often this resource is not fully tapped into—especially in times of difficulty or crisis, when support and strength are most needed. The first step to uncovering our own power demands that we recognize a power greater than ourselves—and lean on it with deep faith.

Spirituality and faith provide us with a deep unwavering belief in something bigger and more powerful than ourselves. Spiritual practices such as prayer and meditation can help develop a quiet and peaceful mind. And spirituality can help us understand that we're here to learn important lessons and open our minds and hearts to what life and God are teaching us. Belief in the Lord can help us to accept or make sense of things we don't understand; it means we believe that a divine plan is at work in our life.

Prayer was the first action on my journey to getting my life back. My faith in Jesus Christ has provided the strength, courage, and confidence to get through every obstacle that has come before me. It provides the ability to move beyond fear, knowing that I have someone with me with unconditional love, limitless strength to support me, and wisdom to guide me.

Even though I had known that the Lord was always with me, and his hand could lift me up from the darkness and numb pain of PTSD, somehow, I did not feel worthy to be anywhere else but where I was. I was not worthy of feeling happiness or joy. I felt guilty because of my anger and resentment. These feelings were so far removed from the essence of who I was, yet they continued to build a wall to keep me from returning to where I belonged.

I had become paralyzed by my fear and the uncertainty of the future. I believed that the circumstances in my life were out of my control. It was then that I returned to God's promises and my heart was reassured.

The moment I realized that I was worthy of God's help and God's forgiveness everything changed. With the Lord's help I was able to begin moving forward and restoring my life.

We learned earlier in the book the role that PTSD can play for our veterans in the area of spirituality. In the same way, spirituality plays an important part in our lives. Having a deep, unwavering faith in something bigger and more powerful than ourselves provides us with the opportunity to embrace the love, gratitude, values, and hope that will lead to a fulfilling life.

Here are some questions you can ask yourself to see where you are in terms of using spiritual strength to uncover your power:

1. Are you allowing spirituality into your life?
2. What steps can you take to seek the Lord's help?
3. Do you know where you can find spiritual support?
4. Could you benefit from learning and having a greater spiritual understanding?
5. Do you have someone in your life with a strong faith that you reach out to and ask for help?

"For I know the plans I have for you," declares the Lord. "Plans to prosper you and not to harm you, plans to give you hope and a future. Then you will call upon me and come and pray to me, and I will listen to you. You will seek me and find me when you seek me with all your heart. I will be found by you," declares the Lord, "and will bring you back from captivity."
Jeremiah 29:11-14

Reclaiming Your Self-Esteem

We pay a great price when we try to live with no self-esteem. Physical, mental, and emotional health can be affected, resulting in such things as heart disease, cancer, premature aging, weight gain, and ulcers. There is also the danger of harmful addictions while trying to numb our pain through alcohol, drugs, food, and unhealthy activities. When we don't value ourselves, we also neglect our own needs for health and happiness: eating right, exercising, and seeking regular medical care.

Neglecting close friendships and intimate relationships can lead to a loss of love. It is very difficult to love someone who does not love himself or herself. We soon stop living with a purpose, feeling we have nothing to give or to contribute to others. Not only are we missing out on using our own gifts, gaining the satisfaction of giving freely, but also the positive benefit of taking our focus off our own problems and putting our attention on something positive. We are also denying the world the gifts we have to offer.

You may remember that my wake-up call came from my husband reading a dead-end sign to me—making it sound as if I were the dead end. When I heard my husband's words "Debbie's a dead end," I knew it was time to make a change. I also realized that I could not do this on my own. I had not lost my faith in the Lord's presence in my life, but I felt so overwhelmed in what was happening I began to believe that this was how my life was supposed to be. I simply resigned and accepted this as my fate. I was destined to become a stranger inside my own skin, as I continued to wear the mask of my old self for the world to see, camouflaging the sad and angry person inside.

During the search to reclaim my self-confidence, personal power, and identity, I began looking for resources to help me. I found a number of books written by Dr. Joe Rubino that provided exactly what I needed to begin taking back my life from the grip of PTSD.

Dr. Rubino is an internationally acclaimed expert on the topic of self-esteem, personal development trainer, success coach, and best-selling author of eleven books.

I was honored to interview Dr. Rubino to discuss self-esteem and how we can reclaim it or keep it high when living with a veteran with PTSD. Our interview follows:

Dr. Rubino, can you tell us what your personal definition of self-esteem is?
I have a broader definition than most with respect to self-esteem. For me it's made up of five components, all essential elements to maintain high self-

esteem. If any one of these five elements is lacking, a person's self-esteem is diminished significantly. They include personal power, significance, virtue, confidence, and empathy.

It starts with personal power, which is our ability to influence others. When people with great personal power speak, other people listen. They have charisma; they are able to influence people with their thoughts and their actions.

The second key element is significance. This is our ability to be accepted and have the affection and attention of other people. People who feel significant feel like they matter and that what they do in the world makes a difference. So they're more likely to take risks and more likely to interact boldly with others. That of course is reflected as high self-esteem.

The third area is virtue. Virtue is how we feel about ourselves morally. Do we feel like we are a good person? Are we proud of the things that we stand for in life and the actions that we've accomplished? Or are we ashamed of the person we are? Do we feel sleazy, underhanded, or untrustworthy? Or that we have some significant deep dark qualities that prevent us from being our best?

Those with high virtue also have the ability to be self-compassionate. This is a key component of high self-esteem because, when people make mistakes, which we all do, those with high self-esteem learn from their mistakes. They forgive themselves; they decide to do better next time. They clean up their mess and apologize when necessary. And they learn lessons that they utilize to enhance who they are as a person and how effective they are with others based on those mistakes. So self-compassion is a key component.

Confidence is the fourth component. Confidence is our ability to produce a result with velocity and to be in control of our lives. It's the ability to turn an idea into a confident result, knowing that we can achieve whatever we set as goals, that we can accomplish our vision. Those people who are confident know that they have control and that they can manifest their desired intention by acting intentionally and deliberately. They know that it's going to make a difference, that it's going to matter.

The fifth area, which many people overlook, is our ability to appreciate what it's like in the other person's world. People who possess empathy, who live by the golden rule, who honor others, and who look for win-win scenarios have high self-esteem. People who are based on self-centered, egotistical values do not—they have what I call *high ego*.

So the notion that we have to be careful because we might be creating egomaniacs by helping our children develop high self-esteem couldn't be more false by my definition. By my definition, high self-esteem and egotism are mutually exclusive. If you have high ego, you don't have an appreciation for what it's like in the other person's world. You don't act in that win-win, integrity-type of behavior. You violate others to get ahead yourself, and so your self-esteem is lacking because you don't see abundance everywhere. You don't see there's enough to go around, so you think you have to take from others or take your own first, before others can get theirs.

Having an appreciation for what it's like in the other person's shoes means that you don't take things personally, when people say things you don't immediately agree with. You realize it's their opinion, but you try it on to see if it has any value. If it does, you shift because of your personal development process, and if it doesn't, you release it. So you're not affected by other people's negative words or actions.

So those are the five key components in my definition of self-esteem: personal power, significance, virtue, confidence, and empathy.

Dr. Rubino, that leads right into my next question. Many spouses live with a veteran with PTSD who is often angry, numb, and depressed. Can you explain how living with someone like that may affect a spouse's self-esteem, and give us some suggestions on how we might turn the situation around?

The spouse can take on the vet's PTSD, affected by his words and deeds, or she can detach from them, realizing that the veteran is not seeing the world clearly, rather from a traumatic perspective. We all interact in life from the pictures from which we view our environment, how we see others, and how we see the world in general. And those who suffer from PTSD see the world in a way that says the world is a dangerous place: you have to always be on guard; people are out there to get you; you have to live in fear; you have to react often times with anger or with sadness to what life gives you.

It's a false reality. So when a spouse can realize that the person who suffers from PTSD is not seeing things clearly, then the spouse need not react to the misinterpretations in a way that negatively affects her. The spouse's role can actually be calming, reinforcing, and supportive by saying things such as: I realize that you see things that way; could we look for other interpretations of it? Or, are you open to considering other possibilities?

If I were working directly with a person with PTSD, I would support them to help see that they have made things up about themselves and other people in the world in general based upon their experiences. Their experiences have skewed their perception in such a way that their perceptions no longer support them. It's not that they don't have some validity, because in certain circumstances like war, they are very valid, like when somebody could kill you around the next bend. It's a different scenario than in peaceful coexistence with people who operate from loving intentions, as opposed to murderess intentions. Spouses can help by understanding, having empathy, supporting the person to see that there is another perspective out there.

Here is an example of an exercise the spouse can do to support the veteran when he misinterprets life situations—when someone says or does something in a way that he doesn't feel supported.

Exercise

Ask your veteran to look at what was said or done, and how it makes him feel. Did it make the veteran feel afraid, angry, and sad? What was the emotional response tied into the situation?

You can also support your veteran by asking him to give up the emotion momentarily. To give up his right to be angry, give up his right to be afraid, give up his right to be depressed about what happened.

Help the veteran to have empathy for what it was like in the other person's world. Help create an interpretation that allows the veteran to be in a relationship with the other person. Or create an interpretation about the world situation that supports harmony, supports empowerment, and supports the veteran to move forward in a way that makes his life a better place to live in.

Dr. Rubino, another common reaction for spouses is to automatically think that it must be our fault when our vet's upset—that we must be doing something wrong. Can you give us some tips on how to move beyond that and accept the fact that most of the time, the things they're doing are not about us?

Yes, that is true in most upsetting situations, not just with veterans and PTSD. Ninety-nine percent of an upset is about the person that is upset. Only 1 percent is about the person supposedly causing the upset. So when a spouse can see things clearly, she realizes that although the world of the veteran is chaotic, stressed, and full of dysfunction, she is not the cause. She cannot be the cause of how other people see the world.

What she can do is create room for the veteran to be who he is. Within that space, she can gently offer him alternative ways to see a situation, supporting him with love to understand her perspective. She can become a guiding light for him in the way she supports him to reinterpret interpretations of the moment, manage negative emotions, manage negative self-talk, and build constructive intuition. And as trust is built, the veteran can gradually re-acclimate to a normal perception, a normal way of seeing the world and other people.

When you're in a traumatic situation like a war zone, you constantly have to be on guard, so your negative self-talker is on overtime. That negative self-talker is meant for your survival. It's crucial in that situation when you don't know who's your friend, who's your enemy, or what's going to come around the next bend. But those same survival skills that were valuable in a war zone are now detrimental in real life because they prevent relationships. They kill harmony. They don't allow for happiness. They don't allow for a peaceful, fulfilling life. They don't allow for charisma and personal effectiveness in relationships.

And all of those things need to be developed to be able to see the world more accurately, instead of misinterpreting life's signals in a way that's well-intentioned to keep you alive, but not effective in harmony, happiness, relationships, and all the things we want in regular life.

Dr. Rubino, that sounds like a big shift, working together with our veterans to make some positive changes.

Absolutely! Having patience, empathy, and understanding [is a key]. And realizing that your veteran is not acting crazy, angry, or divisive intentionally, but rather is acting out of survival techniques learned to keep him alive in a very stressful situation. His brain has adapted to survival mode and has not been able to transition back. The signals his brain is giving off are still in that survival, high-intensity stressful mode—and your calming, soothing, reassuring patience will do much to help him see that you are his friend, there to support him. You understand what he went through. You're not judging him harshly. You understand he has the equivalent of a broken arm in his brain, that he needs to heal, and you're going to support him to heal. PTSD is no less real than a broken bone, but it's so much harder to get our hands around, because it seems irrational and ludicrous to somebody who doesn't suffer from it.

Yes, Dr. Rubino, that is so true; the invisible wound of PTSD is so difficult for the outside world to see and understand. Many spouses that live with a veteran with PTSD feel very vulnerable. How can that vulnerability be used as a source of power?

We typically hold vulnerability as a weakness; however, vulnerability can be the source of our greatest strength. I hold vulnerability as transparent communication, in other words, not withholding, not hiding who we are, but allowing people to see who we really are. It's when our thoughts, words, and deeds are congruent. It's when we make the choice to act with integrity, as opposed to hiding things and not being willing to share our thoughts.

And, of course, we can always share our thoughts in a responsible manner, where we keep the other person whole rather than making him wrong, invalidating him, or acting with anger. This is possible as long as we always act from love, as opposed to anger, sadness, or fear. When we understand that our veteran has gone through some very real traumatic stress, we have the ability to support him, rather than allow him to pull our strings or press our buttons, and avoid getting sucked into the same negative emotion he's experiencing.

Dr. Rubino, often when living with a veteran with PTSD it is necessary for us to create a life that appears abnormal to the outside world. We often get people commenting about this in what seems like a critical way. For instance, I've had people ask me why I chose to go on separate vacations and go by myself to social events. When the values of other people are imposed on you, how can that affect a person's self- esteem?

Well, you have to remember that no one can damage your self-esteem but you. So if you allow people to denigrate your self-esteem, then that is your responsibility. If you are acting with sound logic and you are coming from a place of love to make life work optimally for you, then you can listen to other people's opinions if you choose—and realize that everyone will have an opinion.

They need not influence you. Try on their opinion to see if, like a coat, it fits. Is there some value in what they're saying? Is there another possibility that would serve me better? And, if so, then you adapt, you change, you transform in a way that you didn't see something before and now you have insight. So you act differently. If you analyze their opinion, try it on, and see they don't understand what the situation is—I've tried that and it doesn't work and this way is a functional way for us to survive and thrive—then you don't have to wear the coat. Take the coat off because it doesn't fit.

It's critical that people have high self-esteem in dealing with veterans that have PTSD. Because if not, you are going to get sucked into all the dysfunction that the veteran is experiencing. You will also be sucked into the dysfunction of all your friends and family who really don't know what it's like living with a person with PTSD.

But it's very easy for people to want to help and to lend their opinion. Sometimes those opinions are valuable and sometimes they are not. But we have to remember that we always have the ability to trust our intuition, to listen to others, to thank them, and know they are coming from great intentions most of the time. At the same time, we don't have to be affected by their thoughts, their opinions, or their words. We can be strong and know that everyone else has an opinion, while remembering that we get to evaluate what's best, what works, and what doesn't work in our life, free from other people's opinions.

Dr. Rubino, often when we begin caring for our veteran with PTSD, we neither expected it nor were prepared for it. In my case, PTSD came to visit over thirty years after the Vietnam War. For our younger spouses and veterans, they fell in love with one person who has now come home from the war and suddenly becomes a stranger. Some spouses feel they're caring for their veteran out of obligation, rather than by choice, which can cause resentment. What can you say to these spouses?

We always have a choice. Every one of our actions is a choice. We can choose not to file our income tax, and [if we do] we know there are repercussions to that choice and we could go to jail. With respect to a spouse's decision, a spouse can do whatever it takes to support her veteran with empathy, forgiveness, and understanding. But the veteran has some obligations as well. There will be veterans who absolutely refuse to be helped. They'll refuse therapy, counseling, or any type of treatment.

So the spouse has to make up her mind as to what will serve the relationship, the veteran, and herself the best. Sometimes the answer is not suffering in silence. Any relationship involves two parties; it's a dance. There's responsibility on both parties. When one party is ill, the other party needs to have compassion and understanding, needs to be supportive, and needs to put structures in place to support the health and well-being of that person.

But there comes a time when she also has to make her own decision as to what the rest of her life is going to look like. Personally I don't advise anyone to live her life in resignation, as a martyr, or to live in abject sadness and depression because of the situation she's in. The whole concept of responsibility isn't about blame and fault; it's about the ability to respond in a way that serves you. So do whatever it takes to support your veteran, support the relationship, and get help for yourself. And if there comes a time when your spouse is not willing to be helped, then you have to make your own decision as to what serves you best.

Dr. Rubino, how difficult is it to learn new behavior in order to improve our self-esteem?

It can be done as quickly as flicking on a light switch. It's something everyone can do; what it takes is courage. I believe in a three-part self-esteem system: healing your past, honoring your values, and designing your future.

It takes courage to give up the right to be right, and to give up the right to be addicted to your emotional interpretations, which don't support you anymore—two key components to completely **healing your past** so you are no longer subjected to the effects of misinterpretations, challenges, problems, and things you or others have done in your past.

When your history is complete, you are no longer subject to the effect of the decisions you or others have made. You no longer operate from mistaken perceptions that you made up as a child or during a traumatic situation like war. You are complete. You embrace the process of personal development. You honor your values. You evaluate what's right now, in your current situation. You look at what's working and what's missing—what, if put in place, would have your life work more optimally in all six areas of life. [The six areas Dr. Rubino is referring to are: 1. Physical, Mental, and Spiritual Health, 2.

Relationships, 3. Career, 4. Finances, 5. Recreations and Passions, 6. Personal Growth and Development.]

You also have the ability to look at what **values you honor** and what would be necessary for you to honor those values. Our core values are those threads that form a fabric, that make up who we are at our inner sole, our core. When those threads are pulled, we shut down in our communication and we become angry. When our life doesn't work, we become apathetic, resigned, and we give up . . . hopeless, what's the use?

We have the ability to honor our values at all times. We have the ability to live from a declaration that says, "I declare that these are the qualities that I'm going to be known for. I'm going to be in development every day of my life. I'm going to look for problems, welcome them, embrace them, and know that every problem has a gift that is there for my edification. So that I can grow and learn and become happier, fulfilled, abundant, self-actualized, and at peace every day of my life."

We can look for our gift. We can develop those gifts. Most people don't know what their gifts are. Most people don't develop them or share them fully with the world; they allow them to go undeveloped. When we don't live from a life purpose, we declare we have a default: this is what life gave me; I'm a victim. When we give up our right to be a victim, anything's possible. That's when we can live from responsibility. We can act in line with our commitments. We can embrace problems and look for the gifts they have. We can allow life to train us day by day when we live from that empowering perspective.

The third part of the self-esteem system is that we get to **design a future**. We have a choice to design a future that aligns with our life purpose. A life purpose is something that gives us passion and makes life worth living, as if we were to live another 400 years. It's consistent with the vision we have for every aspect of our life: who we are, what we do in work and play, the key people in our lives, what we have around us, toys and abundance, fun and recreating, personal and spiritual development, family and friends, health and appearance, wealth and finances, and all the things we want as a part of a vibrant life.

We get to take responsibility by taking action. Detailed specific action on a daily, weekly, and monthly basis that aligns with our goals. Actions that are consistent with our vision and that align with our life purpose. As we are taking those actions, we have a personal development plan so that we're not at the mercy of what life gives us. You transform and your veteran transforms when he sees life differently.

Information about Dr. Joe Rubino's books and programs can be found at www.theselfesteemsystem.com.

Communication Tips to Protect Your Self-Esteem

Here are some tips to help you incorporate Dr. Rubino's information during communication with your veteran:

- Use empowered listening skills to keep your mind open to learn something new.
- Think about what it's like in the other person's world, without attachment to or judgment about what's being said.
- Avoid "automatic listening" by avoiding thoughts such as, *I already know that*, or wondering, *Do they like me?*
- Be conscious of your inclination to be looking for opportunities to be offended by what is being said. Avoid listening simply from the point of: *I agree, I disagree, they're right or they're wrong.*

Only you can diminish your self-esteem and only you can restore it.
Freedom comes with nonattachment to whatever another says or does.
Dr. Joe Rubino

Exercise

During the next week notice each time your veteran says something that makes you feel angry, wrong, or put down in some way. Write down each negative thought or feeling that you have about yourself when this happens. Also, write down what was said in black and white—the exact words, not your interpretation. See if you can reinterpret what was said based on the tools and knowledge you have learned in this chapter.

The Power to Choose

In step 1 we discussed how accepting the reality of any situation allows us to be aware of our options and to prepare for the future. When you continue to live your life from the view of how it should be, rather than how it is, you continue to be stuck. You live your life from a feeling obligation, so resentment grows. And by doing this you remove your responsibility for making a choice and eliminate your opportunity to be proactive, designing a life of your own choosing that honors your needs, values, and essence.

As Dr. Rubino said, you always have a choice. A powerful shift is possible in your life when you are able to move from *I have to* to *I choose to*. Here are some choices you can make to begin re-designing your life:

- Rather than being drawn into the negative and angry emotions of your veteran's PTSD, choose to help him out of that place by your example. The more positive, loving, and confident you can be, the more your veteran will begin feeling that way himself—a shining reflection of you.
- Being positive and staying positive is a choice that is open to every one of us. Living in the world of PTSD can and will pull you down. But just as our soldiers go to battle with weapons and armor, you can choose to develop your own tools to protect yourself. You can learn to use the right "weapons" and wear "bulletproof armor" by changing your attitude, behavior, and thinking.
- Be patient and loving with yourself during the process of change. It took time to develop the negative feelings, thoughts, and actions you have about your veteran and PTSD, and it is going to take time to turn them around. But it will be worth it.
- Self-empowerment comes from self-acceptance and contentment. Choose to love who you are.
- You are in charge of your own joy and happiness. Only you know what you need, but sometimes others can overpower your thoughts. Choose to trust in your own instincts.
- Learn to distinguish facts (black-and-white, exact words and actions) from *interpretations* of facts. This is especially important when you're feeling stressed, angry, sad, or afraid.

- Let go of perfection—an unattainable goal. Work towards acknowledging your special gifts, and being satisfied that your best is enough.
- Stop comparing yourself to others. This blinds us to our own strengths and amplifies our weaknesses.
- Revise your concept of failure. When we consider failure as something that makes us look bad, it's easy to think we should avoid it at all costs. This makes us give up on our life and our dreams.
- Give yourself credit for having the courage to step forward, rather than criticizing yourself for taking a step forward and not succeeding.
- Honor your wins and acknowledge your losses by looking at how you might learn and improve next time.

Uncovering Your Essence

In order to build your self-esteem and become empowered, it is important to uncover and embrace your true essence. Essence is the purest sense of who you are at the deepest level. It is your authentic, genuine self. It is what makes you uniquely you.

Do you know what your true essence is? Or have you lost your essence? Are you defining yourself by your relationships, your work, or your roles? These are not your essence. If the purest sense of who you are has disappeared, buried in the volcanic ash of PTSD, then it is time to uncover *you*.

Think about your essence like a forest after a wildfire. It looks as if it's been completely devastated and will never return to the lush green forest it once was. But come spring, if you revisit the forest, you will find that new life is beginning to return. Bright green seedlings are beginning to sprout up through the charred ground. Our essence is like the seeds buried on the forest floor—it is always there inside us, even though at times it seems to have been destroyed.

Values make up the essence of who we are. Thus, failure to honor our values, as Dr. Rubino pointed out, adds to low self-esteem and loss of our identity. In fact, key values exist at the center of our being, so when our values are violated, we struggle. We feel angry, resentful, and negative about ourselves.

Life is meaningful and we are the most happy when we can honor our values. To make sure we're honoring our values, it's a good idea to do a "values checkup" every once in a while. Here are some questions you can ask yourself to see if you're living in alignment with your values:

- What key values are essential to you? (Some common values are love, safety, security, happiness, peace, integrity, respect, and belonging.)
- Which of your values are you not living fully, or living without?
- How is this affecting you?
- What action can you take today to begin honoring your values?

★ ★ ★ ★ ★

When we have become lost at the hands of the stranger, mired in the mirror effects of our veteran's PTSD, it can seem as if there's no way out. But there is!

Start by connecting with your spiritual source. This alone will uncover a new strength within you, as you realize you are not alone.

Check in with yourself about yourself. Does your self-esteem need a booster shot? Take a closer look at Dr. Rubino's three-part self-esteem system in this chapter: healing your past, honoring your values, and designing your future—and see what changes feel reasonable and doable to you.

Begin to redesign your life, using the tips in this chapter. There's a bright future waiting—and it starts now.

And finally, touch base with your values to help you find *your own essence*.

Uncovering your power will not only help you break the stranger's mirror, but embrace life in a whole new way.

Action Step

What is one step that you can take immediately to begin uncovering your power?

1. _____

CHAPTER 27

STEP 3:
UNVEILING YOUR
SUPPORT SYSTEM

I have seen that in any great undertaking it is not enough
for a man to depend simply upon himself.
Lone Man (Isna-la-wica) Teton Sioux

In step 1 we looked at the importance of knowledge, understanding, and acceptance of what your future holds for you living in the world of PTSD. In step 2 information and tools were provided to help you recover your essence and unleash your power so you could move forward. We also discussed the importance of seeking help and support, starting with spiritual support. Step 3 will help you learn to better utilize your existing support system, as well as identify additional sources of support available to you.

Seeking support is an essential step in taking your life back. Asking for support may have been difficult when you did not feel deserving and you were allowing your situation to control you. But part of taking control of your life is to recognize and ask for the help that you need. Because PTSD is not widely understood, it can feel impossible to find people with the empathy, compassion, and knowledge to help you.

But the good news is there are thousands of other spouses just like you that do understand, as well as many people who may not fully understand your situation but are willing to support you in other ways. In this chapter we will learn new ways to look at and build an effective support system based on your needs, current resources, and untapped possibilities. We will also look at treatment options for secondary PTSD and learn the warning signs that this help is needed.

Identifying Existing Support

Living in the world of PTSD is not easy, but reaching out and receiving support from multiple sources can help you to continue to grow, rid you of feelings of isolation, and assist you to begin living the life of your creation, rather than a life that PTSD dictates for you.

Are you feeling lonely? Isolated? Unsupported? Do you feel as though you are the only one in the world feeling the way you're feeling? Do you feel lonely even when your veteran is in the same room? How about when you are in a room full of people, family and friends…do you still feel lonely? I did. And many other women feel that same way. You are not alone.

You may be thinking, "I have no one to support me, there is no one that understands." I understand how the pain of your loneliness and the frustration that no one around you understands PTSD can paralyze you from taking action. When you are unable to move forward, it is impossible to reach out and to see the possibilities all around you.

What if I told you that you could begin feeling supported right here, right now? You don't even have to leave your home, pick up the telephone, or turn on your computer. Feeling supported comes from both the heart and the mind; it's having the comfort of knowing that someone always has your back. I'd like to do an exercise with you to help you see how well you are being supported right this moment, and every moment of your life. And how you are being unconditionally supported in ways that you take for granted and probably never even question.

Exercise

I would like you to start by sitting down in a chair with your feet on the ground and your arms resting beside you. Now close your eyes and lift your legs up off the ground. How do you feel? Are you afraid that the chair will not support you? Or are you sitting there calm and confident that you are safe? Feel the weight of your body on the seat of the chair. Is the chair moving or rocking? Or is it firmly in place and unwavering? When you sat down in the chair, did you have any worry that the chair was not going to support you? Or did you fully trust that it was there to support you whenever you needed it?

Now step outside and feel the earth beneath your feet. Have you ever worried that the ground would not hold you up? Now how can you transfer the faith that you have—that the chair will hold you and the earth will not engulf you—and trust that there is always support all around you?

The earth supports you every day in ways that we simply take for granted. When is the last time that you worried about having air to breath? Or water to drink? Or food to eat? If God has provided all the things that you need to sustain your life, why would you doubt that he would not also provide the emotional support you need? How can you shift your mindset from believing that you are totally unsupported, to seeing and feeling the numerous ways that you are being supported each moment of your life, with little thought or appreciation for that support?

★ ★ ★ ★ ★

The first step in shifting your mindset and unveiling your support system is to identify the support you are already receiving. Here's how you can do that:

- Think about how are you are currently being supported by people in your life—things being done that you simply "trust" will happen. How is your family supporting you emotionally? Your veteran? Friends? Co-workers? And even your pets?

- Think about the spiritual support that you are receiving. Who is providing spiritual support? What are they providing?
- Think about the physical support that you are receiving. Who is helping to support your physical needs? What are they providing?

Appreciating Your Current Support System

In order to open the door for additional support, it is important to begin to appreciate those who are already giving you support. I learned a rule early in my business career: it's much easier and more cost effective to keep your current customers than trying to find new ones. That works with your support system as well.

It is not enough for you to silently appreciate them. If you haven't been doing this, it is time that you begin to verbally express your appreciation for not only the things that you ask them to do, but also all the things that are happening "automatically," which you may have forgotten to appreciate. Thank-you's and appreciation keep the door open for next time. It is much easier to ask for more support when you are continuing to show appreciation.

Identifying Areas Where Support is Needed

In order to find support where you need it, it's important to assess where you are today. Below is a tool to identify and assess how you're doing in terms of support in major life areas. The scale includes seven common areas in which you may need support while caring for your veteran.

Fill out the following scale to help assess the areas in which you might need support and how well you feel those needs are currently being met. Rate each need on a scale of 1 to 10, using number 1 as the lowest level of satisfaction and number 10 as the highest level. (Write N/A if it does not apply.) This scale is meant to cover general categories, so feel free to add additional areas to meet your specific needs. And once you determine your top areas of need, write specific needs/tasks for each need.

Current Support Satisfaction Assessment: *Rate from 1 - 10*

Emotional support   _____
Spiritual support   _____
Financial support   _____
Household chores   _____
Help with children   _____
Caring for your veteran   _____
Help with parents   _____

Now describe specific details about the tasks and needs for the top three areas in which you need more support.

Strengthening Your Current Support System

One common problem that creates a barrier for support is the lack of understanding about our veteran's health problems. He may be viewed as "having nothing wrong with him" or "lazy" for no longer doing things he did in the past. No wonder support is not being readily given. How can others support us if they can't even acknowledge that our veteran has a problem?

I realize how frustrating it becomes when no one around you understands or believes that PTSD is a life-changing event. After years of having my family close their eyes to my husband's problems, I finally found the words that worked for me.

It was another family dinner that my husband did not to attend. The empty chair and untouched table setting emphasized Randy's last-minute failure to appear. My family sat mutely, their disapproval showing on their faces.

I decided it was time to break the silence. To make one more attempt to help them understand why once again Randy was not feeling *well*.

"I want to tell you about Randy," I began. "You know he receives permanent Social Security disability. The VA has also determined that he is

100 percent disabled and unemployable, so they provide him with disability payments as well.

"I understand that you cannot see the wounds from the eighteen months he spent in Vietnam. But the Social Security Administration and the VA go to great lengths to determine disability benefits. They do not approve benefits lightly. Many people take part in the approval process, and Randy was examined by numerous experts that had to agree on their findings. Randy would not be receiving disability compensation from both SSA and the VA if there was not something wrong with him."

I stopped and did not try to explain any further. No one spoke or asked questions. However, the faces around the table had changed. They were no longer showing disapproval. The blank stares that I had experienced on previous occasions when I had attempted to "teach" them about PTSD were absent this time. The mood was that of validation. A higher authority had validated that something was wrong with Randy. They still did not want to know or understand about this *taboo mental condition* called PTSD, but their mindset had changed. They accepted that if two government agencies said there was something wrong with Randy, that was good enough for them.

My family may not have understood PTSD, but they finally accepted that Randy had a serious problem. I was no longer questioned when Randy did not go places with me, and support began coming in different ways. Not necessarily emotional support, but support in ways they were comfortable. "Can we run an errand for you?" "Do you want us to check in on Randy while you are away?" "I'm sending our lawn guys over to mow for you today; I know Randy hasn't felt up to it." "Do you need me to get those things down from the attic for you?" "I noticed your gate was broken, so I replaced the latch."

Eventually more conversations opened up: "We saw something on the news about that PTSD thing." "Oh, here's an article we saw in the newspaper." "Hey, the last episode of my soap opera was about PTSD; you might be interested in watching it, so I recorded it for you."

Gradually the road to understanding was opening up, in their way, and at their comfort level.

Think about different ways you may be able to talk to your family and friends about your veteran's PTSD. Is there an approach that might work for them—perhaps using something that they can relate to, that's within their comfort range? It's important to try to meet them where they are, rather than expecting that they will immediately come to where *you* are.

Remember, it took you time to process and accept the changes in your veteran. Allow your family and friends that same opportunity, trusting that they do want to continue to be there for you.

Tips for Strengthening Your Current Support System

- We may wish that our emotional support would come from those closest to us, but often it is emotional support that they just aren't able to give. Don't close the door to these people who love and care for you. Trust that they want to support you, even though that support may not be possible in exactly the way you might expect. Now look again at your list of areas where you need support. And look at those in your support system. This time look at your support team in a new way. Forgive them for not being able to help in the way that you would like, but look at new possibilities of ways they might help you.

- Would your life be easier with one less trip to the grocery store a week? One day free from shuttling your children around? One week without doing yard work? One less repair on your to-do list? Trust that you do have those who want to help; they are there waiting and just need to be given something to do. Learn to determine what help is comfortable for each member of your support team, and learn to ask for the support you need. Remember we each possess unique strengths, talents, and gifts. Let them support you coming from their strengths.

- Appreciate each gift that someone in your support system is able to give, and accept it as a *gift*.

- Understand that in time you may get more emotional support from your immediate family and friends, but for now let them have the time and space to adjust.

Reaching Beyond Your Comfort Zone for Support

It is also time to begin unveiling new sources of support beyond the confines of the stranger's mirror and your comfort zone. You have broken the mirror and now have a clear view of the endless possibilities available to you. But you may still have emotional needs that are not being met, and it's essential that you find support for these needs, in order to have a full and happy life.

Tip: Look outside your personal world and find emotional support from those who are in similar situations. These sources of support will likely be more compassionate and understanding of your emotional needs.

When I considered the need in my life for compassion, understanding, and support to help navigate the difficult road ahead with PTSD, I was reminded of another time in my life when I had had those needs. I was far away from my home and from my support system. I was at U.C. San Francisco Medical Center, where my ten-year-old son, Aaron, had just been diagnosed with a malignant brain tumor. Overnight our life was turned upside down. I was terrified and alone, captive inside the cold gray walls of the pediatric oncology ward.

When I finally took a moment to look outside the numbing disbelief that was fogging my mind, I saw other parents just like me. These parents were on the same journey as I, but some were much further down the road; some had been fighting this battle for years. Their expressions of fear and hopelessness mirrored my own.

I learned that by befriending these parents, I was able to learn from their experiences, their wisdom, and knowledge. They helped me with tips on the practical issues of dealing with what seemed like an impossible journey. They had great understanding and concern for me. Being acquainted with those other parents quickly took me out of the victim role. My eyes were opened up to those around me who were also suffering, and I began wondering how I might offer them support and compassion as well.

In dealing with Randy's PTSD, I felt that isolation again. My friends, and both my family and Randy's family, maintained that there was nothing wrong with him. Even after reaching out to professional therapists, my feelings of being alone were immense. I continued to suffer in silence for many years.

Then, in 2011, while researching information on secondary PTSD, I ran across the website of Family of a Vet, www.familyofavet.com. I was comforted to find that there were other spouses in the same situation who truly understood. When I saw they were looking for volunteers, I immediately offered my help. It was the best thing I could ever have done. Not only did it take away my feelings of isolation, but it also gave me the opportunity to use my gifts to help others. Seeing how many lives were so much worse than mine made a huge shift in my attitude.

My first interaction with Family of a Vet (FOV) was with founder and president, Brannan Vines. Hearing her story pulled at my heartstrings. Brannan has graciously allowed me to share her story with all of you as well:

Like most of us, it began as a love story. Brannan met her husband when she was sixteen. She knew the day they met that he was to be her future husband. They were high school sweethearts, and two years later, they married and began their life together. Brannan had a job with a promising career, and Caleb was in his third year of engineering school. A bright future lay ahead for them.

Then the events of September 11, 2001 happened. On that fateful morning they both happened to be at home sick. As the second plane hit the second tower in New York, Caleb said, "I need to join the service." Brannan sensed his determination to protect his homeland and family no matter what the personal cost. She was proud of his decision and awed by his patriotism. Very soon he was headed to Iraq, where he spent a total of twenty-seven months on two tours.

When Caleb came home, he had a seven-month-old daughter that he had only seen for a few days after her birth. Brannan knew instantly that he had changed. Her family was in crisis, and she began reaching out for help, to the VA and community organizations—but no one had the help she was seeking. Then she ran across a website for Vietnam Veterans Wives, www.vietnamveteranswives.org. She wasn't a Vietnam veteran's wife, but she contacted them anyway. She had a call back from the president and founder of VVW Ferry County Mountain Veterans Center, Danna Hughes.

Danna's words to Brannan were, "Let me tell you what's going on in your house." Danna went on to describe exactly what Brannan's life looked like—the anger, nightmares, reactions. Brannan describes Danna's voice as being *so real*. Danna understood, and she helped Brannan to find her voice and ways to cope. Her advice to Brannan was to find other people to help, to take the focus off her own problems.

Brannan took that advice to heart and decided to start a *little* website, to share what she had learned. That little website changed Brannan from feeling *crushed,* to today feeling *empowered*. Today what began as a *little* website is now serving 40,000 to 60,000 visitors per week. Brannan wanted her life to have purpose—she has fulfilled that goal.

Looking Back to Move Ahead

If you find yourself stuck and unable to move forward, look in your rearview mirror. Reaching back into your past may turn up support from unexpected sources. Look back into the past at friends, neighbors, classmates, work, and church acquaintances. There may be people you haven't thought about in the same situation as you. They may be having the same challenges that you are; together you may find a place for mutual support.

You may have an old friend who is compassionate, kind, and nonjudgmental, who would like to rekindle your relationship. It is easy in our busy lives to let years pass by, and without meaning to, simply lose touch with someone with whom we at one time had a very close connection. And today it is much easier to reconnect with some of those lost relationships with Facebook and other social media.

My biggest support after my son passed away was my old college roommate, Nancy. We had only seen each other a few times in twenty years, but stayed updated with Christmas cards and an occasional phone call. We still felt very close to each other, even though our busy lives got in the way of more frequent contact.

I reached out to her when my son passed away. She had lost her own son a few years earlier. As it turned out, Nancy had not had any moms to talk to that had lost a child, and I was able to provide support and compassion to her as well. Two moms both struggling with the loss of their firstborn child, we ended up providing amazing support to each other.

You may be surprised where your support is found when you begin reaching out. When I began coaching and started a support group in my community, I was surprised and saddened to know that I had friends, neighbors, and business associates that I had known for many years who had been suffering in silence just like me. We now forged a new bond of support and understanding. It's amazing what can happen when you find the strength to step forward and tell the world your story.

Other Sources of Support

If you are having difficulty finding a support group in your area specific to the needs of spouses and loved ones living with the a veteran with PTSD, I would challenge you to start one. You will find information on my website, www.detours2dreams.com, to help you with this process. You can also look for other support groups that may not be specific to PTSD but have people sharing some of the same problems and issues that you are. Some ideas where you might look for support are caregiver support groups and Al-Anon.

Churches can provide a variety of support for you. Many pastors offer individual and marriage counseling for no charge. There are also Bible studies and other types of small group programs where you might have the opportunity to meet people who can provide you with compassion and caring support. Some pastors may have limited knowledge about PTSD, but they're willing to learn. This book is a great place for them to start.

My website also has information on training and materials for Christian-based support groups. Clergy members will have the ability to help you deal with issues such as loneliness, anger, fear, and forgiveness, as well as help you find support in God's words of love and grace, reminding you of the great support that is always available to you through God.

Support Through Giving

We talked earlier about not simply looking for who can help you, but also opportunities for you to help others. The effects of giving are quite amazing and can change your view of your own circumstances. One of the places I found the opportunity to view the lifelong job of caregiving was my volunteer work as a golf coach with Special Olympics.

I have just completed my fourth year as a golf coach with special needs young adults. It has been both heartwarming and inspirational, as well as fun. This experience has opened my eyes to how anything is possible when you open up your heart to love and compassion and accept the challenges as special gifts that God has brought into your life. The joy, laughter, fun, and life lessons that I have been honored to experience through this group—parents who will never know a time in their life when they are not providing care for their children—have been priceless.

I was especially touched by a man who "voluntarily" committed his life to caring for two special needs children when he married their mother. He shared with me that there would never be a time in his marriage when they would not have the *children* (actually young adults) living with them. I have never met a person with more genuine love, compassion, and patience. When I watch him, I am reassured that I can be that person as well—a lifelong caregiver for my beloved veteran.

I am confident that if you open your heart and mind to the endless possibilities available all around you, you will not only find the support you need, but also return that gift to others.

Therefore encourage one another and build each other up,
just as in fact you are doing.
1 Thessalonians 5:11

Professional Help and Treatment Options for Spouses

We discussed earlier that living with a veteran can cause Secondary Trauma Disorder, and some spouses may have full-blown PTSD. Many of the symptoms for spouses suffering from secondary stress disorder are the same as their veterans with PTSD, so many of the same treatment options should also work for them.

But how do you know when you should seek professional help? In addition to the symptoms we discussed in the introduction for part 5, you should also be familiar with symptoms that result from caregiver overwhelm. Here are some signs that you need to talk to a counselor, psychologist, or other mental health professional right away:

- You feel like a bomb ready to explode.
- You feel totally out of control.
- You no longer care about the person you are caring for, and have thoughts of harming him or ignoring his needs.
- You feel hostile, anxious, or lose interest in things that used to be important to you.
- You feel totally overwhelmed.
- You sleep too much or too little.
- You abuse alcohol or drugs, including prescription drugs.
- You feel tired most of the time.
- You are easily irritated or angered.
- You feel sad most of the time.
- You have thoughts of suicide.
- You have frequent headaches, bodily pain, or other physical problems.

Roadblocks to Care

The Croatia study revealed that as many as two-thirds of the wives participating had psychological difficulties and needed professional help; the women agreed that they needed help. Yet only four actually sought help. Why the roadblocks to seeking care?

The Croatia article suggested suggests that this may have been caused by:

- The heavy load that these women were carrying, which made it difficult to find time for treatment and continue with it.

- Guilt for perceiving themselves as not *good enough* to be able to help their veteran.
- The belief that their husbands would return to who they were before their trauma and, therefore, they didn't need help.
- The stigma of admitting the need for psychological help.

Additional roadblocks I have found include:

- Inability to pay for services.
- No insurance coverage for mental health services.
- Veteran will not consent to joint counseling.
- Not being permitted by their husbands to seek care because it may be seen as a negative reflection on the veteran.
- Support groups not available in the spouse's geographical area.
- Spouse does not qualify for mental health services through the VA.
- Locating therapists that specialize in PTSD and/or that understand the special needs of spouses and families.
- Getting the support they need from their veteran to seek help and continue treatment once started.

Solutions

Here are some of the solutions I've found to removing the blocks to spouses getting care:

- Do not overlook the importance of your veteran as a source of helping you get the support you need. Veterans themselves need to understand that having a happy, healthy spouse is good for them as well.
- It is important that the veteran understand that the more his spouse learns about PTSD, the easier his life will be, and the more help his spouse can contribute to his healing.
- There's a lot to be said for the saying "If mama's not happy, then no one's happy."
- We all need time and space to re-create, rest, rejuvenate, and find healing in a supportive environment. Your veteran needs to understand

that when he gives you this opportunity, you will return ready to take on life with renewed energy, emotional stability, and a better outlook on life. It's like the message given by flight attendants every time we fly: parents should put on their own oxygen masks first. This is also true in the case of caregivers.

- Provide more education and training on PTSD and its effects on spouses and families to mental health providers, the clergy, and communities to increase the support systems available for spouses and families.

I hope that you will now be able to see the possibilities for your support system with a fresh view. First, that you feel the strong presence of the Lord and the foundation that is a constant source of spiritual, physical, and emotional support. When these gifts are allowed into your life and embraced, you will have a constant source of support.

Second, by appreciating your current circle of support and providing them the space to give according to their gifts, rather than dictating what they should do, this source of support will be strengthened. Third, widen your support by looking back to people from your past that could be brought back into your life if you called upon them.

And finally, we have endless possibilities in front of us to explore and tap into through both giving and receiving. By frequent, heartfelt appreciation and thanks, and learning to graciously accept whatever gifts are received, our well of support will never run dry.

Become a possibilatarian. No matter how dark things seem to be or actually are, raise your sights and see possibilities—always see them, for they're always there.
Norman Vincent Peale

Action Step

What one step can you take to improve your current support system?

1. _____

STEP 4: LETTING GO OF FEAR, ANGER, AND GUILT & FINDING LOVE, COMPASSION, AND FORGIVENESS

CHAPTER 28

Love is patient and kind; love does not envy or boast; it is not arrogant or rude. It does not insist on its own way; it is not irritable or resentful; it does not rejoice at wrongdoing, but rejoices with the truth. Love bears all things, believes all things, hopes all things, and endures all things. Love never ends

1 Corinthians 13:3-8

D o those words from Corinthians sound familiar? Perhaps they were read at your wedding, or maybe you've seen them inscribed on a card. How are you feeling today? Are you feeling love? Or are you feeling fear, anger, and resentment? What happens when you don't feel so loving towards yourself or your veteran anymore?

In step 3, we discussed the importance of reclaiming yourself. However, if you're still feeling anger, resentment, and fear, it is very difficult to reclaim the true essence of your loving, compassionate, forgiving self. In step 4, you will learn the harmful effects of continuing to live with those feelings that leave you feeling angry, fearful, and resentful. And I will provide you with tools to help you bring love, compassion, and forgiveness back into your life.

Effects of Anger, Fear, and Resentment

As I became more involved with other loved ones of veterans with PTSD, my own feelings of anger and resentment began to feel validated. Yet I was sad to see the anger that consumes so many people living in the world of PTSD, held inside each of us, churning and boiling. We try to hide it from the world, but it keeps us up at night and consumes us during the day.

Where did this anger come from? How did it begin? It began as a deep and wonderful love—but at some point that love began turning into fear.

The strong emotional feeling of fear can protect us in times of danger. It can help us avoid dangerous situations because it triggers our flight-or-fight reaction. But it can also be very destructive, especially if that same response of fear is triggered when no life-threatening situation exists; it becomes a chronic unresolved stress reaction where the brain and body are constantly triggered and never get relief from it.

It is common to become fearful when your life changes because of PTSD. You suddenly find yourself in a new and strange situation. There is fear of the unknown. Fear about the well-being of your beloved veteran. Fear about your own life and what the future will hold. Fear about the uncertainty of the extent of your loved one's illness. Fear of the loss of your spouse, or worse yet, fear of the impact that his illness will have on you and your ability to care for him.

Fear and love cannot co-exist. Fear closes your mind to the opportunities to have a better life. It blinds you to the good things that are around you. If you are not able to calm those fears, that fear can turn to anger…deep, dark anger and resentment.

Other things can also provoke anger. Anger is an emotion brought about when you feel that you're not being treated fairly, especially if you feel powerless to change the situation. Perhaps you're angry with your veteran because he doesn't care as much as you do about his health, his family, or your relationship. Angry that you have the burden of the whole house: cooking, cleaning, laundry, bills, and repairs. Angry that he doesn't care about having a secure financial future for his family.

Angry that he seems oblivious to the anger, frustration, and our plea for help. Angry that while all the burdens of life grow heavier for us, he continues to do less and less to help. Angry when our spouse is noncompliant with the doctors. Angry that our veteran will not acknowledge or seek help for his PTSD, but rather continues to destroy our life as we knew it. Angry with the VA system for not providing the help that we need, or for the delays in getting needed services and financial benefits. Angry that life as you know it is gone, along with your hopes and dreams for the future. And all through no fault of your own.

Often I found myself lying in bed at night much too angry to sleep. Angry that I had to have this life. Angry that the TV was blaring. Angry that I'd take the time to fix a nice dinner and he wouldn't even sit down to eat. Angry that he didn't talk to me anymore. Angry that I always had to walk on eggshells. Angry that the closeness and intimacy in my marriage was gone. Angry that I couldn't even yell at him and express my anger. And all I could do was lie there with that all-consuming anger overcoming my body, mind, and spirit. Then I would feel guilty for feeling that way.

Anger is a harmful emotion to hold onto. Think about the physical things that happen to you when you're angry: tightness or tension in your chest, headaches, upset stomach and digestive system, clenched fists, and a fast heartbeat. Anger also causes mental problems, such as difficulty concentrating, confusion, and problems with your memory.

Have you ever gone to work when you were angry? How did that affect your work performance? An inability to regulate your anger also leads to ineffective and sometimes violent behavior; uncontrolled yelling, swearing, throwing things, door slamming, perhaps even escalating to striking out physically at someone.

Here's an exercise you can do to assess your level of anger and its toll on you. Ask yourself these questions:

- What things about your spouse and/or caregiving situation trigger your anger?
- How do you react when you are very angry?
- How do you feel physically? Mentally?
- What types of actions do you take?
- When was the last time you can think of that you overreacted when you were angry?
- What did you do?

- How did you feel afterwards?
- What other options do you have?
- What would change in your life if you could react in a more positive way?

In caregiving it is easy to begin feeling that you are giving too much, and the injustice of giving more than you are receiving can cause resentment. It is easy to start blaming your partner for your unhappiness. You knew that sickness would come some day, and you vowed to love him in sickness and in health. But not this soon, not right now, not when your dreams are just beginning.

In your heart, you know that it is not his fault. He was so young, a soldier, protecting our freedom. Now you are suffering the consequences, and you are angry. How were you to know that the invisible wound of PTSD would raise its ugly head right in the middle of your happy home—and threaten to destroy your life as you knew it?

You are not alone. Your feelings are common among spouses of veterans with PTSD. It means that your love has turned into fear—and fear breeds anger and resentment. And the price for these negative emotions is high. But there is hope. The Bible says we are to ask for forgiveness:

If he has sinned, he will be forgiven. Therefore confess your sins
to each other so that you may be healed.
James 5:15-16

Transforming Negative Emotions through EFT: Interview with Nancy Forrester

We are now going to learn how to regulate our anger and other intense, upsetting emotions, so that our natural love and compassion may re-emerge. For as Buddha said, "Holding on to anger is like grasping a hot coal with the intent of throwing it at someone else; you are the one who gets burned."

It's time to throw away that burning coal. In chapter 19, we talked with Dr. Dawson Church about the use of the Emotional Freedom Techniques (EFT) with veterans with PTSD. In this chapter, you will learn how to use

EFT for emotions such as fear, anger, resentment, guilt, forgiveness, love, and peace.

Nancy Forrester, mentor, psychotherapist, certified EFT trainer, and master practitioner, will teach you systematically how to use EFT on your own, and how you can easily incorporate it into your daily life with no extra time required. You can even do it while brushing your teeth.

I believe EFT can help with a variety of problems that plague caregivers. Here is my interview with Nancy:

Nancy, I would like to talk in more detail about EFT—what it is and how it is done. Can you give us some basics?

Gary Craig is the founder of EFT. His brilliance was in integrating the work of many wellness researchers and clinicians and developing a very simple technique, one that is not only profoundly effective in the hands of a trained professional, but also an amazingly powerful self-help tool. It involves nine different points on the upper part of the body that we tap on as we're thinking

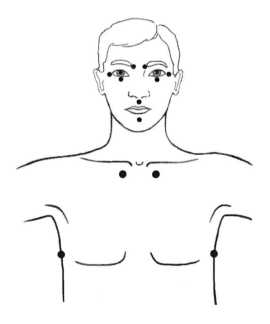

Tapping Points, provided by Dawson Church

about what is causing us to be upset. The first thing I'm going to do is teach you where these points are:

Tapping Points

1. Point number one is called the karate chop point (KC). And as you would expect, it's on the fleshy part of the hand between the wrist and the little finger, right where you would be hitting your hand on a board if you were doing a karate chop to break it. It's a very important point in this whole process. When we tap, we can tap on the karate chop point with our other hand. It doesn't matter which hand you use. Some people actually tap the two fleshy parts of their hands together.

2. Points 2 through 9 are called "reminder" points. For the second point, go up to your eyebrow (EB) above the inner part of your eye just where the hair of your eyebrow starts. It can be on either side, on the left eyebrow or the right eyebrow or it can be both. We tap five to seven times on each of these points. There are no negative side effects of EFT, so if it is feeling good on a particular point, you can just stay there and tap a little bit longer. Often people have a "favorite point" that really helps them feel better.

3. The next point is the side of the eye point (SE). It's on the side of either eye just where the bony part of the eye is—level with your iris on the outside side of the eye.

4. The next point is directly underneath the eye (UE), again on the bone directly underneath your iris. We are tapping at about the heaviness you would use to make a sound on a drum, not too heavy, not too light.

5. The next point is underneath the nose (UN), right between the nose and the lip.

6. The next point is the chin point (CH), and it is between your chin and your lip, right in the middle.

7. Now we're going to drop down to what's called the collarbone point (CB). So find the place where a man would tie his tie, where that knot of the tie would land, right against his collarbone. Then just move

about an inch to one side and tap there. I'm using three fingers. On the upper face points I was using two fingers, but this one has more area, so I use three to tap on that collarbone point.

8. And then the next point—this one gets a little weird, so the kids love this one—I want you to find underneath your arm about four inches down from your armpit (UA). For women it's about halfway down your bra strap. We tap on that point just like we're a monkey. You can imagine what the kids do with this!

9. The last point of the nine is directly on the very top of the head (TH). Sometimes with children, I call this the Pinocchio point, because it's where the string would come out the top of your head if you were a puppet.

Those are the nine physical tapping points, and that's all there is to this part. But it is a huge technique to have in order to calm stress in the emotional brain. I can't overemphasize that just tapping on those physical points while thinking about your issue is really effective.

For example, research shows we can measure the cortisol levels (cortisol is the stress hormone released by the adrenal glands) of someone who's under stress, then tap with them for five minutes, then measure their cortisol again. We see on average a 20-percent drop in their cortisol levels. That's phenomenal.

We have also now identified stress genes in our DNA; we know which genes turn on when we're under stress. We can take a DNA sample from a person, put that in a piece of equipment that can determine which genes are turned on and off, and see that their stress genes are turned on. Then we can have them do this simple physical tapping, get another DNA sample, test it again, and see that the stress genes are turned off. We actually have physical evidence of what's happening in the body when EFT is used.

Tapping is a mind/body technique. We've just done the body piece, tapping on those points over and over again. Five to seven times on each spot, using two or three fingers and just thinking about the upset you're experiencing.

However, we can make this technique even more powerful by focusing the mind (brain) more precisely on what exactly is upsetting us and acknowledging and accepting that as our current "truth." For example, suppose we are really angry at our spouse right now. We tap on the karate chop (KC) and say, "Even though I am really angry right now, I accept that I am feeling this way." We would do that two more times.

Then move through the reminder points saying "I am really angry" as you tap on each one: Eyebrow (EB) I'm angry; Side of the eye (SE) I'm angry; Under the eye (UE) I'm angry; Under the nose (UN) I'm angry; Chin (CH) I'm angry; Collarbone (CB) I'm angry; Under the arm (UA) I'm angry; Top of the head (TH) I'm angry. Then take a deep breath. Check in with yourself and see how angry you are feeling now. If you're still angry, repeat the process as many times as required to feel more calm and peaceful.

Nancy, how often do you need to tap?

What happens with tapping, and what I really want to emphasize, is that in order for it to be most effective, we want to do it on a regular basis. We can't overdo tapping. If we persistently and consistently do this simple technique, what we're doing is interrupting the chronic stress response and teaching the body how to be calm again. Then the body can do what it knows how to do, which is to release the trauma, heal, and feel better.

If words are too much at this point, then drop the words and just do the physical tapping. The body will still respond to that. As we consistently and persistently tap, what happens is that the whole brain and body become more resilient and more flexible. They don't react to stress as often or as deeply and recover more quickly when they do.

Nancy, how long do the effects of tapping last?

This would depend on how long you've been tapping, and also how chronically stressed your body is. Let's take an average person whose been tapping for a while. Research shows that if they spend ten minutes tapping, their immune system is boosted for the next seven hours.

My advice for this stage of the game is to just do it. Even if you have the words all mangled up, it doesn't matter, just do the physical tapping. Try to do it while you're doing some kind of ritual that you already have in your life. That way you can link the two of them together.

For example, many people choose to tap while they're brushing their teeth. We're supposed to brush our teeth for two minutes, so they tap while they're brushing their teeth. Other people have told me that they've set their phone alarm to go off every couple of hours, and every time it goes off, they just do a round of this tapping. Another person said they tap during the commercials on TV. One person taps in her car during red lights.

It seems as if no matter how busy a person is as a caregiver, she could still easily fit this in her day—she really could make tapping work for herself.

Yes, absolutely! We are not asking people to try to fit one more task in; it actually becomes something they do while doing something else. Anything you're doing with one hand, you can do tapping with the other hand. For example, while I'm sitting here on the phone with you, I'm tapping. I like to say to my students, the only time tapping doesn't work is if you don't do it! For example, if I'm needing to have a potentially upsetting conversation with someone, I'll tap on my anxiety about it before the conversation, then I'll be tapping as I'm having the conversation. Things go much better that way!

Can you explain how tapping works?

To begin, one thing to remember is that for years and years, human beings have actually comforted themselves by touching some of these points naturally. For example, if you are surprised and something takes your breath away, your hands automatically go right to the collar bone points that we use when we're tapping; our hands go right to that natural spot.

Or sometimes if we have a headache, we just put our hands over our head to comfort ourselves. Then we're actually covering quite a few of these points, these acupressure points. And so what the originator of EFT did was just organize these points in a fashion so that we're tapping all of them, all the time, to make sure that we're covering whatever the distress is that's been created in that moment.

The underpinnings of tapping have been around since ancient Chinese days. They have known all of these meridians for many, many years. Western medicine is finally getting to the place with our new technology that we are starting to be able see these meridian systems.

Actually, human beings have been using them for a long time, so EFT is just a technique that puts together these comfort points on the body, together with focusing the mind on the upsetting issue and tapping on the points at the same time. What it actually does scientifically is interrupt the neural conditioned feedback loop in the emotional part of the brain. As a result, the body is able to release that upset and replace it with more adaptive learning.

Tapping on these points while tuning into the issue interrupts the stress response, the fight-or-flight-or-freeze response in the body, and brings us back to a place of peace and calm. You can use tapping for any upsetting emotion, body sensation/pain, thought, or less than helpful behavior.

Nancy, what kind of things would you actually tap on?

My answer to that is you tap on whatever you would be telling your best friend. You may be telling your best friend that you're feeling overwhelmed, like you just can't get it all done, it's never ending, there's just too much to do. Or you might be telling your best friend that you're feeling sad or that you're angry and upset about something. So it's a good way to think of it—just what you would tell a friend who gives you a safe place to talk.

The other thing you might be telling your friend is about physical complaints. You may be talking about something that was going on in your stomach. So we can also tap on physical pain. It might be a headache, might be lower back, tension, or it could be tennis elbow.

Generally speaking, with tapping, we want to start tapping on the heavier emotions. The heavier emotions would be shame, guilt, frustration, overwhelm, anger, irritation, anything of that sort. The way this works is those emotions, when I say heavier, actually have a slower vibration to them. So it's no accident that when we're feeling full of shame, we don't want to get up off the couch. It's a very slow, sluggish kind of vibration.

So what happens when you tap on these heavier vibrations is that the energy starts to transform and you feel better and better. So, for example, it is not unusual to have someone tapping on shame and guilt, and the shame and guilt feel better, and now all of a sudden they're angry, because anger has a lot more energy in it. And that's actually great, so then we tap on the anger, and the anger will shift, and then all of a sudden they're feeling better.

The exciting thing about tapping is that we don't have to stop there. Once we're feeling better, then we can start tapping into those wonderful emotions of forgiveness, understanding, compassion, tolerance, and all those lighter, higher vibrations of emotions.

Does that mean that with tapping we can move all the way from our most difficult feelings of anger and shame into a much more loving, compassionate, and forgiving mind?

Yes, what happens with persistent use of EFT/tapping is that the body actually becomes more flexible and more capable of interrupting the stress reaction. It learns to release emotion more quickly. And the body also becomes more resilient to stress—it just doesn't get as upset as often or as deeply.

In other words, the tapping has a lasting effect, and even when those feelings come back again, it's much easier for us to return to that place of peace and calmness.

Yes, and that is such an exciting awareness when we recognize it's happening. There's a real sense of feeling empowered again; we know that it's not such a big deal to be triggered into our anger, because we know how to come out of it faster and faster.

I was talking about the flexibility that this persistent use creates in the brain and the body, but I want to talk about the resiliency. Over time, as we use this technique, the brain also becomes more resilient, meaning that it isn't triggered as often. So what might have bothered me a month ago and made me angry for a couple of days just doesn't bother me after a little while of tapping. It's as if our threshold for stress goes up.

This tapping tool allows that transformation to happen; it literally changes the neuron pathways of the brain. It interrupts that feedback loop so that we do not react. It gives a wonderful sense of control and power in our lives.

It goes to the very heart of trauma, which is that sense of helplessness. There is nothing we can do and there's no plan that we can make—it's just happening to us. Many of the other emotions, anger in particular, are a result of that underlying sense of helplessness and lack of control.

Are there any negative side effects to EFT?

That is the other thing I like about tapping. It's not invasive. There are no known side effects to this. Sometimes when we're tapping we might hit a bubble of emotional intensity. If people have not had experience with this, they might call that a side effect. Actually it's a success, because we are wanting to release that emotional intensity from the brain and body.

Is this something that we need to go to a professional for? Do we need any equipment?

You do not need any special equipment, other than what's at the end of your fingertips, so that also makes it valuable. And we can do this on our own. For the everyday kind of stuff, absolutely, it's a self-help tool like no other.

For deeper issues, my suggestion would be that people find an EFT practitioner that they can build a good relationship with and feel some trust and warmth toward them. Not doing the deeper work may be keeping them stuck and stop them from moving forward. For those very intense emotions, why wouldn't we want to work with a practitioner? Why wouldn't we want to have someone there to hold our hands?

What else is important for people to know?

One of the things I would like people to know is that emotions are energy. Everything is energy, and emotions are energy in motion. So what tapping allows us to do is not get rid of emotions; emotions are good. They're there to give us information about what we don't like, about how we would like life to be different. So none of this is about getting rid of anything.

This is about allowing the energy to move through the body so that it can bring us the information it's meant to. One of the things that sometimes traps people is that they're trying to force something. And that's the exact opposite of what we're trying to do with tapping. With tapping, we want to come into a place of peace and acceptance of what is in that moment. In coming to peace and acceptance, that energy of emotion is resolved from the body; it isn't there anymore.

That is so important, and it makes such a difference when you're living in this world with PTSD—to be able to come to that place of peace and acceptance. It makes a tremendous difference in letting us all move forward in our life with our spouse and be able to deal with our reality.

Exactly. Another benefit of tapping, because it is a mind/body technique, is clarity of mind. When we are in the midst of heavy emotions like anger, guilt, and powerlessness, we cannot make a good decision about how to move forward. When we choose to tap on those emotions and resolve them, we are able to come into this place of acceptance and peace. From there we get a clarity that allows us to decide what is best for all involved and how we should behave in this circumstance.

Nancy, I really appreciate you giving me the opportunity to experience tapping first hand, working with your mentee Mary Surette, for six sessions. I found that tapping gave me the opportunity to stop, to reframe the way I was looking at a situation. That made me able to be more compassionate and really understand from a different point of view what was happening. That was very powerful in transforming those feelings of anger and resentment that I was holding. I am so excited to have the firsthand experience and to share this tool.

I am happy that you were able to have the experience. Another point I want to make is this: just because we are not acknowledging emotions, it doesn't mean they're not there. Every human being has emotions. They're simply chemicals that the body creates, so it is impossible not to have emotions. Oftentimes people will say to me, you know I'm just not feeling anything. Well, numb and frozen are emotions too. We're always having this emotional experience. Now the choice comes to shut that emotional experience down and to keep the emotions stuffed in the body, rather than letting the flow of it come through.

One other point I want to make, which is really important to me, is that relationships are contagious. So if you have a relationship where one partner is irritable, critical, or angry, that has an impact on the rest of his or her family. We have an impact on each other through our emotions. So someone who makes the courageous decision to adopt a tapping ritual to deal with their own emotional well-being is going to have a phenomenally positive impact on the rest of their family as well. I think that's important to know.

Nancy Forrester has provided us with instructions and tapping dialogues. The first tapping exercise is for shame, guilt, and powerlessness. The second dialogue is for courage, acceptance, love, compassion, peace, and forgiveness. Additional dialogues for anger, tension, and resentment; anxiety, fear, and overwhelm; and grief, hurt, loss, regret, and loneliness are available at www. detours2dreams.com.

Instructions Before Starting to Tap

If intense feelings come up, that is a "success." It means that emotional tension that has been trapped in your body is being released. Keep tapping and breathing, and the emotion will eventually flow through. Often when you hit one of these pockets of trapped emotion, you will not be able to speak. That is okay. Keep tapping, take deep breaths when you can, and when the emotion has passed through, you can pick up the dialogue where you left off.

Sometimes it is helpful to move around and shake your body, your legs, and your arms especially. This often will assist the emotion to release. You'll want to have a glass of water available. The body has high water content, and staying well hydrated helps the energy and the emotion in the body to move freely. Tissues will be handy to have too!

If it has been a while since you were able to have these kinds of releases, it might be a good idea to limit the amount of time you spend each day doing this tapping. Perhaps twenty minutes, and then do the "sneaking away" exercise below. Come back to it the next day. After a few days, if you don't notice the feelings getting lighter, that's when you might want to reach out for help to someone experienced in these tapping techniques.

Sometimes, a particular phrase may not apply to you. That's okay, just say it anyway; you won't be doing any harm by including it in your dialogue. And sometimes we're surprised that something we didn't think applies to us—does!

Each round starts with a "test" to measure the intensity of the feelings in that round. After tapping through the phrases, you'll test again to measure progress. Depending on how your body and mind have processed the tapping, you'll either redo the round or move to the next one.

When you have finished your tapping for the time being, if you have upsetting feelings left, the "sneaking away" exercise is a good one to finish with.

ROUND ONE: Shame, Guilt, and Powerlessness

ROUND ONE TEST: Say the following sentence and ask yourself how true it is for you right now. Rate it on a scale of 0 – 10, where 10 means it is completely true for you and 0 means it is untrue.

I accept myself for doing the best I can, even though sometimes I'm not loving and accepting toward my partner.

Tapping on the Karate Chop (KC) point about 7 times for each sentence:

KC: Even though part of me is ashamed about how I'm handling this PTSD situation in my family, I'm willing to do this tapping technique just in case it might help us.

KC: Even though I feel guilty about some of the things I'm thinking and feeling and I could never ever tell anybody, I'm willing to do this tapping technique just in case it might help us.

KC: Even though I feel so powerless to control what's happening to my family and myself and sometimes I behave really badly as a result, I'm willing to do this tapping technique because maybe it just might help us.

Tapping on the Reminder Points (points 2 through 9)—one phrase on each point:

Eyebrow (EB): I'm so ashamed of myself for having these feelings about my husband.

Side of Eye (SE): I could never let anyone know.

Under Eye (UE): I'm so cold, irritated, and resentful all the time.

Under Nose (UN): I shouldn't be feeling this way.

Chin (CH): If anybody found out, I'd be so embarrassed.

Collarbone (CB): I have to keep it all hidden and pretend I'm doing fine.

Under Arm (UA): It's really hard to do that though.

Top of Head (TH): Does that mean that I'm a bad person and partner?

Take a breath and then continue with the reminder points.

EB: I feel so guilty.
SE: I'm supposed to be compassionate and caring.
UE: But I'm not.
UN: I'm supposed to be more accepting and forgiving of my partner and myself.
CH: The truth is, I'm not.
CB: Does that mean that I'm a bad person and partner?
UA: I feel so guilty.
TH: Nobody else would be feeling this way.

Again, take a breath and then continue with the reminder points.

EB: They'd be more understanding and loving, but I just don't feel that way all the time.

SE: I'm ashamed of myself for having such terrible thoughts.

UE: Sometimes I just want to escape from it all – just up and leave them all.

UN: Shame on me for being stuck here and not being able to fix all this.

CH: It's not his fault – he didn't ask for this.

CB: Am I a bad, uncaring person for feeling this way?

UA: I'm so guilty that I can't be the partner he needs me to be.

TH: Other people have it much worse than I do – at least my partner is alive.

Take a breath and continue.

EB: I'm really angry with myself for feeling this way.

SE: I should be able to control myself better.

UE: I should be more tolerant.

UN: I just can't control what's going on.

CH: There doesn't seem to be anything that I can do.

CB: My partner and my family need me to be strong and I'm being so self-centered.

UA: I feel guilty for not always being there for them.

TH: I should be handling this a lot better.

Take a breath and continue.

EB: But I just feel helpless to change it.

SE: I've read so much about all of this.

UE: But I still can't figure out how to fix it.

UN: What's the matter with me?

CH: Why can't I be more tolerant?

CB: I feel badly for how I behave toward him and my family.

UA: I just can't seem to help it.

TH: If anyone found out the truth, I'd be so humiliated.

Take a breath and continue.

EB: I have to keep it all hidden and wrapped up in a pretty package.

SE: I'm so tired of the energy it takes to do that.

UE: What if I could just let myself know how I really feel?

UN: That would be such a relief.
CH: I'd love to stop pretending – at least to myself.
CB: What if I could just acknowledge what it's really like for me?
UA: I think I'd feel some relief.
TH: What if other people feel this way? What if these reactions are normal in this situation?

Take a breath and continue.

EB: What if I'm not alone in all these reactions?
SE: There would be some comfort there.
UE: Maybe I can let myself feel the way I feel – at least when I'm by myself.
UN: I feel some relief as I say that.
CH: It feels good to just acknowledge the truth for me right now.
CB: I'm willing to tell the truth about all this – at least to myself.
UA: That feels a little better.
TH: I feel some relief.

Now take a few deep breaths as your mind and body processes all of this. Take a drink of water too. You may have noticed some yawning, or you took a big sigh, or perhaps your eyes and nose started running. Sometimes the body releases burps/gas as the tension around the digestive system relaxes. These are all positive signs of the autonomic nervous system coming into better balance.

Some nervous systems react quickly to this work; others take a few minutes or hours to process the effects. There is no right or wrong way for a body to release stored tension. It is quite usual to feel drained after doing the tapping. The tension that has been released from the body has been there for a long time; the relief and exhaustion often accompany letting it go after having held onto it so long!

Now, let's go back to the ROUND 1 TEST and compare your result to before doing the tapping.

TEST: Say the following sentence and ask yourself how true it is for you right now. Rate it on a scale of 0 – 10, where 10 means it is completely true for you and 0 means it is completely untrue.

I accept myself for doing the best I can, even though sometimes
I'm not loving and accepting toward my partner.

If you are a 6 or higher, move onto Round 2. If you are less than 6, redo Round 1. Or, if you are out of time for tapping right now, use the Sneaking Away Round below to put some distance between you and the upsetting feelings. When you return, start with Round 1 again.

THE SNEAKING AWAY ROUND

Sometimes we need to stop tapping before we have fully resolved what is upsetting us. When that is the case, we can "sneak away" from the feelings and thoughts and come back to them later.

Tapping on the Karate Chop point about 7 times for each sentence:
KC: Even though I'm still feeling some upset about all of this, I'm willing to put it away somewhere for now.
KC: Even though I'm not feeling total peace at the moment, I'm willing to bundle all the upsetting feelings and store them somewhere far away from me.
KC: Even though there is more tapping required, I'm willing to trust myself to come back to it later and be a little more peaceful now.

Tapping on the Reminder Points—one phrase on each point:
EB: These feelings are still troublesome.
SE: I'm not feeling peace yet.
UE: How can I put some distance between me and these feelings?
UN: How far away do I need to put them?
CH: Maybe another planet?
CB: Maybe another country, maybe in the box underneath the couch?
UA: I'm putting them far enough away so I feel safer and more powerful.
TH: Do they need to be secured with a lock or some rope?
Take a breath and continue with the reminder points.
EB: I'm securing them so I can feel more peaceful.

SE: When it's time, I'll come back and continue with them.

UE: Until then, they are safe and I am safe.

UN: Stretching my body, wiggling my toes, rubbing my hands together.

CH: Feeling where my body touches the chair.

CB: Looking around, noticing what I see.

UA: Listening carefully, hearing what I hear.

TH: Breathing deeply. I am safe in this moment.

Take a breath and a drink of water.

ROUND 2: Courage, Acceptance, Understanding, Compassion, Love

(There is no Karate Chop point for the following statements.)

Tapping on the Reminder Points—one phrase on each point:

EB: I'm proud of myself for doing this tapping.

SE: I'm pleased that I've taken this step toward feeling better.

UE: I can feel that it is making a difference.

UN: I feel more alert and present, a little more relaxed.

CH: And I like those feelings.

CB: I feel a bit more like me.

UA: What if I could feel even better?

TH: I'm willing to feel even better.

EB: Maybe more hopeful.

SE: Maybe a little safer.

UE: What if I could move toward accepting this situation even though I don't like it?

UN: What if I could have a little more peace around it?

CH: I'm willing to do that.

CB: In fact, I'd really like to have more understanding.

UA: Maybe some compassion.

TH: We're all doing our best.

EB: Given our experiences and challenges.

SE: I like compassion and acceptance.

UE: I enjoy feeling tolerance and love.

UN: There is so much to appreciate.

CH: So much to be grateful for.

CB: I'm pleased and grateful to be feeling more of these emotions.
UA: Good for me!
TH: Good for me!

Give yourself some full breaths and a drink of water. Smile a little as you stretch your body. These two rounds complete the exercise.

The ability to move away from the constant turmoil and fear of living in the world of PTSD and finding a place of peace does not always come quickly, or easily. I hope that you find these tools useful as a means to begin that journey of finding peace . . . if only one moment at a time.

Finding Love, Compassion, and Forgiveness: Interview with Marci Shimoff

I am now delighted to bring you the *New York Times* bestselling author of *Love for No Reason*, Marci Shimoff. Marci is one of the bestselling female nonfiction authors of all time. She has inspired millions of people around the world as a celebrated transformational leader on love and happiness. Marci has been an inspiration to me through her books, and I have had the honor of having Marci's personal support during my book-writing journey.

Marci, many spouses of veterans suffering from PTSD find themselves having a hard time loving for any reason. I remember feeling that way myself. Your book Love for No Reason *made a tremendous difference in my life. I am so happy to share you and your expertise with other women who find themselves in that same situation. Would you share with us the continuum of love, and what "no love" means? In addition, what are some of the feelings that may be experienced, and what dangers might come from being in that state of no love?*

Yes, absolutely. And just to give a little perspective, there are four levels on my love continuum. The kind of love I'm talking about is not specifically relationship love, but just the love we feel inside ourselves. So on this love continuum, the first level is "no love." When we feel no love, we can feel flat, we can feel empty, we can feel as if life is meaningless, and, in the extreme, we can feel a lot of fear, anger, hate, and resistance. It's when our hearts are shut down.

Another symptom is profound exhaustion, and often we're triggered into the fight-or-flight response. We can feel empty, bored, disengaged, or disconnected. It's really the absence of feeling any juiciness in life, the absence of feeling like life's worth living.

When you are in a severe state of this, a serious type of depression, then I believe professional treatment can be very important. For a lot of people, maybe it's not a clinical depression, it's just a feeling that there's no love, there's no juice, there's no joy, there's none of that great life-force energy flowing freely in their lives. It makes it hard to get up in the morning.

That would be my description of no love. It makes it hard to get through the day. But it doesn't have to be this way, and that's what I'm here to share with people. It can be different.

That's so great, because that's what so many spouses begin to feel when their veteran has PTSD and when they're at the bottom of that cycle. Next on your love spectrum, you talk about "love for bad reason." I know this is when you might use other people to fill a void, and I know this kind of love happens a lot in a caregiver relationship, especially when you're caregiving for a spouse. It's also an example of codependency. Could you share some of the signs that this type of love for bad reason is happening and also what the dangers of this type of relationship might be.

Absolutely. Love for bad reason really isn't love at all. It's what I call no love—but on painkillers. It's us trying to suppress or just not feel the yuck feeling of no love. So we try to get our love from things around us. It can mean any kind of addiction—an addiction to food or to substances, to alcohol, or to people—codependency.

Here are some things to watch for in terms of codependency. You love in order to get love. You give to get. You try really hard to please others so you can be accepted. You feel addicted to the object of your love, whether that be food or alcohol or a partner. It's when you're trying to fill a void inside yourself with something outside yourself—when you feel needy, hungry, or desperate for love.

Trying to control the people that you love or trying to fix your partner or your children is another codependency to make you feel better about yourself. There is always the desire within us to help the person that we love—that's a normal tendency. But when it's a need for them to change, to get fixed in order for us to be okay, that's when it borders on codependency.

Marci, next on the spectrum of love is "love for good reason." In your book, you describe that as being a healthy, mutually beneficial relationship. Often when PTSD enters the picture, that dramatically changes things. Your partner can become a total stranger, cold, distant, and angry. So what guidance can you give us when our love for good reason changes?

Great, great question. That is definitely a very challenging situation, and it can also be the opportunity for us to grow internally. What I've found is that people often have the most profound and positive change in their life when they are in the midst of some kind of crisis. When I give speeches, I often ask people, how many of you have had crisis or a big challenge in your life?—and everybody raises their hand. Certainly having a partner with PTSD would qualify as a great challenge.

Then I ask them, for how many of you did that end up being one of the best experiences of your life because of how you grew from it?—and everybody raises their hand. So the perspective first of all is to look at [how you view the universe] . . . now this is going to sound really, really hard to do, but out of interviewing thousands of people for both *Love for No Reason* and *Happy for No Reason*, I have found that the happiest, most loving people are those who feel that we live in a benevolent, friendly universe.

Einstein said that the most important question you can ask yourself is, "Is this a friendly universe?" And people who are happy always say yes. That doesn't mean that everything goes their way, that doesn't mean that they don't have challenges, but what it means is that they believe that the universe is on their side. If something is happening, even if it is not what you would want to have happen, there has to be a blessing, a lesson, or a gift in it.

So the first thing I would suggest you do in this situation is to just imagine or pretend that this is a friendly, loving universe. And that this situation is happening for a good reason for you. And so ask this question, "If this were happening to serve me, if this were happening for a good reason, for a lesson or a gift, what would that lesson or gift be? If this were happening for a higher purpose, what would or could that purpose be?"

What you might find is that the purpose in this case is forcing you to get even stronger within yourself, to become happier within yourself, to feel more love within yourself. Because I promise you, that is the best way to support your partner suffering from PTSD.

You will not serve him by being dragged into your own unhappiness or despair. So the ultimate lesson of this is to move into what I call the state of "love for no reason," which is the highest level on this love spectrum I talk about. That is the state in which you develop an inner state of love that doesn't depend on a person or a situation or a romantic partner. There are many tools that can help you develop that inner state of love; you'll be able to support and help your partner so much more when you are living more and more in that state yourself.

Marci, thank you so much. That is such important advice for us. Now can you explain what you mean by the state of fear and the state of love being mutually exclusive?

Well, it has been said that there are two main energies in the universe. There's the energy of fear, which causes us to be contracted, and there's the energy of love, which causes us to be expanded. And contraction and expansion are the only two energies. When we're moving in the energy of love, we're moving towards our greatest good and towards our true essence. When we're moving in the energy of fear, we all know how that feels; in fact, fear creates all kinds of chemicals; cortisol and amocicin are the biggest happiness robbers.

There are many, many things or processes that we can do to move out of that state of fear and more into that state of love. May I share a few techniques or tools?

Yes, Marci, please do.

One of my favorite tools is from some research that I find so interesting. This is from a group called the Institute of Heart Math (www.heartmath.com), the world's leading researchers on our heart and love and how that affects our happiness and well-being.

What they have found is that anger, fear, and sadness, what we would call negative emotions, all derive from fear. They all have some element of fear in them. And when we feel any of these emotions, we go into what's called "heart rhythm incoherence," where our heart rhythm becomes very incoherent. If you could see it on a computer screen, you'd see many jagged lines.

When we feel more love, rather than fear, we go into "heart rhythm coherence," in which our heart patterns become very smooth and rhythmic.

When you are in fear or anger, heart rhythm incoherence, it can suppress your immune system. When you're feeling that for just five minutes, it can suppress your immune system for up to six hours. But when you are in that feeling of more love, in heart rhythm coherence, for just five minutes, it can strengthen your immune system for up to six hours.

So these are very different reactions as a result of what we're feeling inside, and they deeply affect our immune system and our health. The state of anger or fear is often called the "stress response." The state of love is often called the "love response."

I'm going to share with you right now a very simple technique that anyone can do to move from the fear response into the love response, even in just a few short minutes. It's three simple steps. I will walk you through these three steps, and you'll see how very easily you can move from the stress response into the love response.

It's called the Inner Ease Technique, and this can be done with your eyes either open or closed. If you're able to, I suggest you close your eyes because it goes a little bit deeper, but even if you're somewhere where you can't close your eyes, you can still do this with your eyes open.

The first step is to simply place the palm of your hand over your heart. That simple act of putting your hand on your heart starts the flow of a chemical called oxytocin, which is dubbed the love hormone. It is what we have when we feel bonded and connected with each other. Just putting your hand on your heart like this right now is stimulating the flow of oxytocin.

Now the second step is to imagine that you're breathing in and out through your heart. So you can either picture or feel that your breath is coming in and out through the center of your heart. Some people do better picturing, some people do better feeling; it doesn't matter, just imagine that you're breathing in and out through the center of your heart.

Finally, the third step is to imagine on each inhale that you are breathing in love, ease, and compassion. You can exhale normally, but on each inhale breathe in love, breathe in ease, and breathe in compassion, then exhale normally. Continue doing this just a few more times, breathing in, taking into your heart the feelings of love, ease, and compassion, then exhaling. Do this at your own pace.

Now take one deeper breath in, breathing in love, ease, and compassion. At your next exhale, you can open your eyes (if they were closed) and take away your hand. Just notice how you feel different in your body, and how you feel different emotionally, just by doing a simple practice that took probably under two minutes.

Debbie, did you feel any different?

Marci, that was amazing! I feel a tremendous difference.

What I love about this is that doing it once feels good, but it doesn't create a lasting change. But if you do this two to three times a day for the next few weeks, you'll start to get in the habit of being in the love response—and that's what we're talking about. As you get more and more in the habit of living in the love response, it becomes more your default state. It becomes more where you live on a regular basis, and you're able to bounce back. It makes you more resilient when challenges come up, because your body is familiar with this love response.

What I love about this also is you can do it anywhere. I do it while I'm standing in line at the grocery store, or sitting on the phone talking to someone, or sitting in a business meeting feeling frustrated or bored. Nobody has to know that you're doing it.

In addition to this, I know, Debbie, that you're very familiar with heart mapping. At Heart Math, they have done a lot of work with PTSD; in fact, I believe they are working in many VA hospitals with PTSD and using this technique with other techniques. They even have a computer program and a handheld device called the emWave that allows you to train yourself to be more and more in this love response. It's cool, like a biofeedback machine for the heart, but it's the size of a credit card. It's a beautiful way to overcome stress and to help heal PTSD symptoms. (See www.heartmath.com/techology-products/emwave-technology.)

It may seem that, when you are bound by feelings of fear, anger, or even hate, there is nothing you can do to move beyond those negative thoughts. But there are many tools available to you. The first step, however, requires you to take action. Only you can decide that you no longer want to remain in this debilitating state of fear.

Action Step

What is one step that you can take immediately to begin shifting from your feelings of fear, anger, or guilt?

1._____

CHAPTER 29

STEP 5: TREATING THE SIDE EFFECTS OF STRESS AND OVERWHELM

The irony is this: Our bodies react to stress in exactly the same way whether or not we have a good reason for being stressed. The body doesn't care if we're right or wrong. Even in those times when we feel perfectly justified in getting angry—when we tell ourselves it's the healthy response—we pay for it just the same.

Doc Childre and Howard Martin

We have talked about the body's normal fight-or-flight reaction in previous chapters. In step 5 we'll look at what happens with that reaction in the face of stress. Specifically, we'll look at the different types of general stress (acute and chronic), caregiver stress, the effects of *overcare*, and tips and tools to avoid and manage caregiver stress.

Stress can be defined as a response or a reaction to any event that requires you to produce energy. The event creating the stress is called a *stressor*. And the behavior displayed when stress occurs is defined as a *stress reaction*. The body cannot tell the difference between an actual stressor, one that it actually needs to respond to, and an imagined one. Have you ever felt exhausted after watching a scary or intense movie? That is because your body does not know the difference between real and imaginary stressors.

Each of us has a different response to stress. What may cause one person stress could have no effect on another person. A certain level of stress is good for you; I'm sure you have known people who say that they "perform better under stress." And this is how stress is intended to work.

When an event happens that causes you to expend more energy, you experience stress. A certain amount of stress, *eustress* (good stress) or productive tension, is good for you. At this stage, hormones are released into your body that provide an energy boost to enable you to respond appropriately to the fight-or-flight response.

But after you have reacted to the event and used the energy, the nervous system needs to return to normal so that the "energy" hormones can dissipate, rather than being stored in the body. Once your body returns to a normal energy level, it's ready for the next stressor in life. At least, that's how it's supposed to work.

But what happens in the real world is that an event occurs that causes your energy level to go up, as your hormones kick in and respond to a stressor. After the response, your body wants to return to a calming place. However, before you can ever get to the place of normal energy, you experience another stressor. Your body responds by another release of energy, and more hormones kick in.

You react to that event, after which, again, there's a natural desire to return to a lower level of energy. But before that happens, you may have another stressor. And before you know it, your hormonal levels remain escalated, as you continuously operate above the productive tension line at a distress level. The results are distress and disease.

The harmful effects of stress are well documented, with numerous studies and reports showing the effects of stress on our bodies. Experts report that stress is the underlying cause of 60–95 percent of all illnesses, including headaches, strokes, heart disease, hypertension, diabetes types I and II, irritable bowel syndrome, asthma, ulcers, fibromyalgia, weight gain, and obesity.

Other problems related to stress include insomnia, depression, anxiety, suicide, lack of energy, irritability, anger, and decreased sex drive. Addictive behaviors, such as alcoholism, drug, and tobacco addiction can also be created by stress.

Acute Stress

Two of the most common types of stress are acute (sudden) or chronic (ongoing). Acute stress is a reaction to an immediate, unexpected stressor, such as:

- Being awakened by your veteran's nightmares.
- Nearly hitting a car pulling out in front of you.
- Hearing a loud noise such as a car backfiring.
- A phone call telling you of an emergency situation.
- Being unexpectedly called on to speak during a meeting.
- An irritated neighbor complaining about your barking dog.
- Waiting for your home inspection during your caregiver screening process.
- Learning that you have no credit left on your credit card.
- Attending your first couples party without your veteran.
- Receiving your benefit approval letter from the VA.
- Waiting in the doctor's office for medical test results.

During acute stress, when the unexpected event occurs, you have the appropriate hormonal response. You respond at a higher energy level, and then, when the crisis is over, you seek out the first chance you can to relax. The body can deal with acute stress in small doses.

Prolonged bouts of acute stress are, however, very taxing and wearing on the body. Rational thinking often becomes distorted thinking, and the rate of accidents and mistakes increases.

Chronic Stress

Chronic Stress is prolonged stress. There seems to be no light at the end of the tunnel. You don't feel any hope for the future and feel that you have no power over the situation. Some situations that produce chronic stress are:

- Being homeless.
- Having no perceived power in relationships or job.
- Dysfunctional families.
- Feeling trapped in a situation or relationship that you dislike immensely.
    For most people though, chronic stress is more often produced by:
- Too much to do, too many commitments.
- Working longer hours on the job with little or no reward.
- Too little sleep.
- Disorganization in one's living and work environments.
- Financial problems without a solution in sight.
- Fear of losing a job.
- Prolonged illness (yours or a family member's).

Caregiver Stress

What is caregiver stress? The simple answer is the emotional and physical strain brought on by constant caring for a person with a chronic illness, physical injury or disability, and/or a mental disorder. But I believe that caregiver stress is so much more than that. It takes chronic stress to a completely new level. My definition is an all-encompassing chronic stress that begins in your heart and radiates outward, incorporating your mind, body, and spirit.

Your heart breaks as you watch your loved one struggle and endure endless pain and suffering—while you stand by, unable to cure him, change him, or control him. But you continue to try. You then feel inadequate that you're not successful and guilty, because you believe that you should be able to provide better care.

You are lonely because caregiving has hurt your social life; you no longer feel that you have the time to get out with friends. You feel lonely even when your loved one is sitting next to you, because PTSD has turned him into an iceberg—often not even noticing that you exist.

You grieve the loss of the person he once was, the relationship that will never be the same, the dreams you shared that are now lost. You struggle to accept your new reality and find a way to love and have compassion for this new person in your life. You feel angry and resentful that the life you had planned has been taken away.

How does caregiver stress affect caregivers? In addition to the problems that we discussed regarding chronic stress, caregivers are also more likely to have:

- Symptoms of depression or anxiety.
- More long-term medical problems, such as heart disease, cancer, diabetes, arthritis.
- Higher levels of stress hormones.
- More sick days.
- Weaker immune system.
- Slower wound healing.
- Higher level of obesity.
- Higher risk for mental decline, including problems with memory and focus.
- Death—It is too early to tell what the consequences will be with our current generation of young caregivers. However, studies of elderly caregivers show that those who felt caregiver stress were 63 percent more likely to die within four years of beginning their caregiver duties than caregivers who were not feeling stressed.
- Suicide—There are no firm statistics on this, but we know it is happening.
- More health problems due to poor self-care.
- Greater neglect in seeking needed professional medical care.
- Failure in getting important health screenings such as mammograms.

Other changes that caregivers reported are that, in comparison to the time before they became caregivers, they're not getting enough sleep, cooking and eating healthy meals, or getting enough physical activity. We will go into detail about the effects of these problems and solutions in step 6.

Overcare

Another common problem many spouses caring for veterans have is *overcare*. I asked our love and happiness expert Marci Shimoff to help us with some tips on this topic:

Marci, can you give us some tips on how to avoid overcare?

Yes, absolutely. You definitely have to pay attention to your own well-being. Obviously, we cannot help others when we are running on empty. So it's critical that we take care of ourselves, and here are three ways that you can avoid falling into the trap of overcare.

The first way is to let go of specific results. When you don't need another person to change in a particular way, when you're not attached to a specific outcome, you are much more able to give freely, and it becomes more enjoyable. I learned a great phrase from my mentor, Jack Canfield: "High intention, low attachment."

What that means, of course, is that you have an intention to help someone, with the intention that they'll get well. But along with that, have a low attachment to the actual outcome. Let go. Do your best and then just let go, so you can give with great enthusiasm, then let the universe take care of the rest, that is, take care of the results.

The second thing to do to make sure you don't fall into overcare is not to expect anything in return. Our giving should be done quite freely. I interviewed a wonderful, well-respected man who studied compassion for many years, named Dr. Steven Post. I'm going to share a quote from him, "We can get hung up on keeping score on reciprocal responses, and that really limits us. It keeps us from being free to love in a way that's uncalculating." We just need to do what a mother that he once interviewed told her son, "Love and forget about it." I love that; our job is to love and not look for any return.

Finally, the third way to make sure you don't fall into overcare is to make sure that your giving doesn't stress, drain, or weaken you. If you are giving in a healthy way, you'll feel good. If you're giving too much, or if you're going into overcare, you're going to go into heart rhythm incoherence. It's going to cause you to feel stressed, burned out, depressed, resigned, or cynical.

So be good to yourself. Pay attention to your own needs. Here's a little exercise I would suggest you do a few times a day. Stop whatever you are doing and ask yourself this question: What's the most loving thing I can do for myself right now? It's a simple question. What's the most loving thing I can do for myself right now? And sometimes the answer might be, I can go get a glass of water, or I can go out and get some fresh air, or it could even be, I can do that Inner Ease Technique that I learned. It doesn't matter what the answer is. What matters is that you pay attention, you listen to your needs, and that you take care of yourself.

It's a way of us reinforcing that we matter to ourselves. We haven't been trained that way, particularly as women. We've very much been trained to take care of everybody else, but not ourselves. And we are suffering from it. One out of four women is on antidepressants. We have an epidemic of unhappiness, particularly amongst women, and I believe that a big contributor to this is our tendency to overcare. So take care of yourself; I promise you it is not selfish. And don't forget to...*love and forget about it.*

★ ★ ★ ★ ★

This information on stress and overcare is provided to raise your awareness about the costly effects of unmanaged stress, especially caregiver stress. The price is high—to your health, your relationships, and your personal well-being. The good news is that there are things that you can do to help prevent and deal with caregiver stress. It's essential to be proactive and to realize the importance of self-care. You can't take adequate care of your loved ones if you don't start by caring for yourself.

It's easy to dismiss your feelings as "just stress." But caregiver stress can lead to serious health problems, and you should take steps to reduce it as much as you can. It is more important now than ever to begin doing whatever it takes to carve out time to begin managing your stress. Research shows that people who take an active, problem-solving approach to caregiving issues are less likely to feel stressed than those who react by worrying or feeling helpless.

Stress Management Tools

Sometimes the most important thing in a whole day is the rest
we take between two deep breaths.
—Etty Hillesum

The best way to manage stress is to make time every single day to relax, refresh, and re-energize. Although you might join a class to help you learn some relaxation techniques, chances are that making it to class will add even more stress, especially if you get to class and your mind is still spinning out of control. In my experience it doesn't matter if you have a ten-minute escape to the privacy of your bathroom, or a four-week respite in the mountains. If your mind is still full of the problems in the next room or around the world, you don't truly get the escape, relaxation, and rejuvenation that our bodies, souls, and minds so desperately need and desire.

I remember how mad I would get when I was able to get away to a Pilates class. After taking the time to wrap up what I was doing in my office, change my clothes, drive twenty minutes to the gym—I'd find that my mind couldn't release the anger I was holding onto. I'd still be angry and rehashing something that had happened at home.

So now he was invading my body and my mind again. I was not fully engaging my body during the class. And my mind couldn't relax either. At the end of one class, for example, the instructor led us in a meditation—but I couldn't visualize anything; my brain was still going a million miles an hour, and I was still tense and angry.

My choices were to use tapping or the Inner Ease Technique from step 4 to immediately shift my anger. Or I could have chosen one of the on-the-spot stress management tools described below. In this section, I'm going to provide tools in three areas: preventing stress, managing stress in the moment, and dealing with the effects of long-term stress.

Tips for Stress Management and Prevention

- Learn to let go of those things over which you have no control.
- Dump the Superwoman cape. Realize and accept your limits.
- Ask for and accept help.
- Put your well-being into the monthly household budget. This investment is the most important thing you can do for your family and your veteran's future. Pay for help—yardwork, housecleaning, etc.
- Invest in respite care, such as adult day health care programs, VAMC, in-home helper/respite care, short-term care in a skilled nursing home or intermediate care facility.
- Take time for yourself to refill your tank. You would never consider running your car very far with the low fuel light on, so why would you do that with yourself?
- Attend a support group.
- Acknowledge your feelings of anger, resentment, and helplessness—they're normal. These feelings do not mean that you are a bad person. Work through them, rather than suppressing them.
- Learn to say no to requests that are too draining.
- Set realistic goals. Break tasks into smaller chunks that you can do one at a time so they do not seem so overwhelming.
- Let go of perfection.
- Prioritize, make lists, and establish a daily routine, but keep flexible for unexpected events with your veteran. Don't let the "little things" stress you out. (We practice "rigid flexibility.")
- Deal with the little stressors as they arrive, so they do not turn into big stressors.
- Get a checkup. Be sure to let your doctor know you're a caregiver, and inform him or her of any symptoms of depression you may be having.
- Make time each day for yourself, even if it's only ten minutes. Make time each week to something that you want to do: lunch with friends, a movie, shopping, a long quiet walk.
- Make it a priority to fit in some type of physical exercise on most days, eat a healthy diet, and get sufficient sleep.

Tips for On-the-Spot Stress Relief

Many stress management techniques can help you maintain a healthy state of being, so that stress does not debilitate you or compromise your health over the long run. Here are four ideas on how you can minimize the negative effects of stress.

Consider these the best of the best stress management techniques. Each of these tips is a powerful tool that will, if consciously practiced on a regular basis, reduce the impact of stress on your body, give you more energy, and help you experience more control over your life.

1. **Breathing techniques**—By engaging in slow, deep breathing, you produce a calming effect on your nervous system. In turn, your stress hormones dissipate and your energy is restored.
2. **Mindfulness**—Mindfulness is paying attention to your feelings, thoughts, sensations, and experiences in the moment. It's a method of focusing only on the moment—what is going on around you. And it engages your senses. Example: Put a mint in your mouth—smell, taste, feel.
3. **Self-talk**—Shift your negative self-talk to this question: "What can I do to make this a good experience?" Be aware of what you are saying to yourself and change any negative language into positive language.
4. **Control vs. no control**—Ask yourself, "Can I control this?" Even though you may not be able to control the situation, what you can control is your reaction.

Make it a priority to set aside time on a regular basis to engage in these exercises.

Managing the Effects of Long-Term Stress: Debbie's Top Ten Personal Stress Tools

1. Walking—anytime, any place, but my favorite is the river trail.
2. Eucalyptus spearmint aromatherapy candle.

3. Indian lemongrass with rosemary hand lotion.
4. Shower with lavender aromatherapy shower gel and body scrub.
5. Dark chocolate—a few ounces satisfies and calms.
6. Dark, quiet nights, moon watching and stargazing.
7. Cuddling with my two cairn terriers.
8. Hot or iced peppermint tea—drinking it mindfully.
9. Pure local clover honey—a spoonful for stress, and it reduces inflammation.
10. Listening to the Beach Boys and Beatles.

Managing your stress is something that will not happen overnight. However, small shifts in your daily routine can begin to make big changes in your life—and your stress level.

Action Step

Review the tools and tips that were provided in this chapter. What three strategies can you commit to begin immediately?

1._____

2._____

3._____

CHAPTER 30

STEP 6: CHERISHING YOU WITH HEALTH AND WELLNESS

Health . . . is not so much a state, but a force: the power
to resist and overcome threats to one's well being.
—Gregory P. Fields

This chapter is not going to be about diets and exercise. There are thousands of books, articles, and TV shows about that. Rather this step is about how you can take three things you do daily that are essential to good health and make optimal use of them. Small shifts in your eating, moving, and sleeping will enable you to perform at your peak and resist the negative effects of PTSD.

As your resistance grows, both you and your family will benefit by you being a healthier, happier caregiver. You'll feel physically and mentally strong. You will be able to give more by maximizing your energy, thus preparing yourself to withstand the rigors of long-term caregiving.

In order to love, honor, and care for your veteran in sickness, you need to begin by honoring and cherishing the body that God has given you. That begins by making the decision to make your personal wellness a priority in your life.

The National Wellness Institution defines wellness as *a process of becoming aware of and making choices toward a more successful existence.* Wellness is about being the best that you can be, obtaining the highest degree of health possible through positive action and creating an environment for healthy living.

I'm not going to ask you to add things that will take more time and money, but rather maximize and make small shifts to what you are currently doing to increase your wellness.

In each step so far, we have stressed the importance of taking time to care for yourself. It is essential that you be at your best to navigate through the difficult times of caregiving. In this step, we'll look at tools to help you become physically capable of handling the demands of life. To become more resistant to illness and disease. To feel better. To look better.

And why wouldn't each of us choose to live our life joyfully, feeling strong, vibrant, and energetic?

Think of wellness as preventive maintenance. We all want our cars running at peak performance, ready to take us anywhere we want to go at a moment's notice. What happens when your fuel light comes on and you simply ignore it? You're going to run out of gas, right? And what happens when you run out of gas? It's inconvenient, stressful, and possibly scary, depending on where you are. It can also damage your engine when you allow your fuel tank to become completely empty.

And what happens if you put the wrong type of fuel into your car? Have you ever heard stories about vandals putting sugar in people's gas tanks? It destroys the fuel system. So it's important to use the right type of fuel for maximum performance. And when the warning light tells you your car is overheating, do you keep going until your engine blows up? Or do you stop at the first opportunity to check your water levels and let the engine cool?

Are you paying attention to the warning signs that your body is sending out when it needs fuel and rest? Our bodies are like cars; they need proper maintenance to run. We normally don't ignore those warning lights on our vehicles for very long. So why is it so easy to let our own bodies go until we are totally depleted?

When we are caught up in the world of PTSD and caregiving, it is very easy to ignore self-care. I was there. Food was my go-to for stress relief. Exercise became a thing of the past. It seemed like overnight I gained almost fifty pounds. My health required numerous trips to the doctor and surgeries with no firm diagnosis as to the cause of my physical pain and symptoms.

I began trying to get better and I struggled, but finally after four years of ups and downs I lost forty-five pounds in time for my daughter's wedding. Then I couldn't manage to keep it off. I gained and lost ten to fifteen pounds over and over and over again. I own every diet book, exercise tape, and a gym membership. I thought that I had all the tools that I needed to get back to a healthy weight.

It was only after I had finished my coaching certification and started coaching other women that I realized I was neglecting my own need for support. I was not following my own rules. I needed help to deal with the emotional aspects of my weight. I needed someone to be accountable to, someone that could help me take responsibility for my own health. I needed to have support from someone who cared and understood the challenges of living in this very difficult world of PTSD. I needed to look beyond food for comfort.

I made the decision to invest in myself and in my health, and I hired a wellness coach. Having support for my mind, body, and spirit made all the difference on my path to wellness.

Roberta Mittman, Wellness Coach

I would like to introduce you to Roberta Mittman, my wellness coach. Roberta is also licensed acupuncturist and nutritional and lifestyle consultant, as well as a holistic mindset mentor. I'm pleased to share with you some of Roberta's wisdom, which has helped me on my journey to becoming happier and healthier.

Roberta, what mental shifts can a caregiver take to start changing the course of their health?

That's a great question, and that's the key to any discussion around caregiving. It all starts with how you're thinking. The way you're thinking about yourself, your situation, and your life, and how successfully you navigate the challenges of your situation determines the outcome in many cases. It makes a difference if you're thinking about how you can make your role and responsibilities a positive experience, as opposed to thinking caregiving is a drudgery, or a sacrifice, or making you a victim. The mindset is so important, because this can be an extremely empowering experience, even though it's challenging.

It is often hard to keep your head above water and think about yourself. So the mindset is an important factor. For instance, one might say, "It's hard to take care of myself when I'm devoting myself to someone who is worse off than I am. How can I be selfish, how can I be self-serving, or how can I have the nerve to be thinking of myself when my job and my role are to take care of somebody else?"

That comes up frequently; there is a lot of shame and guilt around taking care of the caregiver. It is as though your role is to be subservient, to put yourself last, and to make sure that everything is done perfectly for the comfort of the care receiver.

My point is that a caregiver needs to have the wherewithal, the emotional strength, the feeling of deserving and worthiness in his or her own right, in order to really handle this task so everybody wins.

You may be thinking, I can't take time away, because they need me; I am supposed to be here the whole time. We have many self-limiting thoughts about what our role should be. But in many cases, it's based on something that we saw in the movies or something we read in a book. It's not a real life example. What being a true caregiver means is that you need to be a caregiver to yourself first, before you can really give to somebody else. And that gets lost in the equation almost every time.

That is so true. Can you give us some suggestions about how we can start taking small steps towards taking care of ourselves?

Sure, there are so many things we can do to start. Many times they really boil down to some basic awareness of how your body works and what you need to do to feel well, have energy, keep your immune system strong, and keep your spirits up.

Sleep is very important for a caregiver. Many people find that with stress during the day, they have problems sleeping at night. They don't get the rest they need because of their caregiving tasks. It's almost like a parent with a child; sometimes, when the child finally goes to sleep, then it's, *Oh good, now it's my turn; I can do something for myself.*

That can easily backfire because, if you don't get the amount of rest you need, your body does not have a chance for rest and repair, the R&R. This can make you feel exhausted the next day, irritable, cranky, and likely to reach for the wrong foods, because your blood sugar is totally off and your stress level is through the roof. So I would say the most important thing to do is to get the proper amount of rest. Exhaustion will wear down your immune system and make you feel like everything is a burden. It is hard to get through your day when you are exhausted.

Many times your lifestyle and what you are eating dictates how well you feel in the process, and actually how well you can accomplish your tasks. If you're not taking care of yourself from the physical point of view with some of these really basic things, it's going to be much more difficult for you as a caregiver and you will pay the price.

What happens when you don't eat well?

Here's a quick list of some things that can happen to the caregiver if you're not eating well. You can have physical symptoms, such as headaches, muscle aches, neck and back tension. Your pain can worsen. You can have bowel irregularity, stomach and acid reflux, heartburn, insomnia, weight gain, and skin problems.

You can also have mental symptoms, such as irritability, anger, frustration, depression, lack of organization, confusion, distraction, and loss of focus. All these things can come into play when we're not eating well. And it doesn't have to be difficult to change this—we can do it simply by adding more vegetables, fruits, and healthy proteins. Just those three things can make a huge difference.

Can you share more about those three things?

Certainly, when making food choices we should look for simplicity, efficiency, and optimal health. We can accomplish those three goals with these tips:

1. Choose a protein, vegetable, healthy carbs (such as sweet potatoes or quinoa), and healthy fat (such as nuts, olive oil, or avocados).
2. A guideline when selecting foods at the supermarket is to check labels and look for foods that have no more than 5 grams of sugar

per serving, and 2 grams or more of fiber per serving. That's the key to finding foods that aren't too sugary or over-processed. Using these tools helps you make an instant decision—it's yes or no. Because once you bring it into your house, all bets are off.

Can you share some easy steps to begin shifting into a healthier lifestyle?

Absolutely. Some people have the mindset that all this is black or white. This means that if we're talking about nutrition, I can't have any of my favorite foods anymore. I can't enjoy anything anymore. It's going to be very strict, expensive, or difficult. But it's totally just the opposite, because there is a way to incorporate what you enjoy and make easy changes.

The first step I would like to suggest is to take an honest appraisal of what is in your kitchen, because many times we eat food just because it's there. There are many excuses around why we have these foods, but often we won't even miss it if it's gone. So first, get rid of all unnecessary junk food.

The next thing would be to ask for what you need. Many times people feel that they can't find their voice because they're so busy helping someone else. They feel guilt and shame when they say, what about me? If you need to eat, you need to eat. If you need to sleep, you need to sleep.

Also, it's okay to ask your veteran to help you. Often it helps to involve them in the situation. You can ask for help setting the table, or preparing food if they are able to do that. It's important to ask for what you really need and to express what's really important to you, because if your spouse doesn't know, you feel frustrated, used, and abused, and it's easy to get burned out way too fast.

It is easy to neglect your own needs when you get tired. So taking just a ten-minute relaxation break during the day is a great thing to do. Take time out from stress with a quiet meditation, yoga, reading a book, or putting your feet up. Just closing the door to have some privacy and relaxation for ten minutes will really help stabilize your system.

A natural way to boost your energy is exercise. It is important to exercise and keep moving, because it's great for your heart and your lungs. It helps reduce stress, boost your energy, and nurture your immune system. Even on days when you don't feel like it, try to keep an exercise schedule in place—even if it means just walking around the block a couple of times to clear your head or listen to music. Exercise is very important, and it's often the first thing to go when you get busy.

How can a healthy diet help me with my life as a caregiver? And why should I make changes?

Stress can cause people to eat, so it's important to think about the way you can use food as your medicine cabinet. If you're eating well, keeping your body stabilized, balanced, and healthy, you're going to be able to navigate through a lot of frustrations and difficulties and come up with much more resilience than if you ate a sugary junk diet.

Can you give us some tips about what to do with the food once we do get it into our house?

It is important that you store your healthy food choices at eye level, not in the high cabinets or in the lower drawers, or out of sight in the refrigerator. All of your good choices should be at eye level and easy to reach.

Roberta, how about all those things that we still have in the house that we should not be eating?

Out of sight, out of mind. If it is necessary to keep sugary and highly processed foods in your house, use your high cabinets and lower drawers for those.

It is important when you go to the supermarket to have a plan for what you going to buy. (You can find tools to streamline your shopping list in the resource section of Debbie's website at www.detours2dreams.com.)

When you come home, preparation is key. You're going to clean and cut your vegetables, steam them, or do whatever you need to do so they're ready when you need them. They need to be easy to grab, because sometimes it just takes too long and it's much easier to grab the potato chips.

Roberta, I know for all of us it is common to head for the kitchen even when we're not hungry. You have a great acronym that you use to help us change that. Could you share that with us?

We only have a couple of seconds to make the decision, am I really going to eat this? Am I hungry? Why am I eating this? So if you find yourself going back and forth to your refrigerator over and over again, eating mindlessly throughout the day, it's good to stop and say H.A.L.T! Ask yourself, are you hungry, angry, lonely, or tired? That is a good way to decide if you are eating for the wrong reason or eating because your body really needs fuel.

I can personally attest to the effectiveness of all the tips Roberta has shared. They are new habits that I was able to easily integrate into my life. For more information and tips, visit Roberta at www.robertamittman.com.

Tips and Tools for Sleep

Another common problem for caregivers and those living with a veteran with PTSD is sleep. What keeps you up at night? Anger, stress, annoyance at the blaring TV, a brain that won't turn off, worry, your spouse's snoring or sleep apnea, fear, anxiety? For me it was all of these. And the inability to go to sleep or stay asleep created a vicious cycle of more anger, more stress, a lack of focus, loss of work productivity, and more eating. I tried to stay awake and alert during the day, but couldn't exercise because I was too tired. Not to mention the other common side effects of not sleeping such as being cranky, emotional, and stressed.

Not being able to sleep also makes us more vulnerable to disease; we end up picking up every cold and flu that's going around. Not sleeping well also affects diabetes and other diseases. It can make you age faster, gain weight, and increase your risk of depression, alcoholism, and suicide, as well as many other side effects.

I struggled to find something to help me sleep and would like to share with you the things I found useful to me. At times, it would be necessary to use all of these:

- Prayer. This is the first thing I do each night. It provides closure to the day's events, an opportunity for gratitude, renewed support, and the connection and peace of being watched over.
- Darkness. New research shows that the sleep-promoting hormone melatonin is suppressed by light of any kind, but especially the blue waves given off by LEDs. Use a sleep mask and cover every LED light in the room.

- Ear plugs. These are helpful for snoring partners and blaring televisions.
- Chamomile tea. Chamomile is an herbal remedy that has been used for insomnia for thousands of years.
- Lavender aromatherapy. Research has shown that lavender acts as a mild sedative, helping you fall asleep faster and more soundly. There are plenty of ways to use it, including lavender-scented dryer sheets, pillow spray, oils, lotions, and bath products. My favorites are reed diffusers and lavender-scented dryer sheets.
- Melatonin. I first heard about melatonin as a useful sleep regulator to reset your clock after jet lag. My doctor suggested it as a sleep aid, and I have found it helpful; you should discuss melatonin use with your doctor before trying it.
- Oatmeal, bananas. Melatonin is found in both oatmeal and bananas, so eating a snack consisting of one or both of these a short time before bed can be helpful. Bananas also contain potassium and magnesium, two minerals that promote muscle relaxation.
- Yoga. A number of yoga poses help relax your body and mind to help you get to sleep. My standby is the Nighttime Goddess Stretch. Lie on your back with your knees bent. Place the soles of your feet together, then let your knees fall open, forming a diamond shape with your legs. Rest your arms on the bed. If you feel any strain, elevate your legs by placing a pillow underneath each knee. Hold the pose for two minutes.
- Deep breathing. It helps to clear your mind of the clutter when you're able to simply concentrate on breathing and relaxing.
- Journaling. I found it useful to keep a notebook by my bed in order to do a brain dump when my brain would not quit. It all went on paper: my to-do list, my thoughts, my feelings. Much of part 1 of my book was written during sleepless nights.
- Separate rooms. Sometimes there is just no choice but to sleep apart.

I hope you've found some tools and tips that can help you begin making some small shifts towards a healthier life. Remember that we have only one body, and if we don't care for it, the neglect will soon take its toll—not just on us, but also on those we're caring for.

Action Steps

What are three shifts that you can commit to this week to help improve your wellness?

1._____

2._____

3._____

CHAPTER 31

STEP 7: CREATING THE SPARKLE: ADDING FUN, HAPPINESS, AND PASSION

If there is no passion in your life, then have you really lived? Find your passion, whatever it may be. Become it, and let it become you and you will find great things happen FOR you, TO you and BECAUSE of you.
—T. Alan Armstrong

Living a life of fun, happiness, and passion are essential to the quality of your life. Many say these elements are also essential to your health and well-being. Yet, it is so easy to lose sight of the importance of these joys while living in the world of PTSD and caregiving. And when these essentials are overshadowed, life's sparkle is stripped away, leaving behind only the essential of surviving.

This does not have to be the case. Fun, happiness, and living with passion are free, available to everyone who wishes to pursue them. Step 7 will provide you with information and tools to help you bring back fun, happiness, and passion into your life.

Fun

Recreation is an especially important ingredient in the life of a healthy caregiver. Recreation provides an opportunity to rejuvenate and guard against the dangers of caregiver burnout. And it allows us to re-create! Recreation can entail any type of activity that allows the mind, body, and spirit to rest, recover, and re-create.

It doesn't have to be manual labor that you're recuperating from; mental and emotional strain also benefit from recreation. It may be group or individual; what may be fun to you may not be fun to someone else, like stamp collecting or skydiving. The important thing is to find something that brings you pleasure and revitalizes your spirit—and do it.

Fun and recreation are considered essential for patients in skilled nursing homes and many other medical facilities. For over twenty years my job as a recreation therapist consultant required me to visit these facilities. I had to make sure they were complying with the state licensing regulations for their activity programs, offering opportunities for the creative, spiritual, social, learning, and physical aspects of residents' lives. Activity directors had to write goals and objectives and have a plan for each resident. They had to chart their attendance at events and have strategies to encourage participation. It was my job to provide them with assistance to meet these requirements.

I've often thought we should have the same type of regulations for caregivers who are so easily neglected and have long ago given up on leisure activities. When I began working with caregivers, I reflected back on those times and thought, *Who is insuring that our caregivers are getting these important needs met?* Fun is no longer in their vocabulary—yet recreation and leisure are an essential part of healthy living. When you have the opportunity to step away from the rigors and stress of caregiving, you can relax and get a fresh perspective on your life. You're able to return refreshed, mentally and physically, and be a better caregiver and spouse.

Does it seem selfish or not important for you to have fun? How do you feel when you smile? When was the last time you laughed? The feeling provided by fun, laughter, and smiling is one that can't be replicated by anything else you do. Nor does anything else provide the same healing qualities as fun and recreation.

Your life has changed with the new responsibilities of caregiving and living in the world of PTSD. You may not be able to do the same activities that brought you pleasure in the past, but the world is full of endless opportunities for fun. They don't have to be expensive, and you don't even have to leave your home. Think about activities that you could begin today to bring fun back into your life.

Happiness

Happiness is an amazing feeling. Do you think some people are just born happy? What's the secret? I'm honored to have Marci Shimoff, the Happiness expert, and *NY Times* bestselling author of *Happy for No Reason* help answer our questions about happiness and provide tips on raising your own happiness level.

Marci, can you give us some tips on how to begin taking responsibility for our own happiness? Sometimes as caregivers, it seems impossible even to stop for a minute to get that glass of water.

I can totally appreciate what you're saying. What I know is that you are of no help to somebody else until you are feeling full within yourself. While it seems like you don't have time to get that glass of water or take care of yourself, you have to train yourself to do that. You have to train yourself to take care of yourself. And know that that is the greatest service you can give to somebody else.

We often live in our culture with a myth that I call "the myth of I'll be happier when." It's "I'll be happier when I get a better job," or "I'll be happier when I lose twenty pounds," or in this case, "I'll be happier when my partner is doing better." When you base your happiness on anything outside yourself, which is natural because we've all been trained to do that, it is a sure-fire recipe for unhappiness.

So the first thing to do is to recognize that we all have what's called a happiness set point. What that means is that no matter what happens to us, whether it's good or bad, we will tend to hover around our happiness set point unless we do something to change it. Like a thermostat setting, if you want to be happier, you've got to raise your thermostat setting, *your happiness set point.*

There are specific ways that you can raise your happiness set point. What I suggest is that you take ten minutes, and if you can't do ten minutes, then take five minutes. Take five to ten minutes a day, and do something to raise your happiness set point. How about if I share a couple of happiness habits with you?

Yes, that would be great.

One habit has to do with our thoughts: don't believe everything you think. Just because you have a thought, it doesn't mean it's true. The average person has on average 60,000 thoughts per day. Eighty percent of those are negative. And there's a scientific reason for this. We have inherited from our caveman ancestors the tendency to remember the negative more than the positive. Back then it was a survival mechanism. But we no longer need it.

It's what one researcher I interviewed, Dr. Rick Hansen, calls the Velcro/Teflon syndrome. Our minds are like Velcro for the negative, but Teflon for the positive. And what we need to do is reverse that syndrome by releasing the negative. To let them go more easily.

The other side of the coin is that we also need to start to Velcro the positive. Having the positive stick to us more. What's interesting is that it takes longer for a positive event to actually stick and register. It takes about ten to twenty seconds for something good to actually start making changes in the structures of the brain in creating a neural pathway. So that means that we have to notice the good and really take it in, instead of sloughing it off. Let me give you an example here: If you get ten compliments in one day and one criticism, what do you remember at the end of the day?

The criticism, definitely!

Yes, the criticism. So what we need to do to raise our happiness set point is start taking in that good more, start recognizing the positives and allowing them to land in us. So, if somebody says to you "Oh, you did a really great job on this," don't say, "Oh, it was nothing," when you know you worked hard on it. Say, "Thank you, I really did work hard on this and I loved how it turned out. I really appreciate that you acknowledged it as well."

You see, that's a subtle difference, but notice that took about ten seconds to really take it in. Be on the lookout for the good in your life. It's all around you. We only take in a fraction of a percentage of the information that's out there. So what we need to do is shift so that we start paying attention to or noticing the good things.

One great exercise to do is to keep a gratitude journal. That means every day before you go to sleep, write down five things during the day that you are grateful for. What that does is make it stick; it takes those ten to twenty seconds to take the time to remember it. Research shows that just doing this for a month will raise your happiness set point. You will be absolutely amazed how, if you do these simple things even for a few minutes a day over a short period of time, you will start to feel different.

Marci, I am so glad that you emphasized simple things, because that's what I loved about your book Happy for No Reason. *There were so many simple things that I was able to use immediately, and they made such a difference in my life. I am so excited to share you and* Happy for No Reason *with all the other spouses who are really searching for simple tools to change their attitude and begin to find a happier, more positive place.*

I want to emphasize something, because I think that sometimes people get a little confused. They think that I'm saying, oh just decide to be happy. Well, that's where you start, but that's not enough. You can't just decide to be happy and expect to wake up tomorrow morning happier, in the same way you can't just decide to be a great tennis player and wake up tomorrow morning and be ready to play Wimbledon.

If you want to be a great tennis player, you study the habits of great tennis players and you practice those habits. It's the same thing with happiness. Happiness is a habit. So you find out what the habits of happy people are, which is what we found out for you, and you start practicing those habits of happy people.

Like gratitude focusing, there's a saying that "what we appreciate, appreciates." So what we appreciate grows stronger in our life. Where our attention goes, our energy flows. I'm not saying you sweep the bad under the rug and don't pay attention to it. We definitely need to address issues in our life; I'm not talking about going into a state of denial. But I am saying that we can change our neuro pathways so that they are more biased towards the good.

This is the good news! Once you start appreciating the positive and creating more of that Velcro for the positives, it becomes easier for you to notice them because your neuro pathways are structured so that you see what you're looking for. And when we have what I call a stronger positivity muscle being built, then we start noticing and appreciating the positives more.

I love that, strengthening your positivity muscles!

People ask me what's the fast track to greater happiness and love. And I'd have to say if there was one universal fast track, it would be forgiveness. We cannot feel better in our lives when we are holding onto anger, resentment, or grudges. If your life isn't working in some way—and if you're dealing with someone who has PTSD, then you have a challenge going on—my first suggestion to you is to practice forgiveness. And that means forgiveness towards the situation, perhaps forgiveness towards your partner, and forgiveness towards yourself as well.

We all need forgiveness towards ourselves. There are many tools out there for forgiveness, but the one that I like the most is called ho ho'oponopono. It's a simple practice with profound results. I'm going to share with you how to do it.

What you do is, in your heart, you send these four wishes towards the person or situation that you want forgiveness with. The four phrases are: I'm sorry, please forgive me, thank you, I love you. I'm sorry, please forgive me, thank you, I love you. Now it doesn't matter who was right or who was wrong, or even if there was a right or wrong. For some amazing reason, these four phrases are amongst the highest energy vibration phrases in English; the energy will shift.

So if you have anger or resentment toward your partner, or you're feeling guilty for that and angry at yourself, these are all good things to use this practice on. You just close your eyes, you go into your heart, and you feel from your heart. I'm sorry, please forgive me, thank you, I love you. You just repeat that for five minutes or so and you'll notice that things will start to shift. You may need to do this every day for a few weeks before you notice anything, but I promise miracles will happen.

Thank you for sharing that. That is one of the tools that I began using when I read your book for the first time, and it made such a powerful difference in my life. You can find more information and tools at Marci's website: www.happyfornoreason.com.

Passion

Our next topic is passion. I am honored to have Janet Bray Attwood and Chris Attwood, co-authors of the *New York Times* bestseller *The Passion Test: The Effortless Path to Discovering Your Life Purpose*, join me to discuss how caregiving, PTSD, and living a life of passion and purpose can co-exist.

Chris, can you start by sharing your definition of passion?

Passion is that which gives us meaning in our life. If you look at the most successful people in the world, what's common for all of them is that they learn to make significant decisions in their life based upon that definition of passion.

Janet, what is your definition of passion?

Passion is that thing that gets you up out of bed in the morning. That thing that you love so much that you don't even think about how much money am I going to make, you're just loving it so much that it's what you do because it's fun.

Chris, as you know, I work with spouses of veterans with PTSD. Many of them might feel when you talk about following your passion that it's a selfish thing to do. Or they might think it wouldn't be responsible for them to follow their passions or live their passions while they are supposed to be taking care of a family and a wounded veteran. How would you respond to them?

We often get this question. What it requires is to really look at how you serve the people that you love and care about the most. If you care deeply about someone, do you serve them most by caring for them with a long face and a feeling or attitude of obligation? Or are they served the most when they interact with you and you're happy, joyful, and excited?

I would think that when you serve them with joy and excitement and love, it serves them much better than if they feel your resentment about what you're doing.

I've never met anyone that wanted to feel like they were a burden to the people they love. So there is value in getting clear about what matters most to you. When you can engage with them, serve them, support them, be involved, and interact with them from a place of knowing that this is what is really meaningful to you in your life, it can change everything. When you choose to be there, not that you have to be there. You've chosen to be there because it's so deeply important to you.

On the other hand, what if you make a list of your passions—and none of them have anything to do with your loved one suffering from PTSD? Do you think that you are actually serving them by forcing yourself to do something for them in contradiction to what really matters to you?

Chris, I would think that it's very easy for them to pick up those feelings. And hard to hide the feeling that you're not doing what you really want to do. I would think that that would not be a good situation.

That's my experience. The truth is that if you want to condemn the one in your life suffering from PTSD to a life of misery and unhappiness, then force yourself to do things for him that you really don't want to do, or sacrifice things that matter deeply to you.

If you want to serve the person in your life with PTSD, the way to do that is by, number one, being clear about what matters most to you. The passion test, www.thepassiontest.com, as you know, Debbie, is a simple, powerful process to get clear on what five things matter most to you in your life. Once you've gotten clear on those things, make decisions based upon them.

Sometimes it may be a mix. You know that you deeply love this person in your life who's suffering from PTSD, and you have other needs as well. And if that's the case, make sure that you take care of your other needs as well. Because then when you are with them, you're going to come from a place of feeling happy and joyful and being able to give them the best of yourself.

And, if you love someone, my experience is that what you want to give them is the best of yourself. Isn't that true?

That is so true and such helpful advice. Going through the Passion Test can show us that sometimes we get sidetracked and forget what it is that's truly important to us. I think that happens a lot in a relationship when you're caring for someone with PTSD.

Any relationship always between two people is based on giving and receiving. There has to be a giving and a receiving. If your loved one is incapable of giving because of the trauma and horror he's experienced, then what does that mean? It means that you have to give to yourself. Because no one can be part of a relationship where you are only giving. Because what do you think happens, Debbie, in that experience? What happens when you give, and you give, and you give, and you never receive anything back in return?

From my personal experience I would say that you end up getting very overwhelmed. You can end up losing the true essence of who you are. You end up getting angry about the situation, and then you feel guilty about feeling that way. So it's not a fun place to be; there are many negative feelings.

It's called a vicious circle. Imagine that you have a jug full of water and you're just pouring from that water, giving water, giving water, giving water, giving water. At some point that jug is empty, and there's no more water to give, right? That's also true of people. You can give your love, you can give your support, you can give your help, and you can give and give without getting anything in return. Then what's going to happen is that the jug is going to get empty at some point, there's going to be no love, no help, no support to give any longer. And what it will be replaced with are those things you were talking about, Debbie: anger, resentment, frustration. And that doesn't serve anyone.

So it's imperative that the care provider give to himself or herself. As for the issue of being selfish, it is not about being selfish at all, it's about having the ability to give. And we can only give what we have to give. Isn't that true?

Yes, that's true.

And so if we really love someone and they're incapable of giving love to us, then we have to give love to ourselves. And what that means is giving ourselves permission to do the things that bring us joy, to do the things that bring us fulfillment. Even if that other person doesn't understand, even if they are resentful or angry or whatever they may be, you have to know that the only way your jug can be full and able to give to them is if you give that love, that help, that support to yourself, so that in return you can go back and share that with them.

That is such great advice. I love your analogy of the water jug. Do you have any final thoughts you would like to share with us?

Janet and I like to say that your passions are like the pipelines to your soul. So when you can get clear about those passions, the top five passions in your life (the brain can only hold five to seven things at once, which is why we say five things), you can consistently make decisions in your life based upon those passions, based upon those things that you love and care about most.

What will happen is you'll see little by little your life becoming more and more tuned to the things that you really do care about. And with that you will find that life becomes more meaningful, that it feels more purposeful. As that grows, the love in your heart will grow, that experience of connection will grow, and the sense of separation, the sense of danger, this need for fearfulness because there could be someone or something that could hurt me or destroy me in some way or other, that will begin little by little to disappear.

And so if I could leave one thought with everyone, it would be to pay attention to the things you love. If it's useful to you, use the Passion Test to identify your top five passions, the five things you love most, and then, most importantly, make the important, critical decisions in your life based on those. As you do that, you'll find you come to know yourself more deeply and, with that, come to love the people and the situations and circumstances in your life more fully.

Janet, you talk a lot about intention, attention, and no tension in The Passion Test. Could you explain what you mean by that?

It's a formula for living a passionate life. *Intention* is all about being very clear on what your passions are, so you can clearly know what it is that you intend to create in your life.

Attention is simply the fact that all of us are powerful. Attention is all about focusing like a samurai on what it is you choose to create in your life—in other words, what you're most passionate about—then taking action. It's not enough just to say this is my passion, and now it's going to materialize. You can even make a map of action so that you draw to you the people, the places, or the things you need in order to make that passion a reality.

Once you've done everything you know to do, once you've struck like lightning in all directions to really make that passion happen, then there has to be a point where you say okay, that's it, I've done all I can do, I give up, I surrender, I let go.

So intention, attention, no tension is the formula. Once you've taken all the action you can, just let go.

For more information on the Passion Test visit: www.thepassiontest.com

★ ★ ★ ★ ★

Let's follow Janet's lead and set an intention to create a life filled with fun, happiness, and passion. Turn your attention to the details of what it will take to create sparkle in your life, and begin taking action steps. Next, with no tension, sit back and watch the magic happen as your life begins to sparkle.

Action Steps

What three steps can you begin immediately to bring more fun, happiness, and passion into your life?

1._____

2._____

3._____

CHAPTER 32

STEP 8: PUTTING IT ALL TOGETHER: THE GPS TO YOUR DREAMS

If one advances confidently in the direction of his dreams, and endeavors to live the life which he has imagined, he will meet with a success unexpected in common hours.

—Henry David Thoreau

Today is your opportunity to set into motion the shifts and changes necessary to take your life back from the contagious effects of your veteran's PTSD. You are now armed with the weapons and armor to fight the fear, self-doubt, and unawareness that left you imprisoned in the world of PTSD. You now have a new way of looking at yourself, your veteran, and your future.

This detour from the life that you have been living may seem scary. You are about to embark on a new and unfamiliar road. And change produces fear, even when the change has the promise of bringing you something better. But this road is full of endless possibilities and the opportunity for a new and more fulfilling life.

To begin this journey it will be necessary to bring along the lessons that you have been taught. In part 1 you became aware that you are not alone in your struggle of living with your veteran and PTSD. Each family has its own unique situation, with constant problems and challenges. But none of these challenges have to be life destroying. And we all have the opportunity to create our new normal.

In part 2 we learned about PTSD and how the trauma of war has affected our veteran.

Part 3 provided hope that PTSD symptoms can improve with a variety of available treatment options.

Part 4 addressed the unique problems encountered while living with your veteran's PTSD and provided tools to help live a more peaceful existence.

Part 5 is *all about you*—how important it is to cherish your own needs for health and happiness. We learned about the contagious effects of our veteran's PTSD on us and answered the question, what's happening to me?

In the first seven steps, you were provided with information and tools to help you deal with the effects of living with PTSD. You now have the tools and solutions to make shifts and changes in your life in order to:

1. Understand and accept the reality of life with PTSD.
2. Take back your life and uncover your power and your ability to take control, rather than letting the situation control you.
3. Nurture your current support system and find new sources to reach out to for help.
4. Release the anger, fear, and guilt that have been creating pain in your life, and learn new ways to show love, compassion, and forgiveness.
5. Deal with and prevent stress and overwhelm in your life.
6. Begin taking better care of your health by making small shifts in the way that you eat, sleep, and move.
7. Remember the importance of fun, happiness, and passion in your life.

Step 8 is putting everything together that you have learned up to this point and creating the GPS—Goals, Plan, and Support—to your dreams, a life of your own creation. Each couple and family facing life with PTSD is unique, and it will be important to find the combination that works for you.

You have survived everything that has happened to you up to this point in your life. There have been struggles, pain, anger, and fear. There may have been times when you thought it would be easier to simply walk away. There have been days when you thought that you could not possibly endure another moment. But you did! Now, you are here looking for a better and easier way in which you can love, honor, and care for your veteran, while also cherishing your own needs.

You are now ready to create the next chapter in your life. There is a blank page in front of you. Are you ready to begin?

Before we start, I would like to take a moment to congratulate you for making it to this point. In addition, I would like you to honor yourself for the strength and courage that has brought you here. I understand that it has not been an easy journey. Congratulate yourself for everything you have done to keep your life together up to this point and for the courage to keep moving towards a better life.

Steps to Design Your New Life

To begin our next step, I invite you to open up your heart, your mind, and your imagination to the limitless opportunities that lie in front of you for creating a brighter tomorrow.

We will use six steps to put the essential elements together for creating the life of your design:

1. Make the decision to change.
2. Assess where you are today.
3. Decide where you want to be.
4. Visualize your future.
5. Create your personal GPS: Goals, Plan, and Support.
6. Begin.

1. Making the Decision to Change

The first step requires that you make the decision to take back control of your life. You must trust yourself and your ability to create a life that works for you. It may be a life different from those around you, so it's important that you not compare your life to others, which can bring you down. And those around you may not understand your life; it may not look *normal* to them. Keep confident in your ability to know what is best for you and your veteran.

It's likely that you initially envisioned a life with a healthy spouse. That is not the reality of how my life turned out, or yours. Yes, I could have chosen to toss aside my veteran like damaged goods. However, I chose to love him and to love myself. I chose to have compassion for him and myself. I chose to work at creating a new life and pursue my dreams in a different way. I am no different from you. You have the ability to make those same choices.

Do these choices require sacrifice? Yes, but what worthwhile things in life do not require work and sacrifice? Do you value things more that have come easily to you or those things that you have struggled for?

And what if your spouse's life gets better because of the changes that you make in yourself? What if your life becomes better than you ever dreamed possible? How would that feel? How would it feel to have the daily satisfaction of living a life of love, compassion, gratitude, good health, and happiness? A life that is true to yourself and to your values? You may not reach the dream that you first imagined. But you might end up with something even better than you ever thought possible.

And what will you lose by not changing? What will you gain if you do change?

2. Assess Where You Are Today

During this step, look at various areas in your life to see the level of satisfaction that you currently have. This will give you a starting point for what areas are the most important to focus on improving or changing. (Additional resources and planning tools can be found on the book resource page at www. astrangerinmybed.com).

Assessing Where You Are Today

To create your optimal life, it's important to see where you are today. Fill in the blanks below to assess your current situation and determine the most important areas to work on.

Rate each statement from 1–10, using #1 as the lowest level of satisfaction and #10 as the highest level of satisfaction.

Rate from 1-10

1. Knowledge: I have a good overall knowledge of PTSD. _____
2. Understanding: I recognize how PTSD impacts lives. _____
3. Acceptance: I have accepted the changes caused by PTSD. _____
4. Spiritual: I have spiritual support in my life. _____
5. Power: I believe in my ability to make changes in my life. _____
6. Significance: What I do is important and makes a difference. _____
7. Virtue: I am proud of who I am and what I stand for. _____
8. Confidence: I know that I have the ability to achieve my goals. _____
9. Empathy: I can feel other people's pain. _____
10. Values: I respect the things that are important to me. _____
11. Support: I have all the support in my life that I need. _____
12. Fear: I am not stopped from taking action because of fear. _____
13. Anger: I am able to control my feelings of anger. _____
14. Resentment: I am not resentful about my life. _____
15. Love: I do not depend on others to feel love for myself. _____
16. Compassion: I have compassion for my veteran and myself. _____
17. Forgiveness: I give and receive forgiveness freely. _____
18. Stress Prevention: I do things daily to prevent stress. _____
19. Stress Management: I have tools that I use regularly to manage my stress. _____
20. Eating: I make healthy food choices most of the time. _____
21. Sleeping: I get sufficient sleep most nights. _____
22. Moving: I am physically active at least four days per week. _____
23. Fun: I engage in fun activities weekly. _____
24. Happiness: I do things to create happiness in my life. _____
25. Passion: I am fulfilling the passions in my life. _____
26. Purpose: I do things daily to fulfill my life purpose. _____
27. Cherishing YOU: My health and happiness are honored by others. _____

3. Decide Where You Want to Be

Now look at where you want to be. What would make your life fuller and happier? Open up your mind and your imagination to view the limitless opportunities for your future. Begin to fill your blank page with the things you want to include in your life. Begin creating a list of your unique values, needs, wants, and dreams, using these questions to help you:

- What are the eight most important values that you want to focus on in your life?
- What is the most important thing in the world to you?
- What can't you live without?
- What do you need?
- What do you want in your life that you don't currently have?

In order to know where you want to be, it is important to first imagine that something better is possible. When we can imagine, it opens up our mind to the fact that we do have choices. Considering your life purpose and your passions, answer the following questions:

- How do you want to be remembered?
- How can you best use your special gifts?
- What would you like to do in your life that will really make a difference?
- What gets you up in the morning and makes life worth living?

4. Visualize Your Dream Life

Having dreams and goals is directly related to our happiness, our sense of fulfillment, and our success in life. In order to achieve anything it is important that you have a clear picture of what that is. In the last step, you wrote the things that are important to you. The next step is to create your own personal vision of your life. Answer these questions:

- Who do you want to become?
- What would that look like?
- Do you have the skills and competency to achieve your goals?

- When you think about your dream, do you have a positive attitude, and are you confident that you have the ability to attain your goal?
- Your life is filled with limitless opportunities for the future. What would you do if you knew that you could not fail?
- What would a life look like that was fulfilling all your unique needs, wants, and dreams?

5. Your Personal GPS to Your Future: Goals, Plan, Support

Making these dreams come true will not happen without having a detailed picture of what you want your life to look like and how you're going to make it happen. When you take the time to think about your goals, write them down, and create a detailed plan, it will help you to move forward.

In writing goals, it is important that they contain certain elements. S.M.A.R.T. goals have these qualities:

Specific— something concrete and tangible.

Measurable— something that can be quantified so you can see results.

Achievable— something that you're capable of doing and have the resources available to make happen.

Realistic— something you can actually achieve when you look at all the factors in your life.

Time— something with a time limit, a specific period for accomplishing it. It's a good idea to have short-term, medium-term, and long-term goals.

Smart goals help you to be successful. They provide the opportunity to see your accomplishments, a means to check on your progress, and a way to be accountable. Since they are time limited, you have the opportunity to continue your goal, setting another time limit, or revise your goal if it turns out to be unrealistic. You can also continue setting new goals as you find success.

For each goal you should write the action steps necessary to achieve it, as well as the tools, resources, and support that you will need to be successful. It is also helpful to have a target date of when you plan to complete each step.

Planning Your Dream

When you plan how you're going to implement your goal, you need to consider the following:

- What strategy will be used to accomplish your goal?
- What action steps will be required?
- How long will each step take?
- What is your timeline?
- What resources will be required?
- What problems or roadblocks might you encounter?
- What strategies can you put into place to deal with or prevent these problems?

Do not let the obstacles on your road of life become dead ends and roadblocks to your health and happiness. Think ahead about what challenges or problems you might face and come up with strategies to work through these problems. You may be able to anticipate problems based on previous experience. There will be fear, and you may ask, but what if I fail? What if this is the wrong decision? You won't know until you try.

Looking back on your life, what has been difficult for you to change? What strategies, resources, and support could you put into place to make it past the roadblock? How committed are you to the course of change?

The thing with detours is that there are many ways to get to a destination. If you take a wrong turn, or if you don't like the scenery, you can always try a different way. Learn from your journey, and keep moving forward toward your dream.

You may hit a roadblock, a bumpy stretch, and perhaps need to change routes along the way. Practice flexibility. With each change there may be pain, fear, and discomfort. But there may also be a newfound confidence in your abilities. The more you use the tools you've learned and brought along on the trip, the easier it will be to continue moving forward.

Be cautious of the *someday syndrome*, excuses, and roadblocks. One of the top excuses people use for not making changes in their life is that they don't have time. You may have already been thinking *I can't do this; it's going to take too much time. I am too busy.* This is an important strategy to include in your planning. It will be important to make the time available to accomplish your goals by saying *no* and *by letting go*.

Consider this: we are each given the same amount of time each day. We each have 24 hours in a day, 1440 minutes, 86,400 seconds. We are the keeper of our time. Are you being a good steward of yours? Or are there areas where you have given away your control, or are you simply wasting time by not taking control?

What things must you do? What things should do? What things are out of your control? What are your time robbers: TV, magazines, chatting, computers? Are these things providing value to you? Intellectually? Emotionally? Do they release stress, or are they simply adding to your stress? What are you willing to give up to get something that you truly want? What are you doing that could be delegated? Do you believe you are all things to all people? Look at what you have indicated is important to you. Now look at how much time you're spending on it. Are these congruent?

Support

In step 3, we talked about the need for a support system. Having a strong support system will be important as you move forward in creating your ideal life. As you look at your support system, make sure you're surrounding yourself with people who share your beliefs and values, and who will lift you up. Stay clear of the dream stealers and the people who try to bring you down. At times that may mean you will be alone, but be confident that you will find the right people to support you in your dreams.

6. Begin

Simply begin. This often can be the most difficult step of all. But beginning does not have to be scary. It is not necessary to make giant changes all at one time. Every journey begins with the first step. And the size of that step is entirely up to you. A big step or a tiny step is still a beginning.

★ ★ ★ ★ ★

Today is the first day of the rest of your life . . . . Your next chapter begins now . . . . The pages are blank . . . . It is up to you to fill those pages any way that you choose to create new dreams and to fulfill those dreams that you haven't yet accomplished.

You have the power and strength to do and be anything you choose.

Action Step

Select one thing to make a shift or a change—take a giant step or a tiny step. Whatever you decide to do, simply start down the road to a brighter tomorrow!

Today I will begin: _____

AFTERWORD

REFLECTIONS
FROM THE
STRANGER

I joined the Navy in the fall of 1966 to avoid the draft. After processing and returning home to wait for orders, I received a draft notice. *Wow, that was close,* I thought.

My first duty station was Carrier Air Group 12, staff, San Diego, California. Yes, Shore Duty. Having been born and raised in northern California, I had hoped for duty on a combat vessel so I could travel and see the world. I was disappointed. And I was now stuck in southern California, more anxious than ever to do something more fulfilling.

I volunteered for Vietnam. The response was immediate. I received orders to S.E.R.E. School (Survival, Evasion, Resistance, and Escape). I spent time at the Coronado Amphibious Base in San Diego being indoctrinated into the culture and language of survival training. I strongly supported the use of the water board intelligence gathering technique because many of us were shown just how effective it was: you lie down on a board, then they pull your T-shirt over your face and add water. A recipe that will guarantee your cooperation.

Then it was on to Camp Pendleton for weapons training. I was part of a mortar crew, where we threw live grenades and shot every weapon imaginable.

★ ★ ★ ★ ★

As with most memorable experiences in Vietnam, my arrival in the country set the tone for the months to follow. Off the plane, onto cattle cars, and off to the processing center. In route, our convoy had to cross a river. While in the middle of the bridge, the marines responsible for security cut loose, firing into the river below us. Can you imagine fifty FNG's (new guys) diving into the bottom of that transport vehicle? First day, first hour, I was already feeling the fear of war.

I was first assigned to the Coastal River Division, DaNang. We were lodged on the floating support craft, APL-5. Tied alongside were many small craft, including swift boats, a monitor gun ship, and several ammo-filled mike boats ready for transport to forward operating bases.

After settling in and hitting the rack, I eventually fell asleep. I was awakened suddenly by the sound of concussion grenades going off alongside us. Were there suspected swimmers with satchel charges? If so, they were repelled. But can you imagine the added fear to the day's already stressful happenings? I did not sleep the rest of the night. In fact, I haven't slept well since.

Things were not any easier for several months to follow. TET (Chinese New Year) was in full swing. We were subjected to constant small arms fire, and rocket and mortar attacks. One of our support craft took a direct rocket hit, killing four of the crew. The explosion, bright lights, and cooking-off of ammo lasted for hours. A few miles north of us, the Northern Vietnamese Army (NVA) overran the capital of Hue. It took months to take it back.

My next assignment was with the I-Corp consolidated purchasing and contracting office, downtown DaNang. No safe zone, no security, until the office was satchel charged (bombed). Only then were a bunker and an ARVN guard stationed in front of our building. I also worked with the civic action team, teaching conversational English to the children. While driving through a crowded street on my way to class one day, a VC (Viet Cong) grenade was dropped in the back of my jeep. Thank the Lord it did not explode. Explosive Ordnance Disposal rendered it safe, and I eventually came home with a souvenir that my son now displays in his home.

My next experience was not much better. I was in a private residence only two to three blocks away from my office when an attack occurred. Out of respect for the family, I was not armed. I ran out of the home and headed for my office. The sound of bullets zipping by me, ricochets, and a lot of yelling and screaming were just nonsensical, because I don't remember my feet hitting the ground. I felt as though I were running in slow motion.

I blasted in through the front door of 17 Yen Bay Street. Was I safe yet? Not really. I vividly remember the look on the faces of my buddies, as we all geared up with flack jackets, helmets, and jacking rounds in our weapons. The enemy blew by our position, as their objective was the ARVN Headquarters several blocks away. Their efforts were in vain, however, as they were defeated immediately.

At one point during my tour, I was being treated for an injury received during a rocket attack. I was given an injection and immediately went into anaphylactic shock. I was clinically dead. No heartbeat, no breath; my lungs were gurgling. I was gone.

I had an out-of-body experience. I rose to the top corner of the room, where I peacefully watched the doctor and staff frantically moving around working on my lifeless body. I could not hear anything, but what was going on was very obvious to me later. I then moved to the tunnel. Slowly moving through the tunnel, I could see light at the end. There was movement, but I could not make out what was beyond the bright light behind the fog.

As I moved closer to the light, I seemed to slow down, and I remember a very distinct voice in my mind stating, "No, he's not ready yet." The next thing I realized, I was regaining consciousness. The doctor had been performing CPR; he was sweating and very red in the face. He said, "Don't ever let anyone give you this s—t again!

On another occasion during a rocket attack, a round was coming in very close. I hit the ground and curled up. After the explosion, I sat up and regained my senses. I saw a man down not too far from me. He had been wounded and had almost lost one of his legs. I applied a tourniquet, threw him over my shoulder, and took him to medical. I dropped him on the gurney and watched as they checked him out. He was dead. I was covered in his blood and did not feel clean even after a two-hour shower.

These are just a few of my experiences during the TETs of 1968 and 1969. I did not share them with anyone for many years. I had many other unpleasant and outright scary situations happen to me while I was in Vietnam, but I still find it very difficult to share them.

★ ★ ★ ★ ★

Time passed and thirty years later, I met Debbie. There was an immediate attraction, and eight months later, we were married. We were on our way to the happy life, having many wonderful experiences together. She brought me to a Christian way of life, and I came to know my Lord and Savior, Jesus Christ. I was baptized and confirmed in the Lutheran Church.

I had always believed in a higher power of some kind, but never fully understood what or why until I became part of her life and church. Little did I know how the meaning of my out-of-body experience in Vietnam would be revealed to me later on in our relationship.

After a couple years of marriage, I began to have nightmares. Waking with fear and anxiety, I came to realize that I was reliving some of my horrible experiences of the war. My nightmares caused me to fight, swing, and kick hard at my imaginary enemy, yelling and screaming in Vietnamese. I was not aware of what I was doing until I was fully awake.

I became afraid of falling asleep for fear of having another nightmare and possibly hurting Debbie. Deprived of rest, I became very angry, agitated, and argumentative. I began drinking more and took prescribed narcotics to deaden the pain and memories so I could sleep. I did not know what was happening to me. This was not the person that I knew I was inside.

One day I met another Nam vet in a parking lot. We talked a while and he asked me if I was receiving any help from the VA. I said, "What for?" He said that he was sure I had PTSD and should get some help. *Why*, I wondered, *I'm tough and can man-up and will get through this.*

He convinced me otherwise. The next day he walked me into the Veterans Service Office, and I began receiving clinical help for PTSD within the week. It took me some time before I could feel at ease with my therapist, Dr. Chet Sunde. But I realized that I did need help and sincerely wanted to change my behavior. I had put Debbie, her daughter, and others that I loved through living hell.

With Dr. Sunde's help, I have learned how to deal with my issues. I am still working towards better mental health after eleven years. I now say that I am medicated for everyone's protection, including my own.

Here is where my out-of-body experience comes to light. It allows me to see the bigger picture: I was meant to go through everything I went through and to share my pain with Debbie so that she could help others with their pain. Because of Debbie's desire to help me in my time of need, she began researching and learning everything she could about PTSD. She was also overwhelmed from living with my PTSD, and thus began researching and learning about its stressors and how they affected my behavior.

She then started to take on her own symptoms of PTSD. She was losing her own identity. She too became stressed and depressed. She realized she needed help of her own. She was now dealing with the contagious effects of PTSD.

When she first told me that for the first time in her life she was unmotivated and didn't care about her life, I was too numb myself to notice or even care. I told her I couldn't help her. I had too many problems of my own.

So she sought out the help of two psychologists. I went to the second one with her. Neither had any understanding of what she was going through; both advised her to get divorced and move on.

Because of her beliefs, that was not going to happen. Instead, she took many classes, attended seminars, and became a Board Certified Life and Career Coach. In the process of learning to help herself, she also learned how to most effectively help me. She understood what stressors affected me and

*Randy in DaNang, Vietnam with children from the English class
he was teaching as a volunteer with the civil action group*

how. She made my problems easier for me to deal with. She avoided triggers that would cause my bad behavior to surface. That alone was enough to make my life less stressful.

As she studied and learned, she realized that spouses of veterans with PTSD do not have the resources they need to help their vets—and themselves. So she developed her own amazing program to assist spouses and families of combat veterans in dealing with this epidemic of PTSD. Our struggle and pain motivated Debbie to write this book. And my pain and suffering led Debbie, through her faith, to help many, many families suffering the same way we have.

I will be eternally grateful for Debbie and her commitment, not only to me, but to veterans, their spouses, and their families everywhere.

God bless her, and God bless our veterans and their families.

ABOUT THE AUTHOR

 **Debbie Sprague** earned her bachelor's degree in therapeutic recreation, with a minor in psychology, graduating with honors from California State University (CSU), Chico. She also pursued postgraduate work in gerontology at CSU, Chico and University of Southern California (USC), Percy Andrus Gerontology Center. Her master's thesis, a successful grant proposal, brought the first Older America Act funds into Shasta County, California. The program she created has now been providing services to the community of Anderson, California for more than thirty years.

Debbie is also a board certified life/career coach and recreation therapist and holds a community college teaching credential in health and physical care services.

Debbie's life has been dedicated to improving the quality of life for others. She has worked with and/or created social service and health programs for the elderly and disabled, adaptive recreation programs for handicapped children, creative activities for residents in skilled nursing facilities, classes on independent living skills for seniors, and travel companies that specialize in providing escorted tours for senior citizens.

Debbie has personally experienced the challenges of caregiving during her son's losing battle with cancer and caring for her late mother-in-law. In 2004, Debbie's husband, a Vietnam veteran was diagnosed with complications from exposure to Agent Orange and Post-Traumatic Stress Disorder. Life dramatically changed for them, and in 2006, Debbie was also diagnosed with

PTSD. Debbie then used her gift for creating programs to take on the challenge of finding answers and solutions for spouses who become overwhelmed and lost in the world of caregiving and PTSD.

Debbie is a grass-roots volunteer for Family of a Vet, where she is a contributing author for their web site and hosts the weekly blog radio show "Life after Combat – Caregiver Edition PTSD & TBI." She also provides workshops and community education on PTSD and secondary PTSD and is a contributor to the number one international bestseller *Wounded? Survive! Thrive!!!*

Debbie serves as the Vietnam veteran era representative on a focus committee for the National VA Caregiver Peer Support Mentoring Program. She is also an advisory group member for MOAA-Zieders "Warrior-Family Roundtable – Military Caregivers Financial-Legal Guide Advisory Group."

RESOURCES

Congratulations! You have started on the journey to taking your life back. With each step it will become easier to love, honor, and care for your veteran in sickness, while you begin cherishing your own needs for health and happiness.

But you may still have questions or need help to keep moving forward. At times, the road may get rough. But don't worry—you are not alone! I will be here, along with all my experts, to help you along the way. We will be here to continue providing you with help and support to ensure you have a successful journey.

Debbie's Gifts and Programs

- **Complimentary Newsletter and Teleseminars:** Sign-up at www.detours2dreams.com to begin receiving Debbie's weekly newsletter and invitations for free monthly webinars and teleseminars. Keep up-to-date on the latest information, resources, tools, and tips for successful living with PTSD.
- **Workbook:** The perfect companion to *A Stranger in My Bed* is the *8 Steps to Taking Your Life Back Workbook.* Filled with more tools, tips, and questions to enhance your learning experience and help you create the life of your dreams. Available at www.astrangerinmybed.com.
- **Keynotes, Workshops, Seminars, Training, and Presentations:** Debbie would be honored to help your group, organization, or church learn more about PTSD. Whether you want to learn how to support veterans and their families or hold a workshop for spouses and caregivers, she can provide a program tailor-made to fit the unique needs of your group or organization.

- **Online Learning and Coaching:** Customized courses and programs are available to expand on the tools and knowledge you've learned in this book to ensure your success.
- **Individual and Group Coaching Programs:** The opportunity to work personally with Debbie, using her guidance, compassion, and support to help you move more quickly and easily to success.
- **Cherish YOU Cruises and Retreats:** Relax, refresh, and renew in a place that is all about YOU! Join with others who share similar struggles for a time of growing, sharing, and having fun!
- **Consulting and Training Certification:** Training and consulting for helping professionals. Become a certified trainer for Debbie's signature *8 Steps to Taking Your Life Back* program.

Visit Debbie's websites at: www.detours2dreams and
www.astrangerinmybed.com.
To contact Debbie:
Debbie@detours2dreams.com
PO Box 993670
Redding, CA 96099
Telephone: (530) 247-0170

The Experts

Visit our experts' websites for complimentary tips and tools, and more information about their programs and services:

Dawson Church, www.stressproject.org
Dr. John Gray, www.marsvenus.com
Dr. Joe Rubino, www.centerforpersonalreinvention.com
Barbara Stanny, www.barbarastanny.com
Marci Shimoff, www.marcishimoff.com
Nancy Forrester, www.integratedmentoringinstitute.com
Roberta Mittman, www.robertamittman.com
Chris Attwood and Janet Bray Attwood, www.thepassiontest.com
Brannan Vines, www.familyofavet.com

BIBLIOGRAPHY

"A Closer Look: Definition of Recreation."http://reference.yourdictionary. com/word-definitions/definiton-of-recretion.html.

Arloski, Michael. *Wellness Coaching for Lasting Lifestyle Change*. Duluth, MN: Whole Person Associates, Inc., 2007

Attwood, Janet Bray and Chris Attwood. *The Passion Test*. New York: Penguin, 2008.

"Caregiver Stress Fact Sheet." May 1, 2008. http://www.womenshealth.gov/ publications/our-publications/fact-sheet/caregiver-stress.

England, Diane. *The Post-Traumatic Stress Disorder Relationship: How to Support Your Partner and Keep Your Relationship Healthy*. Avon, MA: Adams Media, 2009.

Ethridge, Keith. July 8, 2010. "Spiritual Injuries and Three Key Spiritual Life Tasks." http://www.myhealth.va.gov.

_____. October 13, 2011. "What is the History of Spirituality and Health Care?" University of Maryland Medical Center. http://www.umm.edu/ altmed/articles/spirituality-000360.htm.

Ford, Debbie. *The Best Year of Your Life: Dream It, Plan It, Live It*. San Francisco: Harper Collins, 2005.

France, Betty. September 29, 2012. "Spiritual Alienation Information: A Church Sermon." http://www.ptsdsupport.net.

Frančišković, Tanja and Aleksandra Stevanović, Ilijana Jelušić, Branka Roganović, Miro Klarić, and Jasna Grković. "Secondary Traumatization of Wives of War Veterans with Post-traumatic Stress Disorder." *Croatian Medical Journal* 48 (2) (April 2007) : 177-184.

Gray, John. *Men are From Mars, Women are from Venus: The Classic Guide to Understanding the Opposite Sex.* New York: Harper Collins, 1992.

Hamblen, Jessica. January 2010. "Treatment of PTSD." U.S. Department of Veteran Affairs National Center for PTSD. http://www.ptsd.va.gov.

Handzo, George and Brian Hughes. *Spiritual Care Handbook on PTSD/TBI.* Chaplain Corps U.S. Navy, 2009.

"Helping a Family Member Who Has PTSD." January 1, 2007. National Center for PTSD. http://www.ptsd.va.gov/public/pages/helping-family-member.asp.

Hotakainen, Rob. May 26, 2011. "Concern Grows Over 'Epidemic' Veteran Suicide." http://www.thenewstribune.com.

"How Stress Affects the Body." Heartmath. http://www.heartmath.com/infographics/how-stress-the-body/print.html.

Jayatunge, Ruwan. January 7, 2011. "PTSD Described in the Holy Bible." http://www.Lankaweb.com.

Jeffreys, Matt. January 7, 2009. "Clinician's Guide to Medications for PTSD." U.S. Department of Veterans Affairs National Center for PTSD. http://www.ptsd.va.gov/professional/pages/clinicians-guide-to-medications-for-ptsd-asp.

LeRoy, Andree. "Exhaustion, Anger of Caregiving Get a Name." CNN.com http://www.cnn.com/2007/HEALTH/conditins?08/13/caregiver.syndrome/index.html

Lewis, Libby. September 24, 2007. "'Perfect Storm' Triggers PTSD in Vietnam Vets." www.npr.org.

Livestrong Foundation. "Vitamin Therapy for PTSD." http://livestrong.com/article/367331-vitamin-therapy-for-ptsd.

Luger, Steven. "Flood, Salt, and Sacrifice: Post-Traumatic Stress Disorders in Genesis." *Jewish Bible Quarterly* 38 (2) (2010).

Mason, Florence. *Recovering from the War: A Woman's Guide to Helping Your Vietnam Vet, Your Family, and Yourself.* New York: Penguin, 1990.

Matsakis, Aphrodite. *Vietnam Wives: Facing the Challenges of Life with Veterans Suffering Post-Traumatic Stress.* Baltimore, MD: Sidran Press, 1996.

Mayo Clinic Staff. July 23, 2010. "Spirituality and Stress Relief: Make the Connection." http://www.mayoclinic.com/health/stress-relief/SR00035.

"Aging Veterans and Posttraumatic Stress Symptoms." U.S. Department of Veterans Affairs National Center for PTSD. http://www.ptsd.va/about/ptsd-awareness.

National Center for PTSD Fact Sheet. http://www.ptsd.ne.gov/pdfs/coping-with-traumatic-stress-reactions.pdf.

National Institutes of Health. "Post-Traumatic Stress Disorder Fact Sheet." October 2010.

Nauert, Rick. "Canine Therapy for Military PTSD." http://psychcentral.com/news/2010/07/09/canine-therapy-for-military-ptsd/15444.html.

Nelson-Pechota, Margie. 2004. "Spirituality and PTSD in Vietnam Combat Veterans." http://www.warveteransministers.org.

Office of Public Health. September 2012. "Report on VA Facility Specific Operation Enduring Freedom (OEF), Operation Iraqi Freedom (OIF), and Operation New Dawn (OND) Veterans Coded with Potential PTSD." http://www.publichealth.va.gov/epidemiology.

_____. September 2012. "Analysis of VA HealthCare Utilization among Operation Enduring Freedom (OEF), Operation Iraqi Freedom (OIF), and Operation New Dawn (OND) Veterans." http://www.publichealth.va.gov/epidemiology.

"Physical and Mental Changes to Expect." May 2011. U.S. Department of Veterans Affairs VA Caregiver Support. www.caregiver.va.gov.

Price, Jennifer. December 20, 2011. "Findings from the National Vietnam Veterans' Readjustment Study." U.S. Department of Veterans Affairs National Center for PTSD, http://www.ptsd.va.gov/professional/pages/Vietnam-vets-study.asp.

Price, Jennifer and Susan Stevens. "Partners of Veterans with PTSD: Research Findings." http://www.pts.va.gov/professional/pages/partners_of_vets_research_findings.asp.

"Questions to Ask a Veteran's Health Care Providers." May 2011. U.S. Department of Veterans Affairs VA Caregiver Support. www.caregiver.va.gov.

Rand Corporation. "One In Five Iraq and Afghanistan Veterans Suffer from PTSD and Major Depression." http://www.rand.org/news/press/2008/04/17.html.

Rubino, Joe. *Restore Your Magnificence: A Life-Changing Guide to Reclaiming Your Self-Esteem.* Boxford, MA: Vision Works Publishing, 2003.

———. *The Success Code: 29 Principles for Achieving Maximum Abundance, Success, Charisma & Personal Power in Your Life.* Boxford, MA: Vision Works Publishing, 2007.

Seahorn, Janet and E. Anthony Seahorn. *Tears of a Warrior: A Family's Story of Combat and Living with PTSD.* Ft. Collins, CO: Team Pursuits, 2008.

"Sexual Functioning in War Veterans with Posttraumatic Stress Disorder." *Croatian Medical Journal* 49 (4) (April 2008): 499-505.

Shimoff, Marci and Carol Kline. *Happy for No Reason: 7 Steps to Being Happy from the Inside Out.* New York: Free Press, 2008.

———. *Love for No Reason: 7 Steps to Creating a Life of Unconditional Love.* New York: Free Press, 2010.

"Symptoms of PTSD." May 15, 2012. U.S. Department of Veterans affairs National Center for PTSD. http://www.ptsd.va.gov/public/pages/symptoms_of_ptsd_.asp.

Tull, Matthew. Dec. 20, 2011. "Delayed-Onset PTSD: What is it and Why Does it Occur." http://www.about.com.

———. Jan. 26, 2012. "An Overview of Physical Health Problems in Veterans with PTSD." http://www.about.com.

———. July 27, 2012. "The Relationship Between PTSD and Medication Adherence. http://www.about.com.

———. July 8, 2009. "An Overview of PTSD Symptoms." http://www.about.com.

———. Nov. 22, 2011. "Sexual Problems in Veterans with PTSD." http://www.about.com.

———. July 22, 2009. "Rates of PTSD in Veterans." http://www.about.com.

———. Jan. 29, 2012. "PTSD From the Vietnam War." http://www.about.com."

———. Nov. 5, 2008. "How to Identify and Cope with Your PTSD Triggers." http://www.about.com.

U.S. Department of Veterans Affairs. http://www.va.gov.

"U.S. Veterans Facing 'Major Health Crisis.'" Associated Press. April 7, 2008.

"VA Offering Training for Rural Clergy: Finding New Ways to Connect Rural Vets with VA Services." March 22, 2012. Office of Public Affairs Media Relations. http://www.va.gov.

Zoroya, Gregg. "VA Study: 22 Vets Commit Suicide Every Day." *USA Today.* February 1, 2013.

PERMISSIONS

Grateful acknowledgment is given for permission to use the following materials:

"Secondary Traumatization of Wives of War Veterans with Post-traumatic Stress Disorder," by Tanja Frančišković, Aleksandra Stevanović, Ilijana Jelušić, Branka Roganović, Miro Klarić, and Jasna Grković. Copyright 2007 *Croatian Medical Journal.*

The Beginning, by David Saywell. CreateSpace Independent Publishing Platform. October 2012.

GIVING BACK

In the spirit of giving back,
I am honored to donate a portion of the author proceeds from

A STRANGER IN MY BED

to this very worthy non-profit organization:

PTSD, TBI, & LIFE AFTER COMBAT

FamilyOfaVet.com

Get informed. Get involved. Save a Hero.

CPSIA information can be obtained at www.ICGtesting.com
Printed in the USA
BVOW080159210613

323899BV00004B/23/P